INDIAN BANKING

— PRESENT CHALLENGES —

M.S. SHETTY

ATLANTIC

PUBLISHERS & DISTRIBUTORS (P) LTD

ATLANTIC
PUBLISHERS & DISTRIBUTORS (P) LTD

7/22, Ansari Road, Darya Ganj, New Delhi
Tel.: +91-11-4077 5252, 2327 3880
E-mail: orders@atlanticbooks.com
Web: www.atlanticbooks.com

Published by Atlantic Publishers & Distributors (P) Ltd 2024

Printed & bound in India by Atlantic Print Services

Preface

Indian banking has come a long way since the independence of the country and subsequent banking and financial sector reforms introduced in the year 1991.

Banking activity is vital for any economy and a strong and stable banking structure in the country is essential for the economic growth of the country. The modern world has already moved from cash economy to banking economy. Cash to the maximum extent has been replaced by bank accounts and the cheque economy. It has further moved from a cheque economy to a digital economy now.

These are the trend changes witnessed all over the world. The world is globally connected through trade and commerce. In order to keep up with the global trend in trade and commerce, countries were required to follow certain openness in financial matters to facilitate global trade. Now, it is a foregone conclusion that a country cannot pursue protectionist economic policies and that in order to benefit from the global trade and commerce, it is necessary to adopt global standards in many areas. Globalisation is now not seen as dilution of sovereignty of the country but as a necessary tool to benefit from global trade.

Many countries including our country have learned this lesson the hard way. For quite some time countries have continued with protective covers against global trade. These are mainly in controlling imports and exports, trade policies, controls and permits for manufacturing industries, control on exchange rates of the currency, etc.

In the case of our country, the need to change the then existing protectionist policies were felt in 1990s and we have witnessed opening up of economy and globalisation since then. The financial sector and banking reforms were ushered in by the Central governments led by Shri P.V. Narasimha Rao and then by Dr. Manmohan Singh.

Banking reforms undertaken in the country from 1991 were mainly based on recommendations of Narasimham Committee Reports I and II. From the year 1991 till the year 2014, reform continued and progressed well. Indian banks reached to stable position with low NPA levels. In the year 2013, CRAR of scheduled commercial banks was 13.88%. NPA position of scheduled commercial banks were 3.2% gross NPA, and 1.7% net NPA as on 31st March, 2013.

But, the most important gain of globalisation was in the very healthy foreign exchange reserves of the country. It may be recalled that India's forex reserves perilously stood at USD 5.8 billion as of March 1991 and dwindled further during the course of that year. The country had to ship out its gold to avoid a default. This crisis eventually led to the liberalisation of the Indian economy. Globalisation has helped the country and as per Economic Survey 2014, the country's forex reserves went up to USD 304.2 billion as on 31st March, 2014. Further, as on 10th September, 2021, country's forex reserves stood at USD 641.1 billion (as per RBI). India's total foreign exchange reserves stand at around USD 593.5 billion (as per RBI) on 26th May, 2023, slightly lower than the September 2021 figures.

In the year 2014, a big political change took place in the country. For the first time in the history of our country, Bhartiya Janata Party (BJP) got clear majority in Parliament elections and BJP in alliance with few small parties came to power under the leadership of Prime Minister Shri Narendra Modi. The BJP led government got re-elected again in the 2019 general elections and formed the government again under the leadership of Prime Minister Shri Narendra Modi.

In the first five years of the BJP rule during 2014-19, and second term of the BJP rule from 2019 till Sept 2021, few decisions on economic policies were taken by the government. The important decisions affecting banking sector were:

1. Demonetisation of 500- and 1000-rupee notes on 8th November, 2016.
2. Introduction of GST in the whole of the country and withdrawal of existing multiple taxes on trade and industry from 1st July, 2017.
3. Development in banking industry: The banking industry was doing well till the year 2013 with good growth over past many years. Bank deposits and bank advances grew consistently. Banks NPAs were well under control as gross NPA was about 3.2% and net NPA was 1.7%. But, from the year 2014, the position changed due to down turn seen in the industry and other sectors of the economy. This resulted in steep increase in NPAs of the banks more particularly of public sector banks. In fact, in the years 2015 and 2016, governor of RBI warned that public sector banks were showing stress in their credit portfolio.

   Gross NPA of banks went up to 7.5% in 2014-15 and to 11.2% in 2017-18. This increase in NPA to such a dangerous level was due to loans sanctioned by banks prior to the year 2014 during the Congress regime at the centre, turning to bad loans. Earlier to these developments, RBI had already issued guidelines to banks for implementing Basel III norms for capital measures and banks were to increase their capital to 11.5% on the risk weighted assets by 31st March, 2019.

   The new BJP government from the year 2014 was concerned with the high level of NPAs of the commercial banks. Few large cases of bank frauds involving many thousand crores of rupees were also disclosed by banks. Government took some measures for early recovery of bad loans of the banks by creating a new legislation called 'The Insolvency and Bankruptcy Code, 2016'. This has speeded up the recovery system for bank credit. The Government was also forced to recapitalise public sector banks in order to comply with Basel III norms for capital adequacy.

4. Mergers of public sector banks: The earlier decision of merging subsidiaries of SBI was completed. Even the newly created Bharatiya Mahila Bank was also merged with SBI in 2017. In the year 2018, government also announced the merger of public sector banks—Vijaya Bank and Dena Bank with Bank of Baroda. This indicated that the merger of public sector banks to create large sized public sector bank is on the agenda of the present government. This was followed by another merger announcement by the government in 2019. Public sector banks are reduced in number to 12 after the mergers by April 2020.

   Later, during the budget for 2021-22 presented in February 2021, Government of India announced its intention to privatise few public sector banks. Privatisation of public sector banks is proposed by Central government as its policy to privatise few public sector undertakings and collect resources for funding its future development plans.

5. Monetary policies, RBI and Government relationship: There were occasions when the GOI and RBI had differences in their views on monetary policy related matters and also on some other matters. As RBI is autonomous with mandate to manage monetary policies and control banking sector, whether the GOI shall have a final say in the matter is the real issue involved and debated. To understand this, the role and functions of RBI vis-à-vis GOI's overall authority may have to be understood in correct perspective.

6. BJP government introduced the Financial Resolution and Deposit Insurance (FRDI) Bill in 2017 which had 'bail-in' provisions for the resolution of financial institutes under distress. This bill was withdrawn in the year 2018. A new bill called the Financial Sector Development and Regulation (Resolution) Bill (FSDR) 2019 was proposed to be placed before parliament in 2020. However, this bill is not introduced in the Parliament so far. This may be due to Covid-19 which hit the country in the beginning of the year 2020 and disrupted the economy. This bill will have far reaching implications for the banking system in the country.
7. During the years 2018 and 2019 banking and NBFC sectors faced problems. PMC bank—an urban coop bank and Yes bank—a new private sector bank, faced crisis mainly due to bad loans. IL&FS and Dewan Housing Finance Corporation Ltd. (DHFL)—two leading NBFCs with huge loan outstanding defaulted in their repayments. Both these NBFCs are now being liquidated.

   GOI and RBI had to bail-out Yes bank in the year 2020 and GOI approved reconstruction scheme for this bank. PMC bank issue took longer time and only in January 2022 GOI approved a takeover plan of this bank by the new Unity Small Finance Bank. Yes bank and PMC bank cases are discussed in chapter 2 of this book.

Indian banking industry which was considered robust till the year 2014 came under threat due to increasing NPAs to the extent of over 10% gross NPA level. Government had to take action to improve this position. The Government introduced a new law to speed up the recovery of NPAs from corporates. Banks particularly public sector banks suffered huge losses due to high NPAs from the year 2015 to 2018 and capital base of the public sector banks was eroded. This necessitated the government to provide capital to these banks in order to bring the capital levels of the banks as per Basel accord III. This posed a huge problem for government as it was forced to shore up the capital of public sector banks.

The crisis in PMC Bank in the year 2019 prompted the government to increase deposit insurance limit to ₹ 5 lacs per depositor from February 2020. The limit was just ₹ one lakh till then.

Yes Bank crisis was by far the biggest bank crisis in the history of Indian banking. Though it is a private sector bank, keeping the interest of banking system in the country, GOI bailed out this bank through SBI in March 2020.

Covid-19 hit the country in the beginning of the year 2020. There was a complete lockdown in the nation for some time and lockdowns were continued by the states for most part of the year 2020. This affected the working of banks though banks remained open all the time. But, economic activities were at standstill for the major part of the year.

The impact was felt on the banks in the cooperative sector more, as they are mostly smaller banks. Their financial position deteriorated with the large number of urban cooperative banks showing signs of weakness. As UCBs are the weak link in the banking system of the country, GOI through an ordinance amended the Banking Regulation (Amendment) Bill, 2020 in June 2020. This amended Act gave powers to RBI to supervise UCBs at par with commercial banks.

However, it was expected that Covid-19 effect would be felt on the NPA levels of the banks in the year 2021 and 2022 when NPA levels would go up.

With this background, this book will discuss some of the relevant issues as under:

1. The present structure of banking and different types of banks in the country.
2. Global developments in banking sector. After banking sector reforms were introduced from the year 1991,

many of the recommendations of international bodies were implemented. The impact of these changes on the banking sector of the country is discussed in a separate chapter.

3. RBI is the controller of banking and financial sector. RBI is also the monetary authority of the country and is an autonomous body. The role and functions of RBI in respect of banking sector is discussed in a separate chapter.
4. Though RBI is autonomous, it is a creation of GOI. Will GOI's views on monetary policies and banking sector prevail? The relationship between GOI and RBI matters and in case differences arise: how the matter gets resolved? Many differences have surfaced over the last few years which are discussed in a separate chapter.
5. How the interest rates are decided and what makes them move upwards or downwards.

   Interest rates on deposits and loans are now bank specific. There are many other important interest rates offered by government under various schemes, and offered by other players in the financial sector. This is discussed in a separate chapter.
6. In the year 2016, GOI demonetised 500- and 1000-rupee notes. The purpose for demonetisation and its results are discussed in a separate chapter.
7. Urban Cooperative Banks are the weak links in the banking industry. They are controlled by state governments through Cooperative Societies Acts. RBI control on these banks has increased over the years and in June 2020, GOI amended the banking regulation act giving powers to RBI same as in case of commercial banks. The issues facing UCBs are discussed in a separate chapter.
8. Rural Cooperative Banks are the dedicated banks for rural credit. Though they are credit cooperatives same as

UCBs, their role in the country is directly under control and direction of government. In the year 2006, GOI decided to revive these banks by offering a financial package and bring them up to the standards of other banks in the country. Their present status is discussed briefly in a separate chapter.

9. At present, Deposit Insurance and Credit Guarantee Corporation of India, a wholly owned RBI company, is providing insurance cover of one lakh rupee per account holder of the failed bank up to January, 2020. This is increased to ₹ 5 lakhs in February 2020. The premium for the insurance is borne by the banks.

RBI has asked the banks to educate depositors about the insurance cover available through the passbooks or by other means. Even public sector banks are also doing this. This is now creating confusion and doubt in the minds of account holder that his money is unsafe with the banks including public sector banks. There is a need to enhance the insurance cover to a reasonable limit per account holder to make it a meaningful risk cover. Bank depositors' protection and the insurance coverage available are discussed in a separate chapter.

M.S. Shetty

Acknowledgements

The author acknowledges with thanks the invaluable information provided by Reserve Bank of India in its master circulars, data base, other circulars and guidelines issued from time to time and made available at its website.

Author also acknowledges with thanks various international financial organisations, other entities and banks in India for providing information on various aspects of banking system through their respective web sites. Some important organisations are as under:

- Bank for International Settlements (BIS) and its committees—Basel in Switzerland.
- Financial Action Task Force (FATF), Headquarters: Paris, France.
- Financial Stability Board is an international body promoted by G20 nations of the world in the year 2009 at Basel in Switzerland.
- International Association of Deposit Insurers (IADI) is formed in 2002 to enhance the effectiveness of deposit insurance systems by promoting guidance and international cooperation. It is a body under the aegis of BIS Basel.
- FIU-IND.

Besides, the sources are generally mentioned in the book along with the information or the tables, and we acknowledge with thanks all the sources mentioned in this book.

M.S. Shetty

Acknowledgements

Contents

Abbreviations

Abbreviation	*Stands for*
ALM	Asset and Liability Management
BIS	Bank for International Settlements
BoD	Board of Directors
BoM	Board of Management
CRR	Cash Reserve Ratio
CPI	Consumer Price Index
CRAR	Capital to Risk-weighted Asset Ratio
CAR	Capital Adequacy Ratio
CCB	Capital Conservation Buffer
DCCB	District Central Cooperative Bank
DICGC	Deposit Insurance and Credit Guarantee Corporation
FATF	Financial Action Task Force
FI	Financial Institution
FIU-IND	The Financial Intelligence Unit-India
FSB	Financial Stability Board
FSDR	Financial Sector Development and Regulation (Resolution) Bill, 2019
GDP	Gross Domestic Product
GOI	Government of India
GOVT.	Government

G20 nations	Intergovernmental Forum Comprising 19 Countries and the European Union (EU)
IADI	International Association of Deposit Insurers
J&K Bank Ltd.	Jammu & Kashmir Bank Ltd.
KYC	Know Your Customer
LAB	Local Area Bank
LIC	Life Insurance Corporation of India
LAF	Liquidity Adjustment Facility
MCLR	Marginal Cost of Funds-based Lending Rate
MPC	Monetary Policy Committee
MSF	Marginal Standing Facility
MSME	Micro, Small & Medium Enterprises
NABARD	National Bank for Agriculture and Rural Development
NBFC	Non-Banking Financial Companies
NPA	Non-Performing Asset
PACS	Primary Agriculture Credit Society
PCARDB	Primary Cooperative Agriculture and Rural Development Bank
PCA	Prompt Corrective Action
PMC Bank	Punjab and Maharashtra Cooperative Bank
PMLA	Prevention of Money Laundering Act, 2002
REPO	Repurchase Agreement
RBI	Reserve Bank of India
RCB	Rural Cooperative Bank
RC	Resolution Corporation
RA	Resolution Authority
RLLR	Repo Linked Lending Rate
RRB	Regional Rural Bank
SBI	State Bank of India
SEBI	Securities and Exchange Board of India
SCB	Scheduled Commercial Bank

SCARDB	State Cooperative Agriculture and Rural Development Bank
SFB	Small Finance Bank
SLR	Statutory Liquidity Ratio
StCB	State Cooperative Bank
SIFI, G-SIFI	Systemically Important Financial Institution, Global-Systemically Important Financial Institution
UCB	Urban Cooperative Bank

1

Present Banking Structure in the Country

Banking business in our country is old established and it was with the private hands. They were known as indigenous bankers. Mostly, they were firms owned by individuals. In the 19th century banks as, limited companies came in to existence. Many British agency houses also opened banks. There were also few foreign banks who were handling foreign exchange business related to imports and exports. Then British Govt. started three banks in the presidency towns of Bombay, Calcutta, and Madras to handle govt. business and also to issue bank notes. These three banks were: Bank of Bombay opened in 1840, Bank of Bengal in 1806 and Bank of Madras in 1843. These three banks were later merged to form the Imperial Bank of India in 1921. In the year 1955, Govt. of India created the State Bank of India to take over the business of Imperial Bank of India.

During British rule, some princely states had also created few banks to take care of their treasury. Eight such big banks were converted as seven banks and made as subsidiaries of State Bank of India (SBI) in the year 1959. All these subsidiary banks of SBI were merged with State Bank of India by the year 2018.

British rulers had also created many postal savings banks in the country. This banking business, after the independence of the country, was merged with Indian postal dept.

Private sector banks. Besides, large number of banks in the private sector came up in 19th and 20th centuries. In the year 1947, there were more than 625 commercial banks in the country and during the consolidation period (1950s to 1970s) of banking industry most of them were merged with other banks. Some were liquidated.

In the year 1991, only 26 private sector banks were present. Out of this, 13 of the banks were later merged with other banks during the phase of banking sector reforms started from the year 1991 till the year 2010.

One private sector bank, Lakshmi Vilas Bank was amalgamated with DBS Bank India Limited (DBIL) effective from 27 November 2020.

Public sector banks. Govt. of India, out of the existing private sector banks, nationalised 14 banks in the year 1969 and six more banks in the year 1980. These nationalised banks along with State Bank of India are now known as public sector banks.

Cooperative Banks

Cooperative movement started in the country from the beginning of 20th century and amongst others many credit societies were started. Many of these credit societies gradually became coop banks.

After the independence in 1947, agricultural credit societies which were in rural areas were encouraged by the govt. for providing agricultural loans to farmers. Thus, they were segregated from other credit societies and named as primary agriculture credit society (PACS). Then GOI decided and created three-tier systems in cooperative sector for disbursing short-term loans to farmers. At the village level the primary agricultural credit societies (PACS) were enrolled or created, at district level—district central coop banks were created and at apex level in the states—state coop banks were created. Similarly, the existing land mortgage banks in coop sector were enrolled to extend long-term loans to the farming sector. Some new coop banks were also created. They are renamed as Primary Co-operative Agriculture and Rural Development Banks (PCARDBs). At apex level in the state—State Co-operative Agriculture and Rural Development Banks (SCARDBs) were created. All these cooperative banks engaged in financing agriculture and rural development are called the Rural Coop. Banks.

There were many other credit coop societies existing who were extending loans for other activities and they are mostly located in semi-urban or urban cities. Many of these credit societies became coop banks. These credit societies/coop banks were segregated from the credit societies/coop banks engaged in rural credit and were named as urban coop banks or primary urban coop banks.

Urban coop banks over the years have grown and function like commercial banks in all respect. RBI regulations on them are very similar to the RBI regulations on commercial banks. There are many UCBs now which are comparable in size and business to smaller private sector banks.

Thus, at present coop banks that are present in the country fall under two categories:

(1) Rural coop banks

(2) Urban coop banks

The functions and operations of urban coop banks (UCBs) are similar to commercial banks. However, the rural coop banks are purely dedicated for agriculture and rural development. Rural coop banks are supported and controlled by central and state govts. but registered as cooperative societies under the state acts. Urban coop banks are under private ownership but also registered under cooperative societies acts of the states. The cooperative societies which are functioning in more than one state are required to be registered under The Multi-State Cooperative Societies Act, 2002 which is a Central Act.

The role and present status of these coop banks are given in separate chapters in the book.

Foreign banks. Few foreign banks were present in the country during the British rule. Those banks were then known as exchange banks. Many of them continued in the country. Many newer foreign banks have also started their operation in the country after independence. Now these banks are known as foreign banks.

Foreign banks in India as on July 14, 2020
—Branch/Wholly Owned Subsidiary

Sl. No.	Name of bank	Country	Branches
1	AB Bank Ltd.	Bangladesh	1
2	Abu Dhabi Commercial Bank Ltd.	UAE	1
3	American Express Banking Corporation	USA	1
4	Australia and New Zealand Banking Group Ltd.	Australia	3
5	Barclays Bank Plc.	United Kingdom	6
6	Bank of America	USA	4
7	Bank of Bahrain & Kuwait BSC	Bahrain	4
8	Bank of Ceylon	Sri Lanka	1
9	Bank of China	China	1
10	Bank of Nova Scotia	Canada	2
11	BNP Paribas	France	8
12	Citibank N.A.	USA	35
13	Cooperatieve Rabobank U.A.	Netherlands	1
14	Credit Agricole Corporate & Investment Bank	France	5
15	Credit Suisse A.G.	Switzerland	1
16	CTBC Bank Co. Ltd.	Taiwan	2
17	DBS Bank India Limited*	Singapore	
18	Deutsche Bank	Germany	17
19	Doha Bank Q.P.S.C.	Qatar	3
20	Emirates Bank NBD	UAE	1
21	First Abu Dhabi Bank PJSC	UAE	1
22	FirstRand Bank Ltd.	South Africa	1
23	HSBC Ltd.	Hong Kong	26
24	Industrial & Commercial Bank of China Ltd.	China	1
25	Industrial Bank of Korea	South Korea	1
26	J.P. Morgan Chase Bank N.A.	USA	4
27	JSC VTB Bank	Russia	1
28	KEB Hana Bank	South Korea	2
29	Kookmin Bank	South Korea	1

Sl. No.	Name of bank	Country	Branches
30	Krung Thai Bank Public Co. Ltd.	Thailand	1
31	Mashreq Bank PSC	UAE	1
32	Mizuho Bank Ltd.	Japan	5
33	MUFG Bank Ltd.	Japan	5
34	NatWest Markets Plc	United Kingdom	1
35	PT Bank Maybank Indonesia TBK	Indonesia	1
36	Qatar National Bank (Q.P.S.C.)	Qatar	1
37	Sberbank	Russia	1
38	SBM Bank (India) Limited*	Mauritius	
39	Shinhan Bank	South Korea	6
40	Societe Generale	France	2
41	Sonali Bank Ltd.	Bangladesh	2
42	Standard Chartered Bank	United Kingdom	100
43	Sumitomo Mitsui Banking Corporation	Japan	2
44	United Overseas Bank Ltd.	Singapore	1
45	Westpac Banking Corporation	Australia	1
46	Woori Bank	South Korea	3

Source: RBI.

* SBM Bank (India) Limited (Subsidiary of SBM Group) and *DBS Bank India Limited (Subsidiary of DBS Bank Ltd.) have been issued licence on December 6, 2017 and October 4, 2018 respectively for carrying on banking business in India through Wholly Owned Subsidiary (WOS) mode. They have commenced operations as WOS w.e.f. December 01, 2018 and March 01, 2019 respectively.

Formation of Reserve Bank of India

In the year 1934, the RBI Act was passed by British Govt. and Reserve Bank of India came into existence in 1935 in Calcutta as the central bank of the country. RBI was formed as a limited company. Indian Govt. later nationalised RBI in the year 1949 and converted RBI as statutory bank making it as the central bank of the country and also as the monetary authority of the country.

Regional Rural Banks

Indian Govt. promoted regional rural banks (RRBs) from the year 1975 onwards. The purpose was also overall rural development in the country. These banks were set up as commercial banks in contrast to the rural coop banks created earlier by the govt. These RRBs are in public sector as the maximum capital has been contributed by Central Govt. and State govts. RRBs are sponsored by commercial banks, mostly public sector banks with few exceptions. There were total of 196 RRBs existing in the year 1991. During the reform phase after the year 1991, govt. undertook consolidation of these banks and amalgamated many of them to form lesser number of banks. There were 45 RRBs as at September 2019.

At present, there are 43 RRBs as of 1 November 2020.

List of Regional Rural Banks

	Bank's Name	Established year	Branches	Sponsor Bank
1	Andhra Pradesh Grameena Vikas Bank	2006	755	State Bank of India
2	Andhra Pragathi Grameena Bank	2006	552	Canara Bank
3	Chaitanya Godavari Grameena Bank	2006	219	Union Bank of India
4	Saptagiri Grameena Bank	2006	220	Indian Bank
5	Arunachal Pradesh Rural Bank	1983	30	State Bank of India
6	Assam Gramin Vikash Bank	2006	474	Punjab National Bank
7	Dakshin Bihar Gramin Bank	2019	1078	Punjab National Bank
8	Uttar Bihar Gramin Bank	2008	1032	Central Bank of India
9	Chhattisgarh Rajya Gramin Bank	2013	625	State Bank of India
10	Baroda Gujarat Gramin Bank	2019	489	Bank of Baroda
11	Saurashtra Gramin Bank	1978	259	State Bank of India

	Bank's Name	Established year	Branches	Sponsor Bank
12	Sarva Haryana Gramin Bank	2013	542	Punjab National Bank
13	Himachal Pradesh Gramin Bank	2013	265	Punjab National Bank
14	Ellaquai Dehati Bank	1979	116	State Bank of India
15	Jammu And Kashmir Grameen Bank	2009	217	Jammu & Kashmir Bank
16	Jharkhand Rajya Gramin Bank	2019	443	State Bank of India
17	Karnataka Gramin Bank	2019	1142	Canara Bank
18	Karnataka Vikas Grameena Bank	2005	633	Canara Bank
19	Kerala Gramin Bank	2013	634	Canara Bank
20	Madhya Pradesh Gramin Bank	2019	866	Bank of India
21	Madhyanchal Gramin Bank	2012	454	State Bank of India
22	Maharashtra Gramin Bank	2008	391	Bank of Maharashtra
23	Vidarbha Konkan Gramin Bank	2013	318	Bank of India
24	Manipur Rural Bank	1981	28	Punjab National Bank
25	Meghalaya Rural Bank	1981	87	State Bank of India
26	Mizoram Rural Bank	1983	85	State Bank of India
27	Nagaland Rural Bank	1983	10	State Bank of India
28	Odisha Gramya Bank	2013	549	Indian Overseas Bank
29	Utkal Grameen Bank	2012	442	State Bank of India
30	Puduvai Bharathiar Grama Bank	2008	43	Indian Bank
31	Punjab Gramin Bank	2019	419	Punjab National Bank
32	Rajasthan Marudhara Gramin Bank	2014	715	State Bank of India
33	Baroda Rajasthan Kshetriya Gramin Bank	2013	833	Bank of Baroda
34	Tamil Nadu Grama Bank	2019	630	Indian Bank

	Bank's Name	Established year	Branches	Sponsor Bank
35	Telangana Grameena Bank	2014	421	State Bank of India
36	Tripura Gramin Bank	1976	142	Punjab National Bank
37	Aryavart Bank	2019	1365	Bank of India
38	Baroda UP Bank	2020	2050	Bank of Baroda
39	Prathama UP Gramin Bank	2019	938	Punjab National Bank
40	Uttarakhand Gramin Bank	2012	286	State Bank of India
41	Bangiya Gramin Vikash Bank	2007	587	Punjab National Bank
42	Paschim Banga Gramin Bank	2007	230	UCO Bank
43	Uttarbanga Kshetriya Gramin Bank	1977	142	Central Bank of India

Local area banks. RBI had introduced the Local Area Bank (LAB) scheme in 1996 to encourage financial activities in unbanked areas. The scheme envisaged setting up of LABs with a minimum capital of ₹5 crores, as private sector commercial banks to operate in an area comprising three contiguous districts. Only four local area banks were opened and only two exist now.

1. Coastal Local Area Bank Ltd., Vijayawada, Andhra Pradesh in 1999. The bank has 39 branches.
2. Capital Local Area Bank Ltd., Nakodar, Punjab; in 2000. This is the largest Local Area Bank in the country, with 39 branches.
3. Krishna Bhima Samruddhi Local Area Bank (Karnataka and Andhra Pradesh) in 2001—it has 19 branches at present.
4. Subhadra Local Area Bank Ltd. Kolhapur (Maharashtra), it has eight branches.

Capital Local Area Bank is converted as Capital Small Finance Bank Limited and started operations as India's First Small Finance Bank on April 24, 2016.

The Reserve Bank of India cancelled the banking license issued to Subhadra Local Area Bank vide order dated December

24, 2020 ordering it to be closed. Thus only following two banks under this category exists at present.

List of Local Area Banks (LAB)

1	Coastal Local Area Bank Ltd.
2	Krishna Bhima Samruddhi LAB Ltd.

Later RBI discontinued the policy to issue licenses for this type of banks as it was found that they are not much response for starting this type of banks.

Now under the new policy for starting of small finance banks, RBI has announced that the existing local area banks are eligible to apply for converting to small finance bank. Accordingly, one bank: Capital Local Area Bank Ltd. mentioned earlier is allowed to be converted to small finance bank in 2016.

New Private Sector Banks

After the banking reforms were introduced, RBI, in 1993, issued guidelines for opening new banks, and allowed opening of new private sector banks. New banks like ICICI bank, HDFC Bank, Axis Bank, IDBI Bank, IndusInd Bank and many other new private sector banks came into existence. Many of the new banks were later merged with other banks. Under the 1993 guidelines, RBI had issued the last set of licences in 2001 to Kotak Mahindra Bank and Yes Bank.

In the year 2013, RBI issued comprehensive guidelines for setting up of more new banks by private promoters. RBI now fixed a capital requirement of ₹ 500 crores to start a universal bank. Under this, NBFCs are allowed to convert themselves as universal bank or promote a new bank. Based on this new policy for opening banks, RBI has issued two licenses in the year 2014 to IDFC Ltd.—an infrastructure development company based in Mumbai and Bhandan Financial Services Ltd. Kolkata—the largest Micro Finance Corporation in India.

Thus, two new private sector Universal banks came into existence. IDFC bank started operations on 1 October 2015 (promoted by IDFC Ltd.). IDFC Bank merged with Capital First, a NBFC, to form IDFC FIRST Bank in December 2018.

Bhandan Bank Ltd. was started on 23-8-2015 at Kolkata (promoted by Bhandan Financial Services Ltd.).

List of Private Sector Commercial Banks (March 2021)

	Bank Name	Established	Branches	Total Assets
1	City Union Bank	1904	700	₹352.71 billion
2	Karur Vysya Bank	1916	779	₹576.63 billion
3	CSB Bank	1920	417	₹162.23 billion
4	Tamilnad Mercantile Bank	1921	509	₹322.4 billion
5	Nainital Bank	1922	147	₹7.7 billion
6	Karnataka Bank	1924	858	₹855.81 billion
7	Dhanlaxmi Bank	1927	247	₹122.86 billion
8	South Indian Bank	1929	929	₹743.12 billion
9	DCB Bank	1930	341	₹240.46 billion
10	Federal Bank	1931	1,284	₹1,149.8 billion
11	Jammu & Kashmir Bank*	1938	1038	₹1,089 billion
12	RBL Bank	1943	392	₹486.74 billion
13	Axis Bank	1993	4,800	₹10,600 billion
14	ICICI Bank	1994	5,288	₹14,760 billion
15	HDFC Bank	1994	5,430	₹15,773 billion
16	IndusInd Bank	1994	1,911	₹1,786 billion
17	Kotak Mahindra Bank	2003	1,600	₹2,146 billion
18	Yes Bank	2004	1,119	₹2,578 billion
19	IDBI Bank	2004	1,892	₹3,144.57 billion
20	IDFC First Bank	2015	523	₹1,121.6 billion
21	Bandhan Bank	2015	5,371	₹917.18 billion

Source: Wikipedia.

*Jammu & Kashmir Bank—Central govt./state govt. holds 68.18% share in capital as on June 2021 in this bank. But this bank is treated as private sector bank for some reason.

IDBI Bank which was a public sector bank, after LIC of India took up 51% majority shareholding in the bank in January 2019, it is now treated as a private sector bank. However, LIC of India is a statutory body owned by GOI.

The first 12 banks on the list are banks known as old private sector banks and banks at Sl. No. 13 to 21 are known as the new private sector banks. They are banks started after the banking sector reforms were introduced in the year 1991 onwards.

One old private sector bank, Lakshmi Vilas Bank was amalgamated with DBS Bank India Limited (DBIL) effective from 27 November 2020. DBS bank India Ltd. is a foreign bank as it is the wholly owned subsidiary of DBS Bank Singapore.

Lakshmi Vilas Bank Limited was an Indian private sector bank established in 1926 in Karur, Tamil Nadu. As of November 2020, the bank had 566 branches in 19 states and one union territory. The deposits were about ₹20,973 crore and advances were about ₹10,685 crore.

As per RBI, the financial position of the LVB, has undergone a steady decline, with continuous losses over the last three years eroding the bank's net-worth. Almost one-fourth of the bank's advances have turned bad assets. Its gross non-performing assets (NPAs) stood 25.4% of its advances as of June 2020.

Reserve Bank of India (RBI) had put the bank under Prompt Corrective Action in September 2019. RBI imposed one-month moratorium on LVB from November 17. Shortly after announcing a one-month moratorium for LVB, RBI approved to merge LVB with DBS Bank India. This is the first merger case when an Indian bank is merged with a foreign bank.

RBI has also issued policy (in the year 2014) to start two types of small banks to cater the particular needs of the population segments to improve the banking environment in the country. These small banks are called the 'niche banks', namely the 'payment banks' and the 'small finance banks'.

List of Payments Banks (PB)

	Name	Started
1	Airtel Payments Bank Ltd.	Jan. 2017
2	India Post Payments Bank Ltd.	Sept. 2018
3	FINO Payments Bank Ltd.	April 2017
4	Paytm Payments Bank Ltd.	2017
5	Jio Payments Bank Ltd.	2018
6	NSDL Payments Bank Limited	Oct. 2018

Payments banks. Minimum capital requirement is fixed at ₹100 crores. These banks are allowed to accept deposit up to ₹1 lac from a customer. This limit is recently raised to ₹2 lacs per customer. They are permitted to issue prepaid cards and conduct any payment or remittance services for the customers. However, payment banks cannot give loans. There were six banks in this category in 2020.

RBI had issued 11 in principle approvals licences to different parties to start payments banks. Out of this, three parties have surrendered the licences.

One payments bank, Aditya Birla Idea Payments Bank was started in February 2018. This bank sought for voluntary closure in 2019. The Hon'ble Bombay High Court has passed an order on September 18, 2019 for closure and appointed liquidator.

Further this type of payments banks, for some reason, is not progressing. No new banks are being opened now.

Small Finance Banks. This new type of banks is allowed to undertake basic banking activities of accepting deposits and lending. They are perceived as local banks mainly to provide banking services at hitherto unbanked areas. There is no restriction for the area of their operations but they can only lend to unorganised sectors, to small business units, small and marginal farmers, micro and small industries, etc. Minimum capital requirement is fixed at ₹100 crores which is now increased to ₹200 crores from September 2019. As at March 2021 there were 11 banks under this category.

List of Small Finance Banks (SFB)

Sl. No.	Name of SFB	Started
1	Au Small Finance Bank Ltd.	April 2017
2	Capital Small Finance Bank Ltd.	April 2016
3	Fincare Small Finance Bank Ltd.	May 2017
4	Equitas Small Finance Bank Ltd.	2016
5	ESAF Small Finance Bank Ltd.	March 2017
6	Suryoday Small Finance Bank Ltd.	Jan. 2017
7	Ujjivan Small Finance Bank Ltd.	Feb. 2017
8	Utkarsh Small Finance Bank Ltd.	2017
9	North East Small Finance Bank Ltd.	Oct. 2017
10	Jana Small Finance Bank Ltd.	Mar. 2018
11	Shivalik Small Finance Bank Ltd.	April 2021

RBI is encouraging UCBs to convert as small finance banks. But so far only one local area bank (Capital Small Finance Bank Ltd.) and one UCB (Shivalik Small Finance Bank Ltd.) have voluntarily converted themselves into small finance bank.

Public Sector Banks

Govt. took the decision to merge the seven associate banks of SBI with SBI. This merger was completed in the year 2017.

Bharatiya Mahila Bank (BMB) was a fully owned subsidiary of State Bank of India started on 19 November 2013. This bank was created exclusively for the benefit of women. But soon GOI realised that the concept is not helpful. In view of this, Bharatiya Mahila Bank was also merged with SBI on 1 April 2017.

In the year April 2019, govt. merged three public sector banks. Vijaya Bank and Dena Bank were merged with Bank of Baroda. Further, in the year 2019 govt. also announced the merger of few more public sector banks as under:

- Punjab National Bank to merge Oriental Bank of Commerce and United Bank of India with it.
- Canara Bank to merge Syndicate Bank with it.
- Union Bank of India will merge Andhra Bank and Corporation Bank with it.
- Indian Bank will merge Allahabad bank with it.

Merger of these banks took place on 1 April 2020. After these mergers, the country now has only 12 public sector banks, including State Bank of India as under:

List of Public Sector Banks with Financial Positions as at 31-3-2021 (2020-21)

(₹ in crore)

Sl. No.	Bank	Branches	Government Shareholding	Deposits	Advances	CRAR % (Basel III)
1	State Bank of India	22,219	56.92%	3681,277	2182,516	13.74
2	Punjab National Bank	10,769	85.59%	1106,332	739,407	14.32
3	Canara Bank	10,416	78.52%	1010,875	675,155	13.18
4	Bank of Baroda	8,214	71.60%	966,966	706,300	14.99
5	Union Bank of India	9,315	89.07%	923,805	653,684	12.56
6	Indian Bank	6,007	88.06%	538,071	364,010	15.71

Sl. No.	Bank	Branches	Government Shareholding	Deposits	Advances	CRAR % (Basel III)
7	Bank of India	5,107	89.10%	627,113	401,436	14.93
8	Central Bank of India	4,608	92.39%	329,973	176,913	14.81
9	Indian Overseas Bank	3,217	95.84%	240,288	139,597	15.32
10	UCO Bank	3,089	94.44%	205,919	118,405	13.74
11	Bank of Maharashtra	1,964	92.49%	174,006	107,654	14.49
12	Punjab and Sind Bank	1,531	83.06%	96,108	76,811	17.06

Source: Annual reports of respective banks.

The first six banks in the above list have merged with themselves many other public sector banks prior to 31-3-2020. SBI is the biggest bank in the country. The business figures of these banks mentioned in the table represents their global business as many of these banks have branches in other countries also.

Indian Banking—Present Status

In India, we have many types of banks at present. These banks can be broadly divided into two major categories. They are the commercial banks and the cooperative banks.

Under commercial banks we have following sub-categories:

(1) Public sector banks

(2) Private sector banks (old and new)

(3) Foreign banks

(4) Local area banks

(5) Small finance banks

(6) Payment banks

(7) Regional rural banks

Cooperative banks are further divided into two sub-categories of

(1) Urban coop banks, and

(2) Rural coop banks.

As at the year 2020, the number banks under the above categories are as given in the table below:

1st April 2020		No. of banks
Commercial banks	Public sector banks	12
	Private sector banks	21
	Local area banks	2
	Small finance banks	11
	Payment banks	6
	Regional rural banks	43
	Foreign banks	46
Coop banks	Urban coop banks	1539
	State coop banks	33
	*PACS -97006	
	District coop banks	363
	SCARDBs	13
	PCARDBs	602

* PACs are not banks. They are primary agriculture credit societies and act as an important link to disburse short-term loans to farmers.

Scheduled Banks

Scheduled banks in India refer to those banks which have been included in the Second Schedule of Reserve Bank of India Act, 1934. RBI in turn includes only those banks in this Schedule which satisfy the criteria laid down vide Section 42(6)(a) of the said Act. Banks that are not included in this Schedule are called Non-Scheduled Banks.

The banks which are identified by RBI based on certain criteria fixed as regards capital and compliance are given the status of scheduled bank. This is a compulsory requirement now for all commercial banks (public sector and private sector banks), foreign banks and regional rural banks and small finance banks. For local area banks and payment banks, it's optional. It is also optional for both urban and rural coop banks.

Under coop banks only 54 urban coop banks and 22 state coop banks are in scheduled bank category. Remaining all other coop banks are under non-scheduled category.

BUSINESS SHARE OF BANK GROUPS

All Scheduled Banks

As per RBI, there were 209 scheduled banks out of which 133 were scheduled commercial banks as at 31-3-2021. Other 76 banks which are scheduled banks, other than commercial banks, are from the category of urban coop banks and state coop banks (53 UCBs and 23 state coop banks).

Business figures of Scheduled Commercial Banks and All Scheduled Banks as at March 2021 are given in the table below.

Business share of SCBs and other scheduled banks

(₹ in crores)

	Aggregate deposits	% to total	Total bank credit	% to total
All scheduled banks	15539580	100	11298820	100
Scheduled Commercial Banks	15113178	97.26	10951561	96.93
Scheduled UCBs and state coop banks	426402	2.74	347259	3.07

Source: RBI.

From the above table, we may observe that SCBs account for 97.26% of deposits and 96.93% of bank credits of all scheduled banks. Share of scheduled UCBs and scheduled state coop banks are only 2.74% in deposits and 3.07% in bank credit.

Scheduled Commercial Banks

RBI regularly monitors and brings out information on the working of scheduled commercial banks which are under their direct control and supervision. These banks represent, as stated earlier, bulk of banking activities in the country.

Scheduled commercial banks are a major group of banks in the country. All commercial banks are scheduled banks. This includes public sector banks, private sector banks, foreign banks having branches in India, regional rural banks, small business banks, and only two payment banks (India Post Payments Bank Limited and Fino Payments Bank Limited) are under scheduled category now. This group of banks hold more than 90% business share in banking business in the country.

The table given below gives the important business figures of scheduled commercial banks as a group from the year 2009-10 to 2020-21.

Scheduled Commercial Banks—Select Aggregates

(₹ in crores)

Year	Demand Deposits	Time Deposits	Aggregate Deposits (2+3)	Investments	Food Credit	Non-Food Credit	Total Bank Credit (6+7)
1	2	3	4	5	6	7	8
2009-10	645610	3847216	4492826	1384752	48489	3196299	3244788
2010-11	641705	4566264	5207969	1501619	64282	3877801	3942083
2011-12	625330	5283752	5909082	1737787	81304	4530548	4611852
2012-13	662299	6088155	6750454	2006105	96422	5164037	5260459
2013-14	713921	6991639	7705560	2212821	98447	5895649	5994096
2014-15	794029	7739256	8533285	2491825	94418	6442002	6536420
2015-16	888996	8438294	9327290	2625509	105254	7144361	7249615
2016-17	1281439	9476217	10757656	3030963	53927	7787539	7841466
2017-18	1370282	10055767	11426049	3318454	41989	8583436	8625425
2018-19	1511287	11062484	12573772	3381056	41610	9730112	9771722
2019-20	1617003	11950489	13567492	3747349	51764	10319097	10370861
2020-21	1861193	13252320	15113512	4462526	61524	10887985	10949509

Source: RBI.

Table 1.1: Balance Sheet of Urban Co-operative Banks (At end-March)

(Amount in ₹ crore)

Items	Scheduled UCBs		Non-Scheduled UCBs		All UCBs		Rate of Growth (%)	All UCBs
	2020	2021	2020	2021	2020	2021	2019-20	2020-21
1	2	3	4	5	6	7	8	9
Liabilities								
(1) Capital	4,415	4,467	9,696	9,765	14,111	14,233	3.9	0.9
	(1.5)	(1.5)	(2.9)	(2.7)	(2.3)	(2.2)		
(2) Reserves and Surplus	14,896	15,836	18,423	21,354	33,319	37,190	-10.6	11.6
	(5.1)	(5.3)	(5.5)	(6.0)	(5.3)	(5.7)		
(3) Deposits	2,29,706	2,39,576	2,71,124	2,87,406	5,00,830	5,26,982	3.4	5.2
	(78.9)	(79.5)	(81.4)	(80.7)	(80.3)	(80.1)		
(4) Borrowings	5,003	3,748	334	314	5,337	4,062	-1.0	-23.9
	(1.7)	(1.2)	(0.1)	(0.1)	(0.9)	(0.6)		
(5) Other Liabilities and Provisions	36,950	37,913	33,518	37,471	70,467	75,385	20.4	7.0
	(12.7)	(12.6)	(10.1)	(10.5)	(11.3)	(11.5)		
Assets								
(1) Cash in Hand	1,797	1,676	4,037	4,212	5,835	5,888	8.3	0.9
	(0.6)	(0.6)	(1.2)	(1.2)	(0.9)	(0.9)		

Items	Scheduled UCBs		Non-Scheduled UCBs		All UCBs		Rate of Growth (%)	All UCBs
	2020	2021	2020	2021	2020	2021	2019-20	2020-21
(2) Balances with RBI	9,804	11,121	2,792	3,418	12,595	14,539	-8.4	15.4
	(3.4)	(3.7)	(0.8)	(1.0)	(2.0)	(2.2)		
(3) Balances with Banks	18,526	21,906	47,719	47,694	66,245	69,600	8.6	5.1
	(6.4)	(7.3)	(14.3)	(13.4)	(10.6)	(10.6)		
(4) Money at Call and Short Notice	6,260	5,087	2,135	1,792	8,395	6,879	39.8	-18.1
	(2.2)	(1.7)	(0.6)	(0.5)	(1.3)	(1.0)		
(5) Investments	75,175	80,278	86,328	99,872	1,61,504	1,80,150	3.0	11.5
	(25.8)	(26.6)	(25.9)	(28.0)	(26.0)	(27.4)		
(6) Loans and Advances	1,41,151	1,43,201	1,64,138	1,69,564	3,05,289	3,12,765	0.7	2.4
	(48.5)	(47.5)	(49.3)	(47.6)	(48.9)	(47.5)		
(7) Other Assets	38,257	38,271	25,945	29,760	64,201	68,031	20.8	6.0
	(13.2)	(12.7)	(7.8)	(8.4)	(10.3)	(10.3)		
Total Liabilities/Assets	2,90,970	3,01,540	3,33,094	3,56,311	6,24,064	6,57,851	4.2	5.4
	(100.0)	(100.0)	(100.0)	(100.0)	(100.0)	(100.0)		

Notes: 1. Data for March 2021 are provisional.
2. Figures in parentheses are proportion to total liabilities/assets (in percent).
3. Components may not add up to the whole due to rounding off.

Source: Off-Site surveillance returns, RBI.

During last 11 years the deposits of SCBs have grown by 336% and bank credit has grown by 337%.

Next group of banks are the coop banks. This includes the urban coop banks and rural coop banks shown in the chart above.

Urban Coop Banks

53 UCBs are in the scheduled category and remaining UCBs are non-scheduled banks.

Following data as at 31 March 2020 and 2021 on UCBs are now available.

Deposits of all UCBs as at March 2021 was ₹ 5,26,982 crore and bank credit were ₹ 3,12,765 crore. Total assets as at 31 March 2021 were ₹ 6,57,851 crore.

Rural Coop Banks

Rural coop banks are supported by state and central govts. by capital contribution and also by loans.

Compilation of data on their working results is often delayed. The data given in the table below is of March 2020. 23 out of 33 state coop banks are in scheduled category (as at March 2021) and DCCBs are in non-scheduled category. PACS are not banks but credit coop societies. But they are linked to DCCBs and act as conduit through which agricultural credit is disbursed to farmers. State coop banks and DCCBs provide short-term loans to farm sector. Long-term lending to farm sector is done by SCARDBs and PCARDBs.

Table 1.2: A Profile of Rural Co-operatives (At end-March 2020)

(Amount in ₹ crore)

Item	Short-term			Long-term	
	StCBs	DCCBs	PACS	SCARDBs (P)	PCARDBs (P)
1	2	3	4	5	6
A. Number of Cooperatives	33*	351**	95,509	13	602
B. Balance Sheet Indicators					
i. Owned Funds (Capital + Reserves)	21,900	43,246	43,741	4,859	3,673

Item	Short-term			Long-term	
	StCBs	DCCBs	PACS	SCARDBs (P)	PCARDBs (P)
ii. Deposits	2,10,342	3,45,682	1,65,476	2,409	1,372
iii. Borrowings	85,723	97,448	1,38,571	13,710	16,643
iv. Loans and Advances	1,99,943	2,79,272	2,14,533	20,700	15,819
v. Total Liabilities/Assets	3,40,267	5,35,977	3,25,322	27,104	31,337
C. Financial Performance					
i. Institutions in Profits					
a. No.	32	291	47,027	10	227
b. Amount of Profit	1,740	1,887	6,531	287	86
ii. Institutions in Loss					
a. No.	1	60	37,369	3	375
b. Amount of Loss	16	1,041	8,325	35	657
iii. Overall Profits (+)/Loss (-)	1,724	846	-1,794	252	-571
D. Non-performing Assets					
i. Amount	13,477	35,298	70,160	6,836	6,815
ii. As percentage of Loans Outstanding	6.7	12.6	31.0	33.0	43.1
E. Recovery of Loans to Demand Ratio***(Per cent)	94.4	70.2	69.3	43.1	44.1

Notes: 1. StCBs: State Co-operative Banks; DCCBs: District Central Co-operative Banks; PACS: Primary Agricultural Credit Societies; SCARDBs: State Co-operative Agriculture and Rural Development Banks; PCARDBs: Primary Co-operative Agriculture and Rural Development Banks.

2. (P): Data are provisional.
3. *Data of Daman & Diu StCB (which is yet to be bifurcated completely from Goa StCB) is reported as a part of Goa StCB.
4. **: Excluding Tamil Nadu Industrial Co-operative Bank Limited (TAICO).
5. ***: Denotes the share of outstanding NPAs that have been recovered and on 30 June 2019.

Source: NAFSCOB and NABARD.

Regional Rural Banks

RRBs are also dedicated banks for rural developments but they are scheduled commercial banks. RRBs are a subgroup under Scheduled Commercial Banks. There are 43 RRBs at present and their business figures for years 2019 and 2020 are given in the table below:

Table 1.3: Consolidated Balance Sheet of Regional Rural Banks

(Amount in ₹ crore)

Sr. No.	Item	At end-March		Y-o-Y Growth in Percent	
		2019	2020P	2018-19	2019-20
1	2	3	4	5	6
1	Share Capital	6,73	7,849	4.6	16.5
2	Reserves	25,398	26,817	0.8	5.6
3	Deposits	4,34,444	4,78,547	8.5	10.2
4	Borrowings	53,548	54,393	-7.	1.6
5	Other Liabilities	17,864	25,372	17.3	42.0
	Total liabilities/Assets	5,37,989	5,92,978	6.5	10.2
6	Cash in Hand	2,913	2,860	4.4	-1.8
7	Balances with RBI	17,897	16,744	13.2	-6.4
8	Other Bank Balances	5,469	7,613	-2.5	39.2
9	Investments	2,26,172	2,49,155	1.8	10.2
10	Loans and Advances (net)	2,61,953	2,86,919	10.5	9.5
11	Fixed Assets	1,274	1,226	4.1	-3.8
12	Other Assets #	22,311	28,462	10.1	27.6
	12.1 Accumulated Losses	2,887	6,467	54.7	124.0

Notes: 1. #: Includes accumulated losses.

2. (P): Provisional.

3. Totals may not tally on account of rounding off of figures in ₹ Crore. Percentage Variations could be slightly different as absolute numbers have been rounded off to ₹ Crore.

Source: NABARD.

The data on RRBs are included in the data on scheduled commercial banks.

Thus, we have three broad categories of banks functioning in the country as under:

1. Scheduled commercial banks
2. Urban coop banks
3. Rural coop banks

The business share of these categories of banks as at 31 March 2019, for which data is available, is as under:

(₹ in core)

Category	Total deposits	% to total	Bank credit	% to total
Scheduled commercial banks	125,73,772	92.62	97,71,722	92.54
Urban coop banks	4,84,290	3.57	3,03,005	2.87
Rural coop banks	5,17,377	3.81	4,84,904	4.59
Total	135,75,439	100	105,59,631	100

We can observe that in March 2019 scheduled commercial banks accounted for 92.62% share in deposits and 92.54% share in bank credit. UCBs share was just 3.57% in deposits and 2.87% in bank credit. Rural coop banks accounted for 3.81% in deposits and 4.59% in bank credit.

Public Sector Commercial Banks vs Private Sector Commercial Banks

Indian banking industry was dominated by public sector commercial banks from the beginning. State bank group was old established and had major share in banking business since 1950s. In the year 1969, govt. nationalised 14 major private sector banks and again in the year 1980 nationalised six more banks. These 20 nationalised banks along with state bank and its subsidiary banks came to be known as public sector banks. Public sector banks dominated Indian banking with nearly 90% share in the banking business of the country.

Private sector banks had small share in business along with foreign banks. After banking reforms were introduced in the year 1991, many new private sector banks came to be established. These new generation private sector banks grew very fast and their share in business started growing.

This trend is visible from the tables below:

Market share in deposits (in percentage)

Year	Public sector	Private sector	Foreign banks
2000	81.29	12.63	5.47
2005	78.16	17.12	4.70
2010	77.68	17.31	5.05
2015	76.26	19.44	4.30
2020	64.75	30.35	4.89

(RBI)

In the year 2000, the share of deposits of public sector banks was 81.29%. But after the banking sector reforms were introduced from the year 1991, we can see that the share of public sector banks has gradually reduced to 64.75% in the year 2020. This shows how the private sector banks particularly the new private sector banks have come to garner large chunk of share in deposits. Private sector banks which had 12.63% share in deposits in 2000, now have 30.35% share in deposits. The shift of deposits is more between the years 2016-20.

Market share in advances is given in the table below:

Market share in advances (in percentage)

Year	Public sector	Private sector	Foreign banks
2000	79.41	12.56	8.03
2005	74.25	19.21	6.54
2010	77.24	18.08	4.67
2015	74.28	21.26	4.45
2020	59.80	36.04	4.15

(RBI)

We can observe that market share in advances of public sector banks came down from 79.41% to 59.80% during the period 2000 and 2020. The share of private sector banks increased from 12.56% to 36.04% by the year 2020.

Increase in the share of banking business by private sector banks is mainly due to fact that many new private sector banks established after 1993 have grown very fast. These new private sector banks are: ICICI bank, HDFC bank, Axis bank, IndusInd bank, Yes bank, Kotak Mahindra bank, etc. Even IDBI bank which was a public sector bank earlier, is also now in private sector.

Govt. is now planning to disinvest in few public sector banks and when this happens, we may find that public sector banks and private sector banks may have equal share in banking business. It is also possible that private sector banks overtake public sector banks and become the major player in banking industry.

Future Outlook for Banking Industry in the Country

In April 2021, the structure of banking in India is same as before with commercial banks, urban coop banks and rural coop banks.

Commercial banks are the public sector banks, private sector banks, foreign banks, RRBs, small business banks, payments banks, and local area banks.

Local area banks are encouraged to become small finance banks. There are only two local area banks existing now.

Urban coop banks are now encouraged to become commercial banks under small finance bank category. There are many large urban coop banks and they may transform themselves into commercial banks preferably as private sector banks. Smaller urban coop banks may transform into small finance banks. However, the Banking Regulation Amendment Act of 2020 also provides an option to remain in cooperative sector by allowing UCBs to increase their capital in approved manner and be under the supervision of RBI for all important matters pertaining to their workings.

The rural coop banks are supported by GOI and respective state govts. They are the PACS and rural coop banks like DCCBs, state coop banks, and the two-tier coop banks looking after term lending to rural sector (PCARDBs and SCARDBs). GOI has now approved amalgamation of DCCBs with state coop banks. This will be subject to state govt. consent and RBI approval. Hence, we may see voluntary amalgamations of DCCBs with state coop banks in next few years.

Regional Rural Banks (which are commercial banks) are devoted for rural development. We may not see any changes in the composition and role of these regional rural banks in the near future. They may continue as before. However, there is suggestion that RRBs may be merged with sponsor banks which are all public sector banks. But GOI has not given any indication on this.

One major development in the fiscal policies of the govt. will have bearing on the future of public sector commercial banks. Govt. has already made it known that it will disinvest the commercial organisations that are owned by it. This means govt. will privatise commercial organisations owned by it. This will include public sector financial institutions including commercial banks.

In the year 2021, govt. on the recommendations Niti Aayog (Niti Aayog was established in 2015, by the NDA Government, and replaced the Planning Commission) has decided to disinvest in two public sector banks and one public sector FI. This means that two of the public sector banks in the existing 12 will be privatised. Govt. so far has not indicated the names of two public sector banks it has earmarked for privatisation. The rumour has it that two banks will be from the following six public sector banks:

1. Bank of India
2. Central Bank of India
3. Indian Overseas Bank
4. United Commercial Bank
5. Punjab and Sind Bank
6. Bank of Maharashtra

The other six banks are formed by merging few public sector banks. They are now the bigger banks and it's believed that these six banks will form the public sector in banking industry and may continue in future also as public sector banks. They are:

1. State Bank of India
2. Bank of Baroda
3. Punjab National Bank
4. Canara Bank
5. Union Bank of India
6. Indian Bank

2

Global Developments and its Impact on Indian Banking

BANKS AND THEIR IMPORTANCE TO ECONOMIES

In the modern world, banks are the depositories of public money. Money is invented by human societies to be used as unit of value and as a medium of exchange. Money facilitated to move away from the barter system that prevailed before it. In the process, money also became as storage of value for future use. These three are the crucial functions of money and it enabled human societies to achieve progress in their economic activities.

As the surplus money earned by an individual is stored by him and it enabled him to spend it at some future time when required. Then the business of banking was started. Banks tried to get the money stored by individuals as deposits promising them to repay it when the owner demands for it. Banks used this money collected from the individuals for giving loans. Thus, banks became the financial intermediaries who functioned as a conduit for the money to flow from the owners to the borrowers who needed money.

Slowly the money or cash with the public moved to banks in the shape of deposits and the depositors relied on the reputation of the bank to return it when they wanted it. But if the bank failed then the depositors lost their money as there is no guarantee or security other than the bank's promise.

Banking became an important business in the modern world as it replaced the cash with the public into bank accounts. Banks provided cheque facility which obviated the need to withdraw cash from banks and in its place, cheque is used to settle payments in trade and commerce. Banks' ability to give loan on the basis of money deposited by account holders with it, spurred the economic activities. Trade and commerce progressed in much faster pace than it was before this financial intermediation. Banking has thus become indispensable for the modern economy.

Now the question is that whether the banking system thus evolved over few centuries are dependable and safe? Can the economic activities be conducted on the evolved banking system without any fear of its collapsing and creating economic chaos?

As discussed earlier, banking is also a business mostly in the hands of private individuals. Every business has its inherent risks of failure. There is no guarantee that any business will always remain safe and unaffected. Business is always based on risk taking capability of its promoter. Besides the promoters' capabilities there are also many unknown risks which only the future can reveal. There are also the risks associated with malfeasance by management, staff and others.

Banking business, as any other business also carries its own risk factors. In view of this, bank failures are unavoidable in any society. This has been the experience of all countries in the past and also at present times.

In view of the incidents of bank failures faced by the countries world over, the governments of the countries slowly recognised its seriousness and its adverse impacts on the country's economy. Failures of small banks have been ignored in the past as inherent and unavoidable. Depositors of those banks lost their money but it was not taken seriously as it might have affected only a small section of the population of the country. Slowly the governments realised that bank failures per se are bad for the economy. If a large bank fails today, it will also have cascading effects on other banks and other businesses, and it will upset the country's economy. It may lead to recession in the economy. Governments are now aware that banks have grown big and occupy very important and crucial position in the economy. In the modern world banks have expanded their business to other countries and have financial relationships with banks in other countries. This is necessitated for conducting international trade. Now, if a big bank fails in one country the shock waves will be felt in many other countries also. The classic example of this new threat was seen in Lehman Brothers failure in USA in September 2008. Besides USA, many of the European countries felt the shock and faced trouble in their banking system.

The modern Indian banking system has evolved independently over a period of 100 years till 1990. The developments in banking were specific to the needs of our country. Our country though participated in international trade due to compulsions; there were many controls in place which restricted free trade. International transactions and trade were controlled by The Foreign Exchange Regulation Act of 1947. There were controls on imports and exports.

Due to this, the banking system of our country was insulated from external shocks in the international level. The banking structure in the country was complex with nationalised banks, private banks, foreign banks and rural and urban coop banks. Commercial banks and coop banks are with separate set of controls.

The globalisation of Indian economy was started by the GOI from the year 1991. Globalisation means integrating Indian economy with global economy. This resulted in liberalised industrial policies and reforms in banking and financial sectors.

Reforms in the banking sector made a big change in the banking sector as it necessitated aligning Indian banking practices with international banking practices that was evolving.

International Trends in Banking

Governments all over the world now recognise that stability in the banking system is very important for the well-being of the country. There is unanimity amongst countries in relation to the need for the safety of banking system, and many new measures were introduced to oversee and ensure health of banking system.

The common issues facing countries of the world with regard to international trade and the issues related to it, financial stability, threats of misuse of banking channels for money laundering and terrorist financing, etc., can be better addressed by the countries by cooperating with each other and also by having common practices to deal and manage these issues. Keeping this in mind, many international forums have been created by the countries over the years to discuss and formulate common approaches and practices by all nations. These forums are official forums where the governments or the central banks of the countries are members. Becoming a member of these forums are mostly voluntary but after joining these forums member countries are expected to comply with the views emerging and the documents created by these forums.

The important international forums which have bearing on financial systems and banks are the following:

1. Bank for International Settlement (BIS)

The international body known as Bank for International Settlement (BIS) was formed in the year 1930 at Basel, in Switzerland. The central banks of the countries are the owners and members of this body. BIS was started as a banker to central banks of the countries for settlements of international payments. Slowly BIS became an international forum for the central banks to share and discuss the common issues facing them in the modern era. BIS's mission is to support central banks' pursuit of monetary and financial stability through international cooperation, and to act as a bank for central banks.

In the year 1974, a German bank—Herstatt bank failed. The Closure of this bank caused trouble for many international banks and affected many economies. This bank failure highlighted the settlement risk between banks due to time zone differences prevailing then. This crisis made the central banks of the countries meet and discuss the issue at apex level. Then a committee of central bankers called the Basel Committee on Banking Supervision was formed under the aegis of Bank for International Settlements (BIS).

The committee had published a few papers from the year 1991 onwards emphasising the need to prescribe the best accounting standards for the banks and also to formulate prudential norms to be followed by banks. The committee later formulated 'Core principles for effective banking supervision' in 1996 and published it in September 1997. The document set out 25 basic principles that the Basel Committee believed should be in place for a supervisory system to be effective. After several revisions, lastly in September 2012, the document now includes 29 principles, covering supervisory powers, the need for early intervention and timely supervisory actions, supervisory expectations of banks, and compliance with supervisory standards.

This document is explaining the role, scope and authority of the central bank of the country in supervising the banks in general and banks dealing in international transactions in particular. It also prescribes that the best accounting standards are fixed for banks to follow, which shall include prudential norms for NPAs and provisions for loan losses.

As recommended by this report, the central banks of the member countries were required to frame rules for accounting standards to be followed by the banks in the country and also formulate prudential norms applicable to identify NPAs and to make provisions for bad loans before declaring profit or loss for the year.

In the year 1980, BIS formed a committee known as the Basel Committee to study the capital structure of the banks with international exposures. The committee recommended 8% minimum capital requirement on risk weighted assets for internationally active banks. The recommendations of the committee were accepted by the governing body of BIS and advised the member countries to implement it in 1988. This was followed up by two more Accords in 2004 and 2010. The purpose is to strengthen the capital base of the banks, their internal accounting system, and the supervisory role of the central banks over the banks in their respective countries. These recommendations are discussed a little later in this chapter.

2. Financial Action Task Force (FATF)

FATF was established as inter-governmental body by the G-7 Summit that was held in Paris in 1989, in response to mounting concern over money laundering, and terrorist financing, as well as the financing of proliferation of weapons of mass destruction. At present FATF have 39 members. India became Observer of FATF in the year 2006 and became a member on 24 June 2010.

The FATF recommendations set out a comprehensive and consistent framework of measures which countries should implement in order to combat money laundering and terrorist financing, as well as the financing of proliferation of weapons of mass destruction. Since Countries have diverse legal, administrative and operational frameworks and different financial systems, FATF recommended that the countries take identical measures to counter these threats.

In April 1990, the FATF issued a report containing a set of Forty Recommendations, which were intended to provide a comprehensive plan of action needed to fight against money laundering. Important recommendations are as under:

1. *Assessing risks and applying a risk-based approach**: Countries should identify, assess, and understand the money laundering and terrorist financing risks for the country, and should take action, including designating an authority or mechanism to coordinate actions to assess risks, and apply resources, aimed at ensuring the risks are mitigated effectively.

2. *Money laundering offence**: Countries should criminalise money laundering on the basis of the Vienna Convention and the Palermo Convention. Countries should apply the crime of money laundering to all serious offences, with a view to including the widest range of predicate offences.

3. *Confiscation and provisional measures**: Countries should adopt measures similar to those set forth in the Vienna Convention, the Palermo Convention, and the Terrorist Financing Convention, including legislative measures, to enable their competent authorities to freeze or seize and confiscate the following, without prejudicing the rights of bona fide third parties: (a) property laundered, (b) proceeds from, or instrumentalities used in or intended for use in money laundering or predicate offences, (c) property that is the proceeds of, or used in, or intended or allocated for use in, the financing of

terrorism, terrorist acts or terrorist organisations, or (d) property of corresponding value.

4. *Terrorist financing offence**: Countries should criminalise terrorist financing on the basis of the Terrorist Financing Convention, and should criminalise not only the financing of terrorist acts but also the financing of terrorist organisations and individual terrorists even in the absence of a link to a specific terrorist act or acts. Countries should ensure that such offences are designated as money laundering predicate offences.

5. *Financial institution secrecy laws*: Countries should ensure that financial institution secrecy laws do not inhibit implementation of the FATF Recommendations.

6. *Customer due diligence**: Financial institutions should be prohibited from keeping anonymous accounts or accounts in obviously fictitious names. Financial institutions should be required to undertake customer due diligence (CDD) measures when:

> (i) establishing business relations; (ii) carrying out occasional transactions:
>
> (i) above the applicable designated threshold (USD/EUR 15,000); or (ii) that are wire transfers in the circumstances covered by the Interpretive Note to Recommendation 16; (iii) there is a suspicion of money laundering or terrorist financing; or (iv) the financial institution has doubts about the veracity or adequacy of previously obtained customer identification data.

The principle that financial institutions should conduct CDD should be set out in law. Each country may determine how it imposes specific CDD obligations, either through law or enforceable means.

The CDD measures to be taken are as follows:

(a) Identifying the customer and verifying that customer's identity using reliable, independent source documents, data or information.

(b) Identifying the beneficial owner, and taking reasonable measures to verify the identity of the beneficial owner, such that the financial institution is satisfied that it knows who the beneficial owner is. For legal persons and arrangements this should include financial institutions understanding the ownership and control structure of the customer.

(c) Understanding and, as appropriate, obtaining information on the purpose and intended nature of the business relationship.

(d) Conducting ongoing due diligence on the business relationship and scrutiny of transactions undertaken throughout the course of that relationship to ensure that the transactions being conducted are consistent with the institution's knowledge of the customer, their business and risk profile, including, where necessary, the source of funds.

7. *Record-keeping*: Financial institutions should be required to maintain, for at least five years, all necessary records on transactions, both domestic and international, to enable them to comply swiftly with information requests from the competent authorities.

8. *Politically exposed persons**: Financial institutions should be required, in relation to foreign politically exposed persons (PEPs) (whether as customer or beneficial owner), in addition to performing normal customer due diligence measures, to:

(a) have appropriate risk-management systems to determine whether the customer or the beneficial owner is a politically exposed person;

(b) obtain senior management approval for establishing (or continuing, for existing customers) such business relationships;

(c) take reasonable measures to establish the source of wealth and source of funds; and

(d) conduct enhanced ongoing monitoring of the business relationship.

9. *Reporting of suspicious transactions**: If a financial institution suspects or has reasonable grounds to suspect that

funds are the proceeds of a criminal activity, or are related to terrorist financing, it should be required, by law, to report promptly its suspicions to the financial intelligence unit (FIU).

10. *Tipping-off and confidentiality*: Financial institutions, their directors, officers and employees should be:

(a) protected by law from criminal and civil liability for breach of any restriction on disclosure of information imposed by contract or by any legislative, regulatory or administrative provision, if they report their suspicions in good faith to the FIU, even if they did not know precisely what the underlying criminal activity was, and regardless of whether illegal activity actually occurred; and

(b) prohibited by law from disclosing ("tipping-off") the fact that a suspicious transaction report (STR) or related information is being filed with the FIU. These provisions are not intended to inhibit information sharing under Recommendation 18.

11. *Financial intelligence units**: Countries should establish a financial intelligence unit (FIU) that serves as a national centre for the receipt and analysis of: (a) suspicious transaction reports; and (b) other information relevant to money laundering, associated predicate offences and terrorist financing, and for the dissemination of the results of that analysis. The FIU should be able to obtain additional information from reporting entities, and should have access on a timely basis to the financial, administrative and law enforcement information that it requires to undertake its functions properly.

Source: FATF

After the 9/11 terrorist attacks on US in 2001, the issues were brought to focus once again and all the nations took notice of the seriousness of these terrorist attacks. It was felt that there is a nexus between money laundering and terrorist funding. Though banks were used for these purposes by criminal elements, banks were not in a position to either identify or curb such activities. It was in this background; in October 2001, the FATF issued the Eight Special Recommendations to deal with the issue of terrorist financing. In October 2004, the FATF published a Ninth Special Recommendation, (thus making total of 49 recommendations) further strengthening the agreed international standards for combating money laundering and terrorist financing.

The nine special recommendations are:

I. Ratification and implementation of UN instruments. Each country should take immediate steps to ratify and to implement fully the 1999 United Nations International Convention for the Suppression of the Financing of Terrorism.

Countries should also immediately implement the United Nations resolutions relating to the prevention and suppression of the financing of terrorist acts, particularly United Nations Security Council Resolution 1373.

II. Criminalising the financing of terrorism and associated money laundering. Each country should criminalise the financing of terrorism, terrorist acts and terrorist organisations. Countries should ensure that such offences are designated as money laundering predicate offences.

III. Freezing and confiscating terrorist assets. Each country should implement measures to freeze without delay funds or other assets of terrorists, those who finance terrorism and terrorist organisations in accordance with the United Nations resolutions relating to the prevention and suppression of the financing of terrorist acts.

Each country should also adopt and implement measures, including legislative ones, which would enable the competent authorities to seize and confiscate property that is the proceeds of, or used in, or intended or allocated for use in, the financing of terrorism, terrorist acts or terrorist organisations.

IV. Reporting suspicious transactions related to terrorism. If financial institutions, or other businesses or entities subject to anti-money laundering obligations, suspect or have reasonable grounds to suspect that funds are linked or related to, or are to be used for terrorism, terrorist acts or by terrorist organisations, they should be required to report promptly their suspicions to the competent authorities.

V. International co-operation: Each country should afford another country, on the basis of a treaty, arrangement or other mechanism for mutual legal assistance or information exchange, the greatest possible measure of assistance in connection with criminal, civil enforcement, and administrative investigations, inquiries and proceedings relating to the financing of terrorism, terrorist acts and terrorist organisations.

Countries should also take all possible measures to ensure that they do not provide safe havens for individuals charged with the financing of terrorism, terrorist acts or terrorist organisations, and should have procedures in place to extradite, where possible, such individuals.

VI. Alternative remittance: Each country should take measures to ensure that persons or legal entities, including agents, that provide a service for the transmission of money or value, including transmission through an informal money or value transfer system or network, should be licensed or registered and subject to all the FATF Recommendations that apply to banks and non-bank financial institutions. Each country should ensure that persons or legal entities that carry out this service illegally are subject to administrative, civil or criminal sanctions.

VII. Wire transfers: Countries should take measures to require financial institutions, including money remitters, to include accurate and meaningful originator information (name, address and account number) on funds transfers and related messages that are sent, and the information should remain with the transfer or related message through the payment chain.

Countries should take measures to ensure that financial institutions, including money remitters, conduct enhanced scrutiny of and monitor for suspicious activity funds transfers which do not contain complete originator information (name, address and account number).

VIII. Non-profit organisations: Countries should review the adequacy of laws and regulations that relate to entities that can be abused for the financing of terrorism. Non-profit organisations are particularly vulnerable, and countries should ensure that they cannot be misused:

(i) by terrorist organisations posing as legitimate entities;

(ii) to exploit legitimate entities as conduits for terrorist financing, including for the purpose of escaping asset freezing measures; and

(iii) to conceal or obscure the clandestine diversion of funds intended for legitimate purposes to terrorist organisations, by terrorist organisations posing as legitimate entities.

IX. Cash couriers: Countries should have measures in place to detect the physical cross-border transportation of currency and bearer negotiable instruments, including a declaration system or other disclosure obligation.

Countries should ensure that their competent authorities have the legal authority to stop or restrain currency or bearer negotiable instruments that are suspected to be related to terrorist financing or money laundering, or that are falsely declared or disclosed.

Source: FATF

These recommendations covered 'know your customer'—KYC guidelines, anti-money laundering—AML measures to be implemented by the banking sector. The recommendations also included the creation of legal set-up by the countries to fight and control money laundering and terrorist finance routed through banking channels.

Based on these recommendations of FATF, Basel committee on Banking Supervision also issued guidelines on Sound management of risks related to money laundering and financing of terrorism—January 2014 (rev. July 2020). Customer Due Diligence (CDD) is explained in the guidelines under the customer acceptance policy as under:

Guidelines

Customer Acceptance Policy

12. A bank should develop and implement clear customer acceptance policies and procedures to identify the types of customers that are likely to pose a higher risk of ML and FT pursuant to the bank's risk assessment. When assessing risk, a

bank should consider the factors relevant to the situation, such as a customer's background, occupation (including a public or high-profile position), source of income and wealth, country of origin and residence (when different), products used, nature and purpose of accounts, linked accounts, business activities and other customer-oriented risk indicators in determining what is the level of overall risk and the appropriate measures to be applied to manage those risks.

13. Such policies and procedures should require basic due diligence for all customers and commensurate due diligence as the level of risk associated with the customer varies. For proven lower risk situations, simplified measures may be permitted, if this is allowed by law. For example, the application of basic account-opening procedures may be appropriate for an individual who expects to maintain a small account balance and use it to conduct routine retail banking transactions. It is important that the customer acceptance policy is not so restrictive that it results in a denial of access by the general public to banking services, especially for people who are financially or socially disadvantaged. The FATF Financial Inclusion Guidance provides useful guidelines on designing AML/CFT procedures that are not overly restrictive to the financially or socially disadvantaged.

14. Where the risks are higher, banks should take enhanced measures to mitigate and manage those risks. Enhanced due diligence may be essential for an individual planning to maintain a large account balance and conduct regular cross-border wire transfers or an individual who is a politically exposed person (PEP). In particular, such enhanced due diligence is required for foreign PEPs. Decisions to enter into or pursue business relationships with higher-risk customers should require the application of enhanced due diligence measures, such as approval to enter into or continue such relationships, being taken by senior management. The bank's customer acceptance policy should also define circumstances under which the bank would not accept a new business relationship or would terminate an existing one.

Source: Basel Committee on Banking Supervision.

FATF recommendations had great impact on banker-customer relationship which hitherto was considered confidential and based on practices developed over the years. The money laundering activities which were hitherto hidden by the secrecy clauses of banking practices, and the new menace of terrorism destabilising the peace and progress of the countries, has forced the governments to redefine banker customer relationship and create legal system to fight against them.

All the countries are now made the necessary changes in their legal system and made the banks to follow the new standards of customer relationships. Banks are made responsible to identify and report suspicious transactions to the authorities thereby giving leads which may result in identifying the offences. These changes are in the areas of identification and monitoring of financial transactions in customers' accounts. Commonly these are called know your customer (KYC) guidelines, and anti-money laundering (AML) measures and combating the financing of terrorism (CFT).

The implementations of these guidelines in our country are discussed little later in this chapter under Indian responses.

3. Financial Stability Board

The Financial Stability Board is an international body promoted by G20 nations of the world in the year 2009. Our country is also a member of G20 nations. This Board is at Basel in Switzerland and is formed for the purpose of recommending financial reforms to be introduced by member countries for ensuring financial stability in the global economy. This is considered as important in view of financial crisis of 2008 faced by USA and European countries. This financial crisis which is also known as the Subprime crisis originated at USA.

In USA, banking sector has two segments called the deposit taking banks and investment banks. Deposit taking banks were regulated by the monetary authority but the investment banks which are somewhat comparable to NBFCs of India in their operations, are not regulated to that extent. During housing boom in USA (2001-07), few new derivative products anchored on housing loans were created known as Mortgage-Backed

Securities (MBS) and Collateralized Debt Obligations (CDO) and traded by the investment banks and hedge funds. The investment banks and the hedge funds are called the 'shadow banking sector'. Trading in these derivatives became a huge market but mostly remained unregulated by govt. or monetary authority. The crisis started in this market and then enveloped all financial segments including deposit taking banks.

It started with the Lehman Bros an investment bank and few others. This had a cascading effect on financial and banking system of USA and affected many European countries also, as their financial system was interconnected with USA due to their exposure to securities of US Investment Banks and Hedge Funds.

The subprime crisis in USA started in the financial segments of investment banks and hedge funds and subsequently the deposit banks and insurance companies were also affected. Many financial companies were closed and many are merged with others. US Govt. was forced to provide bail-out packages to few banks and others to save them in order to save the economy. US Govt. approved a $700 billion emergency bailout package in September 2008 to the banking system. Some European governments were also forced to bail-out few banks by providing funds to them to come out of the crisis.

The Financial Stability Board is created to find a solution for this type of financial crisis that may upset the financial world in the future and create recession in the economies of the countries.

Here we must understand that any big financial crisis in any economy will have a crippling effect on the economy. Country's economy cannot bounce back immediately due to many reasons. The reason is that the resolution system in place in most countries moves slowly. The legal system is generally slow to react and set right the wrong doings. When a bank or FI is sick or paralysed, it affects others and unless the problem is quickly resolved, the bad impact on others will linger on and in the process, the economy slows down. This means that the issue of crisis hit bank of FI shall have to be resolved at the earliest. Either it shall be quickly revived by infusing funds, if required, or closed down and quickly liquidated. This type of quick resolution of failed banks or FIs will enable the economy to move on without carrying the burden of failed banks or FI on its shoulder.

FSB has advised the countries to create a proactive system and put it in place to identify the possible risk areas and to mitigate hardships by making the resolution mechanism quick to respond and resolve the issues.

—FSB Press release 12 November 2010

G20 Leaders endorse Financial Stability Board policy framework for addressing systemically important financial institutions The G20 Leaders at the Seoul Summit on 11-12 November endorsed the Financial Stability Board's (FSB) policy framework for Reducing the moral hazard of systemically important financial institutions (SIFIs), including the work processes and timelines set out in the report submitted to the Summit.

SIFIs are financial institutions whose disorderly failure, because of their size, complexity and systemic interconnectedness, would cause significant disruption to the wider financial system and economic activity. FSB jurisdictions have agreed to put in place the policy framework to reduce the risks and externalities associated with domestic and global systemically important financial institutions in their jurisdictions.

As the report states:

The policy framework for SIFIs should combine:

- a resolution framework and other measures to ensure that all financial institutions can be resolved safely, quickly and without destabilising the financial system and exposing the taxpayer to the risk of loss;
- a requirement that SIFIs and initially in particular global SIFIs (G-SIFIs) have higher loss absorbency capacity to reflect the greater risks that these institutions pose to the global financial system;
- more intensive supervisory oversight for financial institutions which may pose systemic risk;

- robust core financial market infrastructures to reduce contagion risk from the failure of individual institutions; and
- other supplementary prudential and other requirements as determined by the national authorities.

Additionally, home jurisdictions for G-SIFIs should:

- enable a rigorous co-ordinated assessment of the risks facing the G-SIFIs through international supervisory colleges;
- make international recovery and resolution planning mandatory for G-SIFIs and negotiate institution-specific crisis cooperation agreements within cross-border crisis management groups;
- subject their G-SIFI policy measures to review by the proposed Peer Review Council.

The report issued today contains further recommendations and timelines for putting this framework into place. The FSB and national authorities, in consultation with relevant standard setters, will determine by mid-2011 those institutions to which the FSB G-SIFI recommendations will initially apply. The Peer Review Council will conduct its initial assessment of national G-SIFI policies by end-2012.

Source: Press release by FSB.

When we go through the above press release by FSB, we can observe that the Board has come out with a concept of SIFI and G-SIFI which is defined as—SIFIs are financial institutions whose disorderly failure, because of their size, complexity and systemic interconnectedness, would cause significant disruption to the wider financial system and economic activity. Hence it is important to identify such financial institutions in the country and monitor them more closely. FSB is also considering enhanced capital requirement prescriptions for them so that they have better capability to withstand the loss.

Further on 15 October 2014, FSB communicated to all member countries "The Key Attributes of Effective Resolution Regimes for Financial Institutions" for implementation.

The Key Attributes set out by FSB have twelve essential features that should be part of the resolution regimes of all countries. They are:

1. Scope
2. Resolution authority
3. Resolution powers
4. Set-off, netting, collateralisation, segregation of client assets
5. Safeguards
6. Funding of firms in resolution
7. Legal framework conditions for cross-border cooperation
8. Crisis Management Groups (CMGs)
9. Institution-specific cross-border cooperation agreements
10. Resolvability assessments
11. Recovery and resolution planning
12. Access to information and information sharing.

Under the 'scope', member countries are required to identify the different types of financial institutions existing in the country. This shall include all types of banking, insurance, and other financial institutions. All of them shall be brought under the resolution regime. This also requires identifying systemically important financial institutions (SIFIs) in the country. SIFIs are financial institutions whose failure will create significant and critical impact on the economy of the country.

Countries are required to create a 'resolution authority' to deal with the resolution matters of the financial institutions under stress. The resolution authority shall have the necessary powers to handle the cases depending on their present status. The powers of resolution authority shall also have powers to carry out 'bail-in'.

Resolution mechanism means a system in place to take care of failed or weak financial institutions quickly and in time bound manner. A weak financial institution shall not be allowed to continue and shall be quickly put back to health, if possible, or closed down quickly so that the financial system of the country is not burdened with its continued sickness that may affect the whole system.

All these developments at international level have substantial effects on the banking system. We can find that the measures taken by the central banks and the governments of the countries reflect the changed perception about banking and its importance to the economy. Governments cannot secure all banks in the country and provide guarantee to the public for the safety of their money in the bank. But governments have moral responsibility to ensure that the banking sector in the country is managed properly to safeguard the interests of the public.

The statement of bank of England given below definitely reflects the present view of the central banks:

> People rely on banks in their day to day lives, whether it's for looking after their money or helping them pay for things.
>
> Not surprisingly, then, if banks stopped working, the entire economy would grind to a halt. It's the Bank of England's job to make sure that banks (and the entire financial system) continue to work in a safe and sound way.
>
> As part of this, we put a lot of effort into reducing the chances of a bank getting into financial difficulty in the first place.
>
> But it is not possible to prevent all banks from ever failing.
>
> Just like any other type of business, it is important that a bank that doesn't make a profit is able to fail. (Bank of England)

Thus, the trend and changes that have taken place in the international level and the recommendations of the international forums discussed herein above can be listed as under:

1. Introduction of KYC norms for bank accounts and the safeguards against the menace of money laundering and terrorist funding, using banks as the medium.

2. Best supervisory practices by central banks—Prudential norms for banks and best standards of accounting system.
3. Capital prescriptions for banks.
4. Resolution mechanism to take immediate effective steps to resolve weak financial institutions.

Indian Response to the above Developments

India moved towards globalisation of our economy from the year 1991 onwards. Till the year 1990, India was isolated and had insulated itself from the global changes taking place. Our financial system and banks were isolated and were following own experiences to propel growth of the economy. But once the GOI has decided to globalise our economy all the above noted changes became necessary to be implemented in the country in order to follow the best standards accepted by the global community. GOI had constituted many committees to study into these issues and recommend transition to globalisation. The First Narasimham Committee (*Committee on the Financial System—CFS*) 1991, set up by GOI made its recommendations that the RBI and the banks in India should adopt the best practices for banking as developed and adopted globally.

Let us now study the past practices/experiences and the transition of Indian banking to global standards.

Our country-initiated reforms in the banking sector from the year 1991 onwards. In the process, Indian banks are made to adopt the international standards in their working. These standards are mainly in the following area:

1. KYC Norms

Financial Action Task Force (FATF) an international body of Nations made certain recommendations to control such menace by better control on banking operations and by legal provisions to bring the culprits to books in 1990. The Basel Committee on Banking Supervision also issued a paper on Customer Due Diligence (CDD) for banks, with indicative suggestions. Banks have been advised to ensure that a proper policy framework on

'Know Your Customer' and Anti-Money Laundering measures is formulated and put in place.

International community is concerned with money laundering and terrorist activities since long. After the 9/11 terrorist attacks on US in 2001, the issues were brought to focus and all the nations took notice of the seriousness of these maladies. It was felt that there is a nexus between money laundering and terrorist funding. Though banks were used for these purposes by criminal elements, banks were not in a position to either identify or curb such activities.

In view of the above, GOI enacted Prevention of Money Laundering Act 2002 (PMLA 2002), a new legislation to fight against money laundering and created FIU-IND (Financial Intelligence Unit of India), a statutory body under Ministry of Finance to implement the provisions of PMLA. This Act defined the offence of money laundering as under:

What is a Money Laundering offence?

1. A person shall be guilty of offence of money-laundering if such person is found to have directly or indirectly attempted to indulge or knowingly assisted or knowingly is a party or is actually involved in one or more of the following processes or activities connected with proceeds of crime, namely: (a) concealment; or (b) possession; or (c) acquisition; or (d) use; or (e) projecting as untainted property; or (f) claiming as untainted property, in any manner whatsoever.
2. The process or activity connected with proceeds of crime is a continuing activity and continues till such time a person is directly or indirectly enjoying the proceeds of crime by its concealment or possession or acquisition or use or projecting it as untainted property or claiming it as untainted property in any manner whatsoever.

Source: FIU-IND

RBI issued guidelines to banks on 'Know Your Customer' (KYC) in 2002 and issued detailed guidelines in the year 2004 advising banks to have 'Know Your Customer Policy' based on guidelines.

RBI has stated the objectives of the guidelines as under:

> The objective of KYC guidelines is to prevent banks from being used, intentionally or unintentionally, by criminal elements for money laundering activities. KYC procedures also enable banks to know/understand their customers and their financial dealings better which in turn help them manage their risks prudently.

The effect of KYC norms introduced in banking has been that the holders of black money or illegal money cannot deposit these monies in the bank for the fear of detection. Similarly, persons cannot hold benami accounts in the bank and park their unaccounted money in those accounts.

Banks are now duty bound to check the financial transactions that are taking place in the accounts and are required to submit report on suspicious transactions and some other transactions to FIU-IND.

At present the following periodical information are submitted to FIU-IND by banks and others:

What type of information is required to be furnished under PMLA?

Every reporting entity is required to furnish information about:

- all cash transactions of the value of more than ten lakh rupees or its equivalent in foreign currency;
- all series of cash transactions integrally connected to each other which have been individually valued below rupees ten lakh or its equivalent in foreign currency where such series of transactions have taken place within a month and the monthly aggregate exceeds an amount of ten lakh rupees or its equivalent in foreign currency;
- all transactions involving receipts by non-profit organizations of value more than rupees ten lakh, or its equivalent in foreign currency;

- all cash transactions where forged or counterfeit currency notes or bank notes have been used as genuine or where any forgery of a valuable security or a document has taken place facilitating the transactions;
- all suspicious transactions whether or not made in cash;
- all cross-border wire transfers of the value of more than five lakh rupees or its equivalent in foreign currency where either the origin or destination of fund is in India;
- all purchase and sale by any person of immovable property valued at fifty lakh rupees or more that is registered by the reporting entity, as the case may be.

Source: FIU-IND

In our country, terrorist activities come under the purview of UAPA 1967 (Unlawful Activities (Prevention) Act, 1967). In view of increased threats of terrorist activities around the globe and in view of many resolutions passed by Security Council of United Nations, The Unlawful Activities (Prevention) Act, 1967 (UAPA) has been amended by the Unlawful Activities (Prevention) Amendment Act, 2008. Government has since issued an Order dated August 27, 2009 detailing the procedure for implementation of Section 51A of the Unlawful Activities (Prevention) Act, 1967 relating to the purposes of prevention of, and for coping with terrorist activities.

Section 51A in The Unlawful Activities (Prevention) Act, 1967

[51A Certain powers of the Central Government. —For the prevention of, and for coping with terrorist activities, the Central Government shall have power to—

(a) freeze, seize or attach funds and other financial assets or economic resources held by, on behalf of or at the direction of the individuals or entities listed in the Schedule to the Order, or any other person engaged in or suspected to be engaged in terrorism;

(b) prohibit any individual or entity from making any funds, financial assets or economic resources or related services available for the benefit of the individuals or entities listed in the Schedule to the Order or any other person engaged in or suspected to be engaged in terrorism;

(c) prevent the entry into or the transit through India of individuals listed in the Schedule to the Order or any other person engaged in or suspected to be engaged in terrorism.]

UAPA deals with terrorist activities, financing of terrorist activities and provides for punishment and also seizure of terrorist proceeds or assets.

At present all the recommendations of FATF have been implemented by GOI and RBI in the country.

2. Prudential Norms

Prudential norms are the accounting standards adopted by banks based on which they report their financial status/ accounts. Earlier to the introduction these norms, each country had followed different standards to publish financial accounts.

In line with the international practices and as per the recommendations made by the Committee on the Financial System (Chairman Shri M. Narasimham), the Reserve Bank of India has introduced, in a phased manner, prudential norms for income recognition, asset classification and provisioning for the advances portfolio of the banks so as to move towards greater consistency and transparency in the published accounts.

Prudential norms (also known as income recognition and asset classification—IRAC norms) pertaining to income recognition, asset classification and provisioning for banks were introduced for the first time by Reserve Bank of India during financial year 1992-93, i.e., year ended 31st March 1993 in line with the international practices. (These norms are discussed under chapter—functions of RBI)

RBI guidelines defined NPA and prescribed rules for income recognition and provisioning as under:

Non-performing assets and assets classification. An asset, including a leased asset, becomes non-performing when it ceases to generate income for the bank. A 'non-performing asset' (NPA) was defined as a credit facility in respect of which the interest and/or instalment of principal has remained overdue for 90 days (w.e.f. March 31, 2004). RBI also issued guidelines for classifying the loan assets into standard, substandard, doubtful and loss assets.

Income recognition. The policy of income recognition has to be based on the record of recovery. Internationally income from non-performing assets (NPA) is not recognised on accrual basis but is booked as income only when it is actually received. Therefore, the banks should not charge and take to income account interest on any NPA.

Provisions for NPAs. RBI has issued detailed instructions to banks for making provisions for NPAs. Instruction as to when NPA shall be considered as doubtful or loss asset has also been prescribed.

RBI introduced these norms as per the requirement under Basel Committee report on 'Core principles for effective banking supervision'. BIS also advised the central banks to prescribe prudential norms in the working of the banks so that the working of banks becomes more transparent. Prudential norms are defined as the general norms issued by the central bank of the country for the proper and accountable functioning of banks.

These are the stringent norms trying to make the financial statements of the banks transparent. The financial statements thus will show the actual level of bad loans and the actual profit or loss for the year.

Prudential norms have made a big difference to banking system in our country. Till then banks were liberal in identifying bad loans and their financial statements generally did not reveal the strength of the bank or its weak loan portfolio. Prudential norms of income recognition coupled with asset classification norms made it incumbent on the banks to reveal the correct position as there is no scope for avoiding the norms. Ninety days default norm for a loan account is specific with no room for anyone to interpret it differently. The loan shall be classified as NPA and the unrecovered interest charges in such accounts cannot be taken as profit for the bank. This norm made the bank to suffer twice for the loan account becoming NPA. Bank cannot book the interest on accrual basis but take it only on actual recovery basis. Further as the loan account is now to be identified as NPA, the rigors of provisioning norms will apply. Bank shall have to make provision for the NPA out of current years earning.

It took more than a decade for Indian banks to recover from the shocks. When the prudential norms were introduced first time, it changed the perceptions about banks. Many banks that were considered as big and leading banks commanding good market reputation became weak banks overnight once the true level of their NPAs were made public. Some banks were in serious trouble and went into red due to loss of income and new requirements for provisions.

Prudential norms have become very important now to identify the strong and weak banks. Banks with huge NPA are the weak banks as their profitability is seriously impacted due to loss of income and requirement of bad loan provisions. This also eroded their capital base making them as weak banks. Further constant vigil by the bank managements became necessary as the results of their loaning activities are reflected immediately in their yearly balance sheets. Indian banks which were hitherto unmindful of their capital funds suddenly woke up and realised the importance of capital funds. If the bank is continuously in red then its capital will be eroded or wiped out and may be forced by market forces or the supervisory authority to close down.

Prudential norms have definitely changed the perceptions of govt., RBI, market and others about the health of the banks and also forces govt. and RBI to take timely corrective actions to safeguard the health of bank thus safeguarding bank depositors.

After the banking reforms undertaken in our country from the year 1991, workings of the banking sector were streamlined and made responsive to weak areas in their workings. We can observe that the performances of banking sector as a whole improved after the year 2000 and this buoyancy remained till the year 2014. Banks had minimum NPAs and banking growth was very good on all parameters. But from the year 2015 NPAs of the banks started rising to an alarming level in few banks. Credit expansion by banks till 2014 started showing stress situation. There were few misdeeds also which accentuated the situation. Suddenly many banks ran in to trouble as their NPAs shot up due to some large loan accounts are declared as NPAs. RBI and govt. have reacted to these developments and have taken many measures to control the damage to banking system.

Thus, the prudential norms are responsible to identify weaknesses in banks' loan assets to enable RBI and govt. to take corrective steps and control the situations. Ultimately this measure goes to safeguard the interest of bank depositors.

3. Basel Accords for Capital Structure of Banks

As stated earlier the Basel Committee on Banking Supervision was formed under the aegis of Bank for International Settlements (BIS). The recommendations of the committee were accepted by the governments of participating Central Banks and came to be known as Basel Accords.

The first Accord known as Basel Accord I was reached in the year 1988 and it has attempted to take in to account the credit risk and market risk faced by the banks. This international Accord identified that the capital base of a bank is crucial for it to withstand any adverse developments and for its survival. It prescribed that bank shall have minimum of 8% capital to their risk weighted assets. These minimum capital requirements are applicable for the banks participating in international trade.

Risk weighted assets means the loan assets or any other type of assets of the bank valued by taking into consideration of the credit risk involved and the security available to secure the loan. It also involves credit rating of the borrower, value of securities, availability of collateral securities to secure the loan, unsecured portion of loan, etc. RBI has prescribed rules and norms based on which the loan and other assets of the banks are valued and total risk weighted assets of the banks are arrived at. It will be different from the balance sheet figures.

Basel I norms were introduced in the year 1993 along with Prudential Norms for the first time in the country. RBI has fixed 9% minimum capital on risk weighted basis as against 8% stipulated by the Basel Accord I. RBI has allowed five years' time to banks to comply with the new capital requirement. Indian banks were found to be weak in capital. Even for public sector banks GOI had to infuse large amounts of additional capital to increase the capital base to the desired level. India became Basel I compliant in the year 1999.

Basel Accord I was followed by two more Accords namely Basel Accord II (2004) and Basel Accord III (2010). These Accords were the further improvements over Basel Accord I based on some new developments necessitating improvements in the Accord.

Basel Accord II

Basel Committee on Banking Supervision issued fresh set of guidelines in June 2004. These guidelines are known as Basel Accord II. This was issued in continuation and as further refined and improved guidelines given in Basel Accord I. Though the basic theme for capital requirement for banks at 8% is same, there are certain improvements over the Basel Accord I in view of this, and it replaced the Basel I.

Basel II besides adding the operational risk for determining the level of capital required also made some major changes in the manner in which the banking sector is supervised and monitored by central banks. It gave more importance to the supervisory role of the central banks in evaluating and monitoring the risk profiles of the banks.

Basel II spelt out the approach for bank strengthening as three pillars requirement:

1. **Capital requirement**: Under the first pillar, capital requirement for credit risk, market risk, and operational risk is to be provided. Newly added Operational risk is defined as the risk of loss resulting from inadequate or failed internal processes, people and systems or

from external events. Operational risk also includes legal risk, like; exposure to fines, penalties, or punitive damages resulting from supervisory actions, as well as private settlements.

2. **Supervisory review:** Under second pillar, supervisory review and internal control of banks are given due recognition. Controllers and management are advised to review the adequacy of systems and control and decide on the level of capital requirement for the bank. Controller can demand a higher level of capital for a bank based on its review of the bank, if considered necessary.
3. **Enhanced disclosure:** Under the third pillar, enhanced disclosure of more relevant areas/information about the bank and also observance of market discipline was prescribed for the banks. Transparency is considered very essential and banks shall have to follow internationally accepted accounting standards and make the information available to the public. This is to make the bank management more responsible and open for appraisal and criticism by public and this will act as a check on the banks.

Basel II is the transformation of original Basel I guidelines as Basel I was basically about capital requirement of banks on two risks: credit risk and market risk. It was more of a mathematical formula. But the Basel II is more of supervisory control and improvement in banks internal management. The capital requirement under Basel II remains unchanged at 8% on risk weighted assets. Though under Basel II, three risks: credit risk, market risk and operational risk are specified for capital requirement, the pillar two widens the scope to further capital requirement for many other types of risks depending on the central bank's views on the matter. It enjoins the Central Banks and the banks to develop risk management capabilities in-house, so that the banks are adequately protected against financial crisis.

Basel II was issued in the year 2004 and all the member countries were to implement the Accord and make necessary changes by the year 2008-09. Our country has adopted the Accord immediately and RBI has announced that commercial banks in the country will be Basel II compliant by March 2009.

RBI had prescribed minimum capital adequacy ratio of 9% for Indian banks. The CAR of banks in India from 2009 to 2011 is given in the following table which shows that the banks in the country have complied with the requirement and are comfortably capitalized.

Table 2.1: Average CAR for Banks as per Basel II: From 2009 to 2011

Capital Adequacy (%)—Basel II as on March 31

Sl. No.	Group	2009	2010	2011
1	SBI & Subsidiaries	13.34	13.51	12.66
2	Nationalized banks	13.22	13.29	13.49
3	Old private sector banks	14.54	14.90	14.15
4	New private sector banks	15.34	17.40	16.28
5	Foreign banks	26.24	26.17	25.90

Source: RBI

Basel III

Basel III is a new global regulatory standard on bank capital adequacy and liquidity agreed by the members of the Basel Committee on Banking Supervision. The third of the Basel Accords was developed in a response to the deficiencies in financial regulation revealed by the global financial crisis. There was a rude shock to the banking sector in early 2008. Subprime crisis in USA erupted and a major investment bank; Lehman Brothers failed and so also few other smaller banks.

This crisis and the episode brought out the disturbing fact that despite Basel Accord compliance, the weakness in the asset liability management of concerned banks was not detected or cleverly hidden. Hence this exposed the limitations of the Accord guidelines which were a serious matter for the Central Banks. This has forced the Committee to revisit the provisions of the Accord and further strengthen it by more stringent norms in the new Basel III Accord.

Basel III has retained the three-pillar approach of Basel II and has improved on it. The committee has kept the capital at 8% on risk weighted assets which takes care of credit risk, market risk and the operational risk as in Basel II. But there are certain major changes now prescribed. The important changes are Basel III proposed to strengthen the capital base 8% by adding capital buffers of 2.5% thus making the total capital requirement to 10.5%. Basel III also introduced new regulatory requirements on bank liquidity and bank leverage.

The new leverage and liquidity ratios were introduced as a measure to supplement the risk-based minimum capital requirements and to ensure that adequate funding is maintained in case of crisis.

Bank for International Settlements (BIS) has stated that:

"Basel III" is a comprehensive set of reform measures, developed by the Basel Committee on Banking Supervision, to strengthen the regulation, supervision and risk management of the banking sector. These measures aim to:

- improve the banking sector's ability to absorb shocks arising from financial and economic stress, whatever the source;
- improve risk management and governance;
- strengthen banks' transparency and disclosures.

Main Features of Basel III

1. The components of tier 2 capital have been streamlined.
2. Tier 3 capital has been eliminated.
3. Additional capital charge in the form of Capital Conservation Buffer (CCB) of 2.5% has been introduced. It is prescribed that the banks shall build this buffer in good years so that in the years of stress it will provide relief to the banks. The additional capital charge has to come from common equity tier 1 capital. This effectively increases the total capital requirement to 10.5% (8% + 2.5%) as against 8% in Basel II.
4. Committee has specifically prescribed Liquidity Ratios and Leverage Ratios for the banks (which were already a subject of second pillar under Basel II).

This was necessitated as it was observed that even the strong banks failed because of weakness in their liquidity management.

5. Basel III has re-emphasized the supervisory role of the central banks under pillar 3 to strengthen regulation review and supervise the bank's capital adequacy and bank's practices and preparedness and prescribe if felt necessary higher level of capital requirement for a bank.

The G20 leaders have officially endorsed the Basel III framework on 11-12 November 2010. G20 is the group of 19 major countries of the world and the European Union. India is also a member of this group. The final guidelines have been issued by Reserve Bank of India for implementation of Basel III guidelines on 2 May 2012.

Implementation of Basel Accord for Capital of Banks

RBI has issued guidelines in 2012 making it effective from January 1, 2013 for complying Basel III guidelines in a phased manner, to be completed by March 2019. Indian banks were already Basel II complaint in 2009.

The CRAR of Indian banks group wise at 2013 was as under:

Average CRAR (Capital to Risk Weighted Assets Ratio) for All Banks—March 2009 to March 2013

Sl. No.	Group	2009	2010	2011	2012	2013
	All SCBs	13.97	14.54	14.19	14.24	13.88
1	SBI & Subsidiaries	13.96	13.46	12.25	13.70	12.67
2	Nationalized banks	13.24	13.18	13.47	13.03	12.26
3	Old private sector banks	14.74	14.85	14.55	14.12	13.73
4	New private sector banks	15.33	18.03	16.87	16.66	17.52
5	Foreign banks	14.32	17.26	16.97	16.75	17.88

Source: From a profile of banks, 2012-13 by RBI.

The above table depicts comfortable position of Indian banking system as the average CRAR of all scheduled commercial banks is at 13.88% (regulatory capital requirements is 9%) at March 2013, but due to changes in the components of tier 1 and tier 2 capital and also the proposed increase in CET 1 capital required additional capital. From the year 2015 to 2018 public sector banks faced steep increase in NPAs. This has affected the profitability of these banks and also the bad loan provision has gone up. GOI had to infuse sizeable additional capital in public sector banks.

As per information available, GOI has provided additional capital to public sector banks from the year 2010 to the year 2019 as under:

Financial year	₹ in crores	Financial year	₹ in crores
2010-11	20117	2015-16	25000
2011-12	12000	2016-17	24997
2012-13	12517	2017-18	90000
2013-14	14000	2018-19	65000
2014-15	6990		
Total	65624	Total	204997

Source: RBI

CRAR of Indian commercial banks as at March 2019 and March 2020 were as under:

As at March 2020 scheduled commercial banks as a group had CRAR of 14.7% under Basel III framework. This is as against the minimum prescription of 11.5% (9% + 2.5% capital conservation buffer). RBI has prescribed minimum 9% capital for Indian banks as against the Basel Committee stipulation of 8%.

Further 11.5% is the minimum level and the banks will require higher percentage of capital for growth and leverage. Public sector banks CRAR was 12.9%. This is after the infusion of capital by GOI. Hence it is expected that public banks may require more capital infusion in the next few years.

4. Financial Stability Board Recommendations

Banking sector stability in the country—Past experience of our country about bank failures

In the history of banking in India in 19th and first half of 20th centuries, banking business was mainly in the hands

Table 2.2: Component-wise Capital Adequacy of SCBs

(As at end-March)

(Amount in ₹ crore)

	PSBs		PVBs		FBs		SCBs	
	2019	2020	2019	2020	2019	2020	2019	2020
1. Capital Funds	6,38,553	6,99,872	6,01,046	6,54,772	1,69,598	1,88,660	14,09,197	15,43,304
i) Tier I Capital	5,18,963	5,65,830	5,27,007	5,80,718	1,59,184	1,72,883	12,05,154	13,19,431
ii) Tier II Capital	1,19,590	1,34,042	74,039	74,054	10,413	15,777	2,04,043	2,23,873
2. Risk Weighted Assets	52,32,524	54,46,253	37,39,838	39,56,956	8,74,432	10,65,869	98,46,793	1,04,69,078
3. CRAR (1 as % of 2)	12.2	12.9	16.1	16.5	19.4	17.7	14.3	14.7
Of which: Tier I	9.9	10.4	14.1	14.7	18.2	16.2	12.2	12.6
Tier II	2.3	2.5	2.0	1.9	1.2	1.5	2.1	2.1

Source: Off-site returns, RBI.

of private individuals and firms known as indigenous bankers. Later at the end of 19th century, many banks incorporated as limited companies came into existence. There were few govt. banks like Bank of Bombay, Bank of Madras, and Bank of Calcutta.

In the history of banking in India, similar to the history of other countries, bank failures were a regular feature. During the great depression and two world wars, many banks have failed. The depositors of the failed banks lost their monies. The concept of central banking authority came up in most of the countries only during the beginning of 20th century.

In our country, RBI was established in the year 1935 as the central bank of the country. Over the years RBI has been vested with many powers over the banking industry for the purpose of safeguarding bank depositor's interest and also to maintain stability in the economy. The real authority of RBI on banking sector became effective in the year 1949, after nationalization of the RBI and after passing of Banking Companies Act, 1949 (later renamed as Banking Regulation Act, 1949). From the year 1960, RBI was given authority to merge weak banks with stronger banks either through persuasion or by forced mergers.

Till the 1960s bank failure was a regular feature in India as can be seen from the table below:

Years	No. of banks failed
1913 to 1922	123
1923 to 1936	357
1937 to 1939	255
1940 to 1946	392
1947 to 1951	242
1952 to 1953	62
1954 to 1959	106
1960 to 1966	48
Total	1585

Bank failures were mainly due to weak financials and poor and mismanagements of these banks. Further, due to the effect of First World War, the Great Depression, Second World War, and the partition of country, large number of banks failed. During the period 1913 to 1966, total of 1585 banks failed as above.

In the year 1938 a major Kerala based—Travancore National and Quilon Bank (TNQ Bank) was liquidated on the orders of Dewan of Travancore. This bank was formed in the year 1937 by amalgamating two banks—Travancore National Bank (established in 1912) and Quilon Bank (established in 1919) which was considered as greatest banking amalgamation in south India. The failure of this bank created a scare in south India, and the role of RBI came under public and media gaze. This also led to the collapse of more than 60 small banks at that time.

Again, in the year 1960 two more fairly big banks failed. They were; Palai Central Bank in Kerala and Laxmi Bank of Akola.

Palai Central Bank was founded in 1927 as a commercial bank with its headquarters in Palai, Kerala. This bank grew up to become the biggest bank in Kerala and the 17th largest among the 94 scheduled banks in India. It was ordered to be liquidated in 1960 by Kerala High Court on a petition moved by the Reserve Bank of India.

Failure of these two banks in 1960 triggered some action by the govt. RBI was given powers to enforce merger and amalgamations of banks to protect the depositors. RBI started using its authority to merge banks from the year 1961 onwards.

The policy of strengthening of the banking sector through compulsory amalgamation and mergers helped in consolidating the banking sector. Between the years 1961 and 1966 RBI managed to merge nearly 202 banks and streamlined the banking system. As a result of this, number of banks in 1967 came down to 91 from 566. Thus, RBI kept bank failures under check. After 1967 no commercial bank was closed and RBI managed to merge weak banks with strong banks.

Another positive outcome of the failure of these two banks in 1960 was the starting of deposit insurance scheme in the country. Deposit Insurance Corporation of India was started in the year 1962 as a subsidiary of RBI, to protect depositors of banks by providing insurance cover. This deposit insurance scheme is discussed later in a separate chapter.

Govt. of India nationalised 14 banks in the year 1969 and six banks in 1980. However, the objective of nationalisation of these banks was not for the purpose of protecting the interest of depositors. Nationalisation was part of govt.'s move to exercise social control on these banks and to ensure that the bank lending is directed to the sectors to support the govt. policies to develop the country. However, as the govt. became the owner of these banks, govt. is morally bound to protect the interests of the depositors of these banks. Though this is an unwritten guarantee from the govt., it has helped these banks to attract huge deposits and grow very fast. Deposits in these banks are perceived as backed by sovereign guarantee.

After these nationalised banks came on the scene, RBI found it easier to merge troubled banks with them. RBI managed to merge many weak banks with nationalized banks. From 1969 to 2010, 38 banks were merged with other banks. Two of the subsidiaries of SBI were merged with SBI in 2008 and 2010, which was a strategic move by SBI.

Other 36 mergers were initiated by RBI. Most of these mergers were forced mergers and weak banks were merged with nationalised banks to protect the depositors of the weak banks. There was one nationalized bank, New Bank of India, which became weak and was merged with PNB a bigger nationalized bank in 1993. Only five mergers have been voluntary when weak banks were taken over by bigger private sector banks.

Few more banks were merged between the years 2010 to 2017. ING Vysya Bank was taken over by Kotak Mahindra Bank in 2014. SBI merged six of its subsidiary banks with it in 2017.

Few more mergers of public sector banks initiated by Govt. of India have taken place in the year 2018 and 2019. (This is discussed in the earlier chapter—present banking structure)

Hence after the merger authority was given to RBI, no commercial bank was closed. RBI always managed to merge the weak commercial banks with stronger public sector or private sector banks. This has imparted some stability to banking system in the country.

Bank Failures in Cooperative Sector

However, bank failure in urban coop sector is still a continuing problem as RBI could not merge weak coop banks and protect depositor's interest. This was mainly due to dual controlling system on these banks by RBI and the state governments. In view of this, many urban coop banks were closed. Depositors of these banks have lost their monies and the failures in UCBs are continuing.

As per DICGC it has paid claims to 351 failed urban coop banks since its inception in 1962 to March 2019.

Failures of urban coop banks are not making national news as they were small in size and with limited area of operation in some districts. However, in the year 2001 failure of Madhavpura Mercantile Coop Bank in Ahmedabad which was a fairly big bank made big news. This bank was ultimately closed and the depositors have lost some portion of their deposits. This coop bank was involved in financing a big share market operator Harshad Mehta.

In the year 2019 a large urban coop bank, Punjab and Maharashtra Coop Bank ran into trouble and this necessitated the intervention by RBI in restricting the bank in its operations. RBI has placed some restrictions on the depositors of the bank for withdrawing their deposits. This matter is now resolved. (PMC Bank case is discussed below in this chapter)

The status of urban coop banks in Indian banking and the latest development regarding steps initiated by the authorities is discussed in a separate chapter.

Resolution of Bank Failures—Present View of Developed Countries

Government's world over some times have been, forced during financial crisis, to bailout banks or financial institutions from collapsing with a purpose to save the economy. US Govt. did this in the aftermath of subprime crisis and failure of Lehman brothers in 2008. So did many other European countries. The experiences of the countries are that in case of failure of a major bank or financial institution, the governments are forced to step in and save the economy from the aftermath of such failure of the bank or FI. Governments are forced to bail out such bank or FI to save their economy from recession. Most of the developed countries are free economies where the banking and financial institutions are in private sector. Despite this, governments are forced to extend bail-out packages to such private banks and FIs to save the economy. This predicament of the governments of developed countries has given rise to debate to address this issue. Governments generally feel that the tax payer's money should not be used to bail-out private organisations and some alternative measures need to be put in place.

This has resulted in setting up of Financial Stability Board. FSB has finalised a policy framework in November 2010 and conveyed it to member countries as mentioned in the press release by it given earlier in this chapter.

FSB report recommended creation of a resolution framework and other measures by the member countries to ensure that all financial institutions can be resolved safely, quickly and without destabilising the financial system. Further it makes it clear that the resolution of distressed financial institutions shall be without exposing the govt. (taxpayer) to the risk of loss. This means that the resolution system shall not look for govt. bail-out as it is felt that tax payers' money shall not be used to bail-out financial institutes in distress as is done by many governments in the past.

Since it is observed that at present the resolution of financial institution is a long-drawn process in many countries and also that it has many legal hurdles for its quick resolution, FSB has recommended that the resolution shall be quick and the countries shall create necessary legal framework to make it possible. This may involve creating new laws or amending the existing laws by the countries. It envisages setting up of Resolution Authority with necessary powers and authority to manage the failure of a financial institution, in a way that ensures continuity of its critical functions. The resolution authority shall have following powers:

- Transfer ownership or assets, rights and liabilities, without the consent of shareholders or creditors, to achieve the sale of all or part of the failing FI, transfer of the FI's critical functions to a temporary bridge institution or transfer of non-performing assets to a management vehicle.
- Write down unsecured liabilities or convert them to equity with the purpose of absorbing losses or providing capital ("bail-in").
- Impose a temporary stay on early termination rights under financial contracts.
- Liquidate all or part of the FI, with timely pay-out or transfer of insured deposits and prompt access to client funds and assets.

We may understand that Resolution of a financial institution in distress has many options. They are: providing funds to tide over the difficulties either short-term (bail-out) or long-term basis (additional capital), mergers, and liquidation. Generally, these are dependent on the nature and level of distress. Merger is generally a quick solution. If the financial institute is just short of funds but capable and its future outlook is good then funding is a good option to save it. Bail-out is generally considered as an option and depending on the importance of the financial institution for the economy; govt. is forced to bail-out as there is no other option immediately available. Bail-out saves the situation and the financial institution can function normally without any break in its functions.

Now FSB has taken a stand and made recommendation that there shall be no bail-out by govt. as it means diverting tax payers' money. Because of this stand, it is proposed now that in the place of bail-out there can be bail-in, a relatively new concept. Under Bail-in the unsecured liabilities can be written down or converted to equity with the purpose of absorbing losses or providing capital. This has serious implications particularly for banks and its depositors. Deposits with banks are unsecured liability for banks and hence it can be written down or converted as capital by the resolution authority. The implications of these recommendations of FSB on our country are discussed below in this chapter.

Indian Response on FSB Recommendations

The subprime crisis of 2009 had no impact on Indian banking or financial system. Indian banking system was in fact appreciated by the international community then, for remaining unaffected by the crisis.

This was due to few reasons peculiar to Indian financial system mentioned hereunder:

- Indian banking is dominated by public sector banks which are the backbone of the economy. Off-balance sheet exposures of Indian banking system are minimal. They are not into handling large derivative products.
- The shadow banking system of investment banks and hedge funds in USA who caused the crisis is absent in India. India has non-banking financial companies who also function similar to banks in giving loans. NBFC segment is not a competitor to banks but are playing a supplemental role.
- The financial market in India is not very active in derivative products like in the US and European markets.
- Indian insurance sector is also stable as they mainly deal in life and general insurance business. Generally, they do not have any exposure to hybrid or derivative financial products.
- In India since 1966 there has been no major banking crisis. RBI has managed to avoid closure of commercial banks and ensured that the weak banks are merged with strong banks. Bank depositors are protected.
- Govt. ownership of the major banks has imparted security to the depositors. However, bank failures are seen in urban coop banking sector. These were small banks and in all the cases the deposit insurance claim has been given.

When we consider the above features of Indian economy, we will observe that the factors that led the developed countries into subprime crisis have no relevance or applicability in Indian context.

But the country faced the problem in the year 2019 when two big NBFCs failed and PMC bank, an urban coop bank faced a crisis. In the year 2020, country faced Yes Bank crisis. Yes bank is a private sector bank and is a big bank. GOI had no option but to save it by providing a bail-out package. (Yes bank case is discussed below in this chapter)

These developments in 2019 and 2020 clearly indicated that FSB recommendations are very relevant for the country as financial sector stability is essential to save the economy.

Further India is a member of G20 nations the recommendations is applicable to our country also. So far, these recommendations are not implemented in our country (till August 2021). However there have been some moves by the govt. for the implementation. Hence it is to be seen how the same will be implemented and to what extent they will be applied to Indian financial system. The developments in this respect are discussed below.

Financial Resolution and Deposit Insurance Bill 2017

In August 2017, govt. placed a bill known as financial resolution and deposit insurance bill 2017, in the parliament which was subsequently withdrawn.

This bill was introduced to provide a framework for the resolution of failures of financial institutions, covering the entire financial sector. It was proposed to bring in all commercial banks, regional rural banks, cooperative banks, insurance companies, payment system operators, Non-Banking Financial Companies (NBFC), mutual and pension funds, and securities firm under the purview of this bill.

The bill proposed to establish a resolution corporation (RC) which will have powers to acquire and transfer the assets or even liquidate any financial service provider in the case of its probable failure.

At present, there are many regulators for the different segments of the financial sectors in India. They are Reserve Bank of India (RBI) for the banks and the NBFCs, Insurance Regulatory and Development Authority (IRDA) for the insurance sector, Securities and Exchange Board of India (SEBI) for securities firms and mutual funds, and Pension Fund Regulatory and Development Authority (PFRDA) for pension funds. Proposed RC will supersede all these regulators for resolution functions.

The bill also proposed to repeal the Deposit Insurance and Credit Guarantee Corporation (DICGC) Act, 1961 and delegate powers of insuring deposits, collecting premium, and compensating depositors, in case of liquidation to the RC.

The management of the proposed RC will have a chairperson, member from the union finance ministry, members each from the RBI, SEBI, IRDA, and PFRDA, and three members nominated by the Central Government and two independent members.

The financial institution which falls into the defined risk category will have to submit a restoration plan to RC and the respective regulator. Once it is under the purview of RC, the resolution process will rest with RC only.

The resolution process can involve transfer or acquisition of assets, merger or amalgamation with another healthy financial firm, or liquidation after obtaining order from the appellate tribunal (National Company Law Tribunal). RC can also use new resolution instruments like 'bail-in' and creation of a "bridge service provider."

The bill also provided for identifying "systemically important financial institutions" (SIFIs) by the Central Government, on the basis of size and other features and based on their importance in the financial system.

Introducing this bill in Parliament became an issue for serious debate and the main concern was on the bail-in provision which enables RC to make the depositors of the banks to bear the loss. It is argued that the public confidence in banks will be seriously eroded due to this change. Further govt. has not proposed any increase in deposit insurance limit and left it to the discretion of RC which makes it uncertain and may turn out to be on case-to-case basis. This again is a big draw back as we have already seen the deposit insurance provisions now available on few of the important countries. Thus, it is argued that the proposed bill is totally against the interests of the bank depositors.

Another serious issue is about the banks in the public sector banks. They have the backing of govt. till now and under this bill govt. can absolve itself of its responsibilities by allowing them to be dealt by the RC. This in fact will be end of public sector bank's identity. For argument's sake it can be argued that govt. cannot do this and still keep these banks under public sector. This is because public sector banks functions on the basis of govt. fiat which makes them to take exposure in areas which the private sector banks are not taking.

It appeared that govt. has not made any in-depth study of the guidelines issued by FSB and its applicability or consequences to the Indian economy.

Govt. subsequently withdrew the bill from the parliament in August 2018 and stated that it will bring a new bill after reviewing the provisions of the bill for resolution of FIs.

(*Source*: by Prasenjit Bose)

Financial Sector Development and Regulation (Resolution) Bill, 2019 (FSDR)

It is now learnt that the new bill in the new name as above is ready and was to be placed in Parliament in the end of 2019. But for some reason it was delayed and it is now believed that this new bill will be introduced in the year 2020. But this bill was not introduced in the year 2020. So far there is no indication about govt.'s intentions on this bill.

Under the new bill the financial sector resolution framework now covers financial entities including banks, insurance companies, financial market infrastructure, payment systems and other financial service-providers (excluding individuals and partnership firms) now it also covers cooperative banks and regional rural banks.

FSDR

Basically, it is revised FRDI bill placed in Parliament in August 2017 for the same purpose of creating resolution framework for the financial institutions in trouble, with some changes.

The salient features of the present bill are said to be as under:

Scope: The financial sector resolution framework will now cover financial entities including banks, insurance companies, financial market infrastructure, payment systems and other financial service-providers (excluding individuals and partnership firms), cooperative banks and regional rural banks.

Resolution Authority (RA): It will be set up and will be based in Mumbai. It will have a representation of all financial sector regulators—Reserve Bank of India (RBI), Securities and Exchange Board of India (SEBI), Insurance and Regulatory Development Authority of India (IRDAI), Pension Fund Regulatory and Development Authority (PFRDA), the Central Government, and will have three whole-time members and two independent members.

Structure: The RA will be self-sustaining and have three types of funds under it.

1. The Resolution Authority Insurance Fund (replacing the Deposit Insurance and Credit Guarantee Authority Act, 1961) for deposit insurance;
2. The Resolution Authority Resolution Fund for covering resolution fees; and
3. Resolution Authority General Fund for meeting RA's administrative expenses.

Systemically Important Financial Institutions (SIFIs): Institutions whose failure may pose a risk to consumers and the overall financial stability of the country will be designated SIFIs by the Central Government.

Prompt corrective action (PCA) framework: The Bill will also provide clearly defined triggers for to bring a problem institution into resolution.

Classifications of FIs: The RA, along with sector regulators, will classify all service-providers into five categories, namely: low, moderate, material, imminent and critical. The classification will take into account several features of the specified service-providers, including adequacy of capital, asset quality, leverage ratio, liquidity and capability of management.

The power of the RA: The powers of the RA come into play when the financial entity is classified under any of the last three categories of 'material', 'imminent', and 'critical' stage. At the 'critical' stage, a receiver will be appointed and payments as well as legal actions/contractual proceedings against the entity stayed as part of the resolution process.

Tools of Resolution: These include the use of one or more of the following:

1. Transferring the whole or part of the assets and liabilities to another entity;
2. Creating a bridge service-provider;
3. Cancellation/modification of liabilities;
4. Merger or amalgamation;
5. Acquisition;
6. Liquidation;
7. Run-off, in case of an insurance company, if deemed appropriate.

Time frame for Resolution: Resolution has to be completed in one year, with the provision for an extension of one additional year, except in the case of liquidation.

Administrator ship: When the resolution process starts, the RA will suspend the board and take over as the administrator. RA is empowered to make executive decisions on behalf of the entity including appointment or removal of managers and act as a receiver. A decision on liquidation, however, has to be cleared by the National Company Law Tribunal—NCLT, which will appoint the RA as liquidator.

It is said that the controversial 'bail-in' provision in the original bill is not in the new bill. But this may be deceptive as the resolution tools in the proposed bill refers to cancellation/modification of liabilities which is same as bail-in. Besides the proposed bill also mentions that its aim as to handle financial sector failures without transferring the burden to taxpayers by establishing a transparent mechanism to deal with such failures.

Deposit insurance of bank deposits is not clear. While the existing DICGC cover is replaced there is no increase in the limit. This is now left to the discretion of RA which is unusual step as it does not specify the insurance cover. It is important that the Deposit insurance limit shall be fixed and made known to the depositors in advance. How the deposit insurance scheme will work is ambiguous.

It is now difficult to comprehend the actual provisions of the bill and if made into legislation without making clear provisions about 'bail-in' and 'deposit insurance' it will definitely have adverse impact on the banking system of the country.

At present there are many other issues also that are not clear. For example; at present govt. has a responsibility for public sector banks and institutions as they are created under specific legislation governing them. For closing a public sector bank govt. will have to amend the relevant legislations. But under the present bill all those acts will be amended and RA will have the authority to deal with public sector banks. It is pertinent to note that the earlier finance minister has made statements that public sector banks will be the responsibility of the govt. Government had recapitalised public sector banks in 2018 and 2019 to make them Basel Accord III compliant. Bringing public sector banks and public sector institutions under the new resolution system is an indication that they will not have any special status. With the powers of RA to write down liabilities, govt. may disown its responsibility for public sector banks in future. Govt. should have made a clear policy about the future of public sector banks so that the public may be aware of it.

Privatisation of public sector banks by any route will be a negative step and the Indian economy may not benefit by it now. It's important to understand the economies of USA and European countries. They are all developed economies and banking and financial sector are all privately owned. Same prescription may not work well in India's case.

It is said that G20 countries of America and European countries have adopted the guidelines including the provision for bail-in. But few countries like China and Japan and some others have not implemented bail-in provision. China also has public sector banks and in fact four of the largest Chinese banks are in public sector and they are ranking in the first ten global banks.

Financial Sector Crisis in the Year 2018 and 2019

While we have been discussing the expected future developments in banking, and the FSDR bill proposed to be introduced in the country, there was a rude shock for the country. In the year 2019 two NBFCs; Infrastructure Leasing & Financial Services (IL&FS) and Dewan Housing Finance Corporation Ltd. (DHFL) a deposit-taking housing finance company, got into trouble. On 1 October 2018, the Government of India took steps to take control of the IL&FS and arrest the spread of the default to the financial markets. The IL&FS group operates over a hundred subsidiaries and it has a debt of ₹ 94,000 crore.

On 20 November 2019, Reserve Bank of India removed the board of directors of Dewan Housing Finance Corporation Limited (DHFL) which had as on July 6, 2019, debt outstanding of ₹ 83,873 crore.

They are big operators and the impact was felt on many banks and other NBFCs. GOI/RBI was forced to change the managements of these two NBFCs for the purpose of resolution.

GOI was thinking in terms of assisting the NBFC sector by providing liquidity support and even asked RBI to consider the requirement to stop the impact of failure of these two NBFCs on others. However, RBI felt that there is no liquidity crisis in the financial sector and that there is no case for bailing out these two NBFCs. Now both these companies are heading towards liquidation.

However, many banks were affected who had exposure to these two companies.

PMC BANK CRISIS

Punjab and Maharashtra Cooperative Bank

On September 24, 2019 the RBI issued a notification to Punjab and Maharashtra Cooperative Bank under sections 35 (A) and 56 of the Banking Regulation Act restricting the amount that can be withdrawn by the depositors to ₹ 1,000 for six months and prohibiting PMC from granting any loans. This was shocking news for the depositors of the urban coop bank and no one in financial world including RBI had any inkling about this crisis. In fact, PMC Bank had finalised its annual financial report for 31 March 2019. Surprisingly PMC Bank's financial position as reflected in its annual report for the year 2019 was quite good. The bank occupied 5th rank in the top ten UCBs.

It is the repeat of similar crisis the country faced in 2001, when a big UCB of that time; Madhavpura Mercantile Coop Bank got into trouble and subsequently went into liquidation. Failure of Madhavpura Mercantile Bank had brought out the weaknesses persisting in the workings of the UCBs and govt. and RBI had taken many measures to ensure that such crisis does not recur in future. But the present crisis in PMC Bank has brought back the issues alive again, that the UCBs are continuing as weak links in the banking system of the country.

PMC Bank was started on February 13, 1984, from Sion, suburb of Mumbai. In the year 2019, PMC Bank had network of 137 branches across seven states.

Bank had consistent growth over the years and has become 5th largest UCB in 2019. It is informed that there were no adverse features observed by auditors and also by RBI during all these years of bank's history. Bank had published its Annual Report for year ending 31 March 2019. Financial results were as under:

(₹ in crores)

	Liabilities	31.03.2019		Assets	31.03.2019
1	Capital	292.61	1	Cash	708.55
2	Reserve fund & other reserves	933.94	2	Balance with other banks	409.69
3	Deposit and other accounts	11617.34	3	Investments	3124.87

	Liabilities	31.03.2019		Assets	31.03.2019
4	Borrowings	305.90	4	Advances	8383.33
5	Interest payable	35.68	5	Interest receivable	63.06
6	Other liabilities	296.44	6	Fixed assets	507.96
			7	Other assets	284.45
	Total	13481.91		Total	13481.91

As of March 2019, its deposits and advances were ₹ 11,617 crores and ₹ 8,383 crores respectively. Total assets were ₹ 13481.91 crores. Its net profit was ₹ 99.69 crore in March 2019. The bank's gross non-performing assets (GNPA) were 3.76% and net NPAs were 2.19% of its advances. It had over 51,000 members and about 9,10,000 depositors.

The bank is patronised, amongst others, by the Sikh community in the country from whom bank received large deposits. It was said that for many depositors this bank is the sole bank with whom they maintained accounts.

Crisis in the Bank

As per reports appearing in the newspapers and other media and also from RBI, it came to light that the bank is in deep trouble. It came to be known that the bank has a huge exposure to Housing Development and Infrastructure Ltd. (HDIL), a major housing development company. HDIL is now facing liquidation proceedings started by a bank for recovery of dues.

It is also reported that HDIL and the management of this bank are involved in fraudulent activities in the sanctioning of loans to HDIL group companies much beyond the regulatory guidelines of RBI by resorting to frauds and fabrication of bank's books to hide these loans. It is claimed that this nexus was going on since past many years and the loans have become NPA. Bank was hiding the true affairs by various means to avoid detection by audit and inspection teams.

The fraud came to light only when the CEO of the bank revealed the fraudulent dealings to RBI as he could not carry on further with the burden of guilt. The managing director wrote to RBI on 21.9.2019.

This letter gave the inside information about the bank, about its initial struggles to survive and its association with HDIL group as dating back to 1986 when HDIL group helped the bank from closing down. Again in 2004 bank faced liquidity problem and there was run on the bank. Shri Rakesh Kumar Wadhavan of HDIL group helped the bank by giving it a deposit of ₹ 100 crores. HDIL group also started banking with the coop bank from this year.

According to the letter the bank started giving loans to HDIL group and the exposure was about ₹ 500 crores in the year 2006-07. HDIL started expanding its business and they also entered into slum rehabilitation related housing projects. They started dealing with other banks as their financial needs have grown in view of their expanding business. They had once closed their loans with PMC Bank but at the request of the bank started availing loans again from them, in addition to few other banks. HDIL had bagged a contract for a slum rehabilitation project near the airport but in the year 2012 it was cancelled. In the year 2013, it was terminated. This affected HDIL and it started having liquidity crunch. The loans given to HDIL became NPAs. As the amount was huge that would have affected PMC Bank, the bank continued to show the loans as standard accounts. These facts were concealed from the board of the bank, auditors and also RBI.

Some of the large loans to the group were not reported to RBI since the year 2008. In the year 2011, the bank had deposits of ₹ 2824 crores and advance of ₹ 2000 crores. Exposure to HDIL was ₹ 1026 crores in 2011. Further fresh advances were made to repay the other bankers of HDIL group to avoid liquidation of HDIL. Bank also resorted to report dummy accounts in place of HDIL group accounts to RBI during its inspection in 2017 and thus hidden the NPAs.

This letter did not inform about the present exposure to HDIL group.

It was stated in the newspaper report that the exposure is about ₹ 2500 crores. Another news report said that the exposure to HDIL group may be over ₹ 6000 crores. On 24.9.2019,

RBI placed PMC Bank under directions and soon other actions like superseding the board of directors and appointment of administrator took place. Criminal actions were initiated against HDIL group and bank management.

In September 2019, the RBI imposed curbs on the bank, saying that depositors would not be allowed to withdraw more than ₹ 1,000 from the bank for six months. The withdrawal limit was raised to ₹ 25,000, and then to ₹ 40,000 in October. On November 5, the RBI again increased the withdrawal limit to ₹ 50,000.

In the PMC Bank case, the RBI has also allowed withdrawals up to ₹ 1 lakh on grounds of medical emergency and hardships. The hardship clause includes marriage, education, and livelihood for senior citizens, etc. But the fate of many depositors with more than ₹ 50,000 in the bank still hanged in balance.

The depositors of the bank are in rude shock as RBI imposed curbs on the bank. This was followed by demonstrations by the depositors of the bank at various places and before various authorities including RBI. It is also reported that few deaths amongst the depositors took place due to this sudden clamping down on their deposits.

PRESENT POSITION

The actual financial position of the bank and its exposure to HDIL group is not yet known till 31.12.2019. RBI governor has stated that it had conducted inspection of the bank and the report is being compiled. The report is expected to be available in next ten days.

Some depositors have moved Mumbai High Court to provide them relief and allow withdrawals from the bank accounts. High court has not considered any relief at this stage. It wanted RBI to come out with the status of this bank. It is reported that RBI has filed affidavit in the high court about the present status. It is reported that RBI has made statement that the management has cheated it by hiding the information and also by faking the information at the time of RBI inspections of the bank.

Now the most important issue is to know the correct exposure of the bank to HDIL group and also to know the realisable security cover available to the bank. This will be revealed when the inspection reports are made public. There is a fear that the exposure to HDIL group is extremely high and it may be to the extent of over ₹ 6500 crores which is about 75% of total loan book of the bank.

PMC bank has published its revised financial report for March 2019 and audited report for March 2020. They are discussed little later.

Future of PMC Bank

What will be the future of PMC Bank? This is a serious issue before the RBI and govt. This bank has deposits of over ₹ 11617 crores as at 31.3.2019. Its advances are ₹ 8383 crores. It is believed that out of the total loans about ₹ 6500 crores are owed by HDIL group. The big question is how much is recoverable from HDIL group. Recovery will depend mainly on the securities bank is having against the loans to the group. This is not yet known. Enforcement agencies have attached some assets and are trying to dispose them.

Revival Option

Reviving the bank is an option if the sickness is curable one, like if the bank is facing problem of liquidity due to losses it has suffered. Here it is important to identify that the loss suffered is due to some isolated frauds or due to some loans going bad in the normal course. In such situation bank can be saved by infusing capital or long-term debt to tide over the crisis. Generally, in such cases the management of the bank if considered capable can be allowed to run the bank may be with certain conditions.

But in the case of PMC Bank, as the things are now revealed, the management is to be blamed and it is found that it is also involved in the fraudulent activities. The board of the bank has been removed. Thus, there is no management available to the bank that can take care of the bank even if it is revived. It will be like starting a new bank. Raising fresh capital will be impossible as the total net owned funds are wiped out due to estimated losses.

Merger Option

There are opinions that PMC Bank shall be merged with some big bank to protect the interest of the depositors of the bank. While RBI has the authority to merge weak commercial banks with stronger banks, it had no authority to do so in case of coop banks. This is because coop banks are governed by the state societies acts. State govt. or Central govt. (for multi-state coop bank) are the authorities to take decisions on this matter. (However, RBI authority on UCBs is now enhanced in the year 2021. This is discussed under the chapter on coop banks.)

Mergers can be with another coop bank or even with a commercial bank. Such mergers are generally considered when a small bank is in difficulty and some portion of its assets is eroded. The acquirer bank that takes over the bank generally bears the cost of loss in assets considering the 'good will' value it will receive by way of number of branches, existing depositors and advances, and the trained staff of the weak bank. When there is good scope for future growth due to merger, the acquirer bank takes over the weak bank even if it has to bear some loss initially. But bigger banks will not agree to takeover weak bank if the erosion of assets of the weak bank is very high as the cost of merger may outweigh the benefits it can derive from the merger.

In case of PMC Bank, if we consider exposure of ₹ 6500 crores to HDIL as reported, that leaves only about ₹ 2000 crores of other advances. Recovery percentage in the loans to HDIL cannot be predicted at this juncture.

Let us compare the financial position of PMC Bank as reflected in its balance sheet as at 31.3.2019, 31.3.2020, and 31.3.2021.

(₹ in crores)

Liabilities	31.03.19	31.03.20	31.3.21	Assets	31.03.19	31.03.20	31.3.21
Capital	292.61	292	294	Cash	708.55	371	377
Reserve fund & other reserves	933.94	(-3132)	(-3542)	Balance with other banks	409.69	379	155

Liabilities	31.03.19	31.03.20	31.3.21	Assets	31.03.19	31.03.20	31.3.21
Deposit and other accounts	11617.34	10727	10535	Investments	3124.87	2326	2350
Borrowings	305.90	279	279	Advances	8383.33	4472	4123
Interest payable	35.68	69		Interest receivable	63.06	45	
Other liabilities	296.44	221	249	Fixed assets	507.96	475	444
				Other assets	284.45	388	366
Total	13481.91	8456	7815	Total	13481.91	8456	7815

Source: PMC bank financial results.

Deposits are shown as ₹ 10535 crores on March 2021 as against ₹ 11617 crores in 31.3.2019. Advances figures are ₹ 4123 crores as at 31.3.2021 as against ₹ 8383 crores in 31.3.2019. Balance sheet is showing a contra entry—Overdue interest recoverable NPA—at ₹ 4582 crores in 31.3.2020 and ₹ 5502 crores in 31.3.2021. This appears to be the reason for steep fall in the advances figures in 2020 as compared to the year 2019. Reserve funds are shown as negative ₹ 3132 crores as at 31.3.2020 and negative ₹ 3542 crore in March 2021. Hence audited net worth is negative ₹ 2840 crores as at March 2020 and negative ₹ 3248 crore in March 2021.

As at 31.3.2021 deposits ₹ 10535 crore are stuck with the bank for more than three years now and the miseries of bank account holders is tremendous and hardly need to be explained.

The auditor M/s R. Devendra Kumar & Associates, Chartered Accountants, for the year ending 31.3.2020 have in their qualified opinion have stated as under:

Basis for Qualified Opinion

Reference is invited to the following notes to accounts in schedule 13B to the Financial Statements:

(i) Note Nos. 1, 9 & 29 regarding Fraud of substantial amount detected at the bank during the year whereby certain advance accounts relating to Housing Development Infrastructure Limited (HDIL) Group having outstanding of ₹ 6212.46 crores and other credit facilities aggregating to ₹ 428.58 crores as on March 31, 2020 remained unreported and were not properly classified in accordance with the asset classification norms issued by RBI.

(ii) The advance accounts relating to HDIL Group and other accounts identified as Fraud, have been classified as Doubtful assets with full provision has been made. These accounts aggregating to ₹ 6641.04 crores should have been classified as Loss Assets. There is however no impact on the provision accounted for these advances.

As per this opinion exposure of the bank to HDIL is ₹ 6212.46 crores and it is categorised as fraud since the bank did not report it and has not properly classified it as per norms issued by RBI.

LATEST DEVELOPMENTS

PMC Bank was trying to rope in parties for taking over the bank and called for the proposals from interested parties in November 2020.

It is reported that according to the EOI issued by the bank last year—"the investors looking to acquire will have to ideally bring in the capital required for enabling the bank to achieve the minimum required capital to risk weighted assets ratio (CRAR) of 9 per cent." "However, the investors may explore the option of restructuring a part of deposit liabilities into capital/capital instruments. The bank may also approach DICGC for its support for payment up to ₹ 5 lakh (insured deposits) to depositors," the EOI said.

Subsequently they received four offers. One offer from Centrum Financial Services Limited dated February 1, 2021 was shortlisted. On 18 June 2021, RBI conveyed it's in principle approval to the offer of Central Financial Services Ltd. to take over the bank.

As per news report, RBI has issued SFB licence on 12.10.2021 to Centrum Financial Services and BharatPe to establish a small finance bank. It is informed that the new SFB has been incorporated as "Unity Small Finance Bank".

RBI has taken many positive steps to save the bank and its depositors. RBI got a revival package for the bank approved by GOI, by which the new SFC created to step-in and take over the PMC bank. GOI has issued notification on 25 January 2022 approving amalgamation of PMC bank with Unity Small Finance Bank. This Scheme is called the Punjab and Maharashtra Co-operative Bank Limited (Amalgamation with Unity Small Finance Bank Limited) Scheme, 2022. As per notification the appointed date is 25.01.2022.

As per details now available it is known that DICGC will immediately pay the insurance claims up to ₹ 5 lacs to all eligible retail and institutional depositors to Unity Small Finance Bank. This claim amount will be released to depositors immediately. Thereafter the remaining deposit amounts will be paid to the retail depositors in instalments spread over ten years' time by the new bank—Unity Small Finance Bank which is taking over PMC bank.

As per the approved scheme, repayments including from the DICGC insurance claim of ₹ 5 lacs, to depositors will be as under:

Due Date of payment	Repayment
For Retail depositors	
Immediate—Insurance claim	Upto ₹ 5,00,000
25.01.2023	Upto ₹ 50,000
25.01.2024	Upto ₹ 50,000
25.01.2025	Upto ₹ 1,00,000
25.01.2026	Upto ₹ 2,50,000
25.01.2027	Upto ₹ 5,50,000
25.01.2032	remaining amount
Interest payment to retail depositors	
	1. No interest on any of the interest-bearing deposits after March 31, 2021 for a period of five years upto 25.01.2027 and afterwards, simple interest at the rate of 2.75% at the end of each year. 2. No interest shall be payable in any current account or any other non-interest-bearing account. However simple interest at the rate of 2.75% after 25-01-2027 shall be paid.

Due Date of payment	Repayment
For Institutional depositors	
Immediate—Insurance claim	Upto ₹ 5,00,000
25.01.2022	Balance remaining— 80% will be converted to Perpetual Non-Cumulative Preference Shares of transferee bank with dividend of one per cent.
25.01.2022	20% shall be converted into equity warrants of transferee bank at a price of ₹ 1 per warrant and these equity warrants will further be converted into equity shares of the transferee bank at the time of the Initial Public Offer when the transferee bank goes for public issue.
Interest payment	No interest on any deposit account after 31.3.2021.

PMC bank crisis which erupted in the year 2019 is finally stands resolved. But there is a lesson to be learnt. It can be claimed that the bank depositors' interest has been protected by RBI. But when we go through the repayment schedule to depositors as shown in the above chart, we can observe that the relief to retail depositors of PMC bank is not adequate. Repayment is extended over a period of ten years. In the first five years only ₹ 15 lacs is returned and they shall wait for further period of five years for payment of remaining amount. Depositors are also losing heavily on the interest earnings.

The institutional depositors are worst hit as their deposits are blocked as equity shares and the recovery of their deposit will be very long process with uncertainties.

Solution worked out by RBI to PMC bank crisis, though it has not provided good protection to PMC bank depositors, it has definitely brought in many changes in the system and legal provisions. GOI has amended the banking regulation act by Banking Regulation (Amendment) Bill-2020, and brought cooperative banking sector under the direct control of RBI same as in the cases of commercial banks. This may help to protect bank depositors in future. Once RBI control on the workings and managements of cooperative banks improves on the lines of commercial banks, the failure of coop banks may be kept under check in future. This development is also discussed in the chapter on cooperative banks in this book.

Another welcome change in the banking system of the country is in the area of deposit insurance scheme. GOI increased claim amount from earlier existing ₹ one lac to the present limit of ₹ 5 lacs. This will provide protection for bank depositors particularly the poor and small depositors.

Further under the newly passed DICGC Amendment Act 2021 (August 2021), DICGC is now mandated to settle claims to bank depositors immediately on failure of banks, within 90 days from the date of issuance of directions on the banks by RBI. This is a welcome development, as earlier to this the claim settlements used to take few years and relief to bank depositors is much delayed.

Amalgamation scheme approved in PMC bank case is also probably a new and unique experiment by RBI and GOI. Under this scheme, the Unity small business bank has taken over the assets and liabilities of PMC Bank. It's similar to takeover or merger of one bank with the acquirer bank. In such case the acquired bank is not considered as closed but continuing under the acquirer bank. Usually, Deposit insurance claim is not paid by DICGC in such cases. All the Deposit accounts of the merged bank will continue with acquirer bank and continue to be secured by DICGC insurance cover as before.

PMC bank case is unique as due to fraud and mis-management of the bank, nearly 60-70% of its assets are wiped out or become doubtful of recovery. Under the circumstances revival of the bank was difficult. It is possible that the depositors of PMC bank may not wish to continue their deposit accounts with the new acquirer bank which is unknown to them. More than ₹ 6000 crores have been lost by PMC bank in bad loans, the chances recovery of these loans is bleak. Acquirer bank would find it difficult to take over without adequate financial resources. In view of this difficulty DICGC is roped in by GOI to make insurance claim payments immediately to part finance the amalgamation. The approved scheme by the GOI requires the acquirer bank to reimburse the claim settlement amount to

DICGC at a later date. The acquirer bank shall have time up to 20 years from the appointed date (i.e., up to 25.01.2042), to repay the amount received from DICGC towards payment to the insured depositors.

Sources: RBI, PMC bank audited reports, news reports and media coverage.

Yes Bank Crisis

Yes bank is a private bank started in 2004. It is one of the new generation private sector banks that are allowed to start banking operations after the banking sector reforms were introduced in country in 1991. The bank had good growth record and became the 5th largest private sector bank in the country. It was said that the bank was quite aggressive in growing its loans portfolio and mainly extended loans to big corporates in sectors like real estate, pharmaceuticals, renewable energy, electricals and media.

It appears that after 2015, the bank had witnessed increase in bad loans. In their annual report of FY 2016, Yes bank has reported the gross NPA of ₹ 748.98 crores but RBI later identified the gross NPA to be very high at ₹ 4925.68 crores.

After RBI's asset quality reviews in 2017 and 2018, Yes bank ran into a trouble as the reviews revealed sharp increase in its bad loans ratio and the bank was struggling to raise the capital that it needed to stay above regulatory requirements. Annual reports of the year ended March 2018 and 2019 are as under:

Yes bank financial position

(₹ in crores)

Particulars	2019	2018
Total Assets	3,80,826	3,12,446
Advances	2,41,500	2,03,534
Deposits	2,27,610	2,00,738
CASA Ratio	33.1%	36.5%
Shareholders' Funds	26,904	25,758
Capital Adequacy Fund	16.5%	18.4%
Net NPA	1.86%	0.64%

Particulars	2019	2018
Gross NPA	3.22%	1.28%
Net Profit	1,720	4,225
Basic Earnings per Share	7.4	18.4
Return on Equity	6.5%	17.7%

Financial Indicators (Annual Reports, 2019)

These figures did not divulge the precarious condition of the bank which was subsequently revealed in RBI inspection of the bank.

Bank in fact had many big defaulters like IL&FS, Anil Ambani group, CG Power, Cox & Kings, Café Coffee Day, Essel group, Essar Power, Vardaraj Cement, Radius Developers, and Mantri Group. This put pressure on the bank as it did not have good deposit base and the capital requirement was going up. Bank was finding it difficult to manage its affairs. Bank was under stress and this led RBI to place the bank under an order of moratorium on March 5, 2020 which is to be effective up to April 3, 2020. Under this order, the depositors of the bank were allowed to withdraw ₹ 50000/- only.

Crisis in Yes bank had all the features to blow up and cause severe damage to the financial sector of the country. RBI and GOI were forced to act immediately and save the bank. This required changing the management and also roping in investors to support the bank. RBI with consultation with GOI, then worked out a reconstruction plan to save Yes bank. Under this plan, the main role was given to State Bank of India, a public sector bank to provide capital and also management of the bank.

This Scheme is called the Yes Bank Limited Reconstruction Scheme, 2020 and it came into force on the 13th day of March 2020.

The reconstruction scheme is as under:

As per govt. notification

Share capital of reconstructed bank. (1) The authorised capital of the reconstructed bank shall stand altered to ₹ 62,00,00,00,000 (Rupees Six thousand two hundred crore only) and number of equity shares to 30,00,00,00,000 (Three thousand crore only) of rupees two only each, aggregating to ₹ 60,00,00,00,000 (Rupees Six thousand crore only).

(2) The authorised preference share capital shall continue to be ₹ 200,00,00,000 (Rupees Two hundred crore only).

The investor bank (SBI) and other investors, shall invest in the reconstructed bank and the reconstructed bank shall allot equity shares of the reconstructed bank, at a price of rupees ten only with face value of rupees two only and premium of rupees eight only.

State Bank of India (SBI) will invest 49 per cent of equity in Yes bank, with other investors also being invited. SBI will hold at least 26 per cent of the 49 per cent of its stake in the private bank for a minimum period of three years. Similarly, the other investors, including the private banks will also be mandated to have a similar lock-in period for 75 per cent of their investment in the bank.

Besides SBI another four top Indian private banks, HDFC, ICICI, Kotak Mahindra and Axis bank have announced investments which is cumulatively ₹ 3,100 crore. ICICI bank was the first private lender to have confirmed its participation in the SBI-led restructuring plan for Yes bank.

Both ICICI and HDFC Bank proposed to invest ₹ 1,000 crore each. Axis Bank and the Kotak Mahindra Bank proposed to put in ₹ 600 crore and ₹ 500 crore, respectively.

Both ICICI and HDFC Bank are likely to have five per cent shareholding each in the restructured Yes bank. In its regulatory filing, HDFC Bank informed that its investment of ₹ 1,000 crore would be completed by March 31.

This scheme was made operational and moratorium earlier put on the bank was removed on 13.3.2020. The financial results for the year ending 31 March 2021 i.e., after one full year of restructuring, revealed that the bank is now safe.

YES BANK LIMITED—Annual Report 2020-21—
Standalone Balance Sheet

CAPITAL AND LIABILITIES	₹ in crore		
	Schedule	31.3.2021	31.3.2020
Capital	1	5011	2510
Reserves and surplus	2	28185	19216
Deposits	3	162946	105364
Borrowings	4	63949	113790
Other liabilities and provisions	5	13451	16946

CAPITAL AND LIABILITIES	₹ in crore		
	Schedule	31.3.2021	31.3.2020
TOTAL		273542	257826
ASSETS			
Cash and balances with Reserve Bank of India	6	6813	5943
Balances with banks and money at call and short notice	7	22496	2439
Investments	8	43319	43915
Advances	9	166893	171443
Fixed assets	10	2148	1009
Other assets	11	31873	33077
TOTAL		273542	257826

*Gross NPA was ₹ 28609 crore and 17.14% of gross advances
*Net NPA of the bank is said to be 5.88%
*CRAR of the bank stood at 17.5%.

It appears that the reconstruction package has worked and the bank is saved. It was possible due to proactive approaches of GOI and RBI and their immediate actions. GOI could ask State Bank of India, a public sector bank, to take leadership in rescuing the bank. However, the bank is still not out of woods as gross NPA is 17.14% and net NPA is 5.88%. It may take couple of more years to recover fully.

Lessons to be Learnt

Failure of two NBFCs and then the crisis in PMC bank and Yes bank discussed above brings out an important issue facing the country. While failures cannot be avoided in future also, and in view of the Financial Stability Board recommendations, what should be the course our country shall take to safeguard against crisis situations in our financial sectors?

It may not advisable to follow the west blindly without understanding the realities existing in our country and the repercussions of the proposed changes.

For example, our banking structure is still public sector dominated. While Private sector in banking is encouraged which was for the purpose of competition and raising the standards of our financial sector, country has not yet decided on elimination of public sector banks and FIs from the financial sectors. However, GOI in last couple of years has shown its inclination to privatise public sector undertakings and the reason stated is to raise funds for the govt.

In banking sector, the depositors are the backbone of the system. In our country financial education is not widespread. Except in few important urban centres, bank deposits are the main avenues for attracting the household savings. Here the need for safe banks is crucial. The system should provide for the safety of bank deposits by overseeing the health of the banks and by providing very reasonable deposit insurance cover. The present insurance cover is not providing safety net for depositors who have entrusted their hard-earned money to the banks. As we are witnessing now, in the case of failure of urban coop banks, the life's savings of poor and middle class is wiped out.

Interest rates offered by banks for deposits are falling now. It may continue to fall in future also. But majority of our populace have no other alternatives available for them to keep their savings. They are not using capital markets, derivative markets, and mutual funds as alternatives to bank deposits as they are not well conversant with these investment avenues. Majority of Indian population will depend on banks for investments. Govt. shall keep this feature of Indian investors in mind before altering the existing systems.

The issue of bail-in provisions proposed to resolve bank failures appears ill conceived for our country. Treating bank deposits by public as liability of the bank and bringing it within the ambit of resolution mechanism can be a retrograde step. In Indian practice bank deposits including term deposits are payable on demand. On this basis, for banks even if they appear on liability side, it's a special and distinct kind of liability. It cannot be equated with other liabilities. In a way deposit of the public with banks are in the nature of money held in trust by banks as per the practice of Indian banks. Under this practice in the country, depositor of the bank may lose his deposit in case the bank closes. This can only be the rule. By making bank depositors liable to bear the loss of the bank for the purpose of keeping the bank afloat as recommended by FSB is an alien thinking.

The proposed bill by the govt. is also silent about public sector banks. We can presume that the status of all banks for resolution purpose will be same. This means govt. will not be responsible for protecting public sector banks. Govt. disowning its responsibility to save its own bank is incongruous as the govt. uses the public sector banks for its sovereign purposes. Govt. may have to privatise all banks so that all banks become equal and are governed by same rules and regulations.

Bail-in is thought as alternative to bail-out. But in fact, it is not so. In a bail-out an outside agency is investing in the bank either as capital or as loan. Most of the time, it is as loan. In maximum cases of bail-out, the bank recovers from its lean period and returns the loan to the bail-out party. In the medium and long run there is no loss to the bail-out party. Bail-out is only considered if there is scope for recovery.

But in the present bail-in provisions proposed, the account holders of the bank are made to bear the loss. There is provision to reduce the liability, or convert some portion of it as capital or long-term bonds. Invariably there will be loss to the deposit holder of the bank. Either he will lose some portion of his deposit and or face the situation of his liquid assets getting blocked for long time. The loss to the bank depositor is irreversible. Even if the bank recovers and make good it's earlier losses, there is no provision or mandate to return the deposit reduced under resolution process.

Bail-in provision for resolution of bank failure is not suitable to our country as at present we have public sector banks. Govt. ownership of banks acts as a stabilizing factor in Indian context. Even in the case of Yes bank reconstruction it is SBI, a public sector bank which could take the responsibility of Yes bank at the behest of GOI.

Indian experience with bank failures is very good with hardly any commercial bank closing down during last about 40 years. But there have been failures of UCBs which were small banks. GOI and RBI need to look into this sector of banks and get them converted as commercial banks at the earliest.

The most important issue is the deposit insurance coverage and GOI should increase it to be comparable with other countries of the world. (This is discussed in a separate chapter.) If the deposit insurance cover is comparable to other countries in the world, then may be more than 70 to 75% of depositors of the banks will be protected in full. In such case, there will be no loss to low- and middle-income groups of our country, in case of any bank fails and closes down.

Conclusion

Resolution regime now proposed will have great impact on Indian bank depositors. The perception about bank deposit may change if bail-in provision is made a law.

We can definitely presume that if deposit insurance is not enhanced and bail-in provision is implemented then it will change the profile of the economy as the bank depositors may look for safer investments like the real estate or gold. Growth of banks will be definitely impacted due to shift in savings preferences to other avenues. This will also result in individuals having multiple banking accounts with more banks to spread their risk against failure of a bank.

This may also eventually lead to privatisation of all govt. banks and govt. financial institutions.

Further, the latest development of Yes bank crisis which necessitated GOI to provide bail-out package has revived the need for setting up resolution authority in the country. RBI Governor has stated that resolution mechanism needs to be put in place to take care of similar issues in future. "We need a structured mechanism with the legal backing to deal with stressed assets," Governor Das said.

The latest PMC Bank rescue in January 2022, in effect, is also a bail-out package. PMC Bank is taken over by the newly created Unity Small Finance Bank and GOI has roped in DICGC to part finance the takeover by releasing the insurance claim amount immediately. We may observe that, in the normal course, insurance claim is payable to bank depositors on closure of the bank and not when it is taken over by some other bank. By making this exception GOI has helped the acquiring bank with funds. Further, the takeover of PMC Bank is approved by the law created by GOI in this case. Though the retail depositors shall be paid by Unity Small Finance Bank in the future years, the payment terms are set out in the law passed by GOI and hence shall be enforceable against GOI even if the Unity Small Finance Bank defaults in future. Hence for all practical purpose PMC Bank case is also a bail-out package by GOI.

However, the controversial bail-in provision should not be introduced for banks till such time there are banks in public sector at least.

3

RBI and its Role in Indian Banking

The Reserve Bank of India is the central banking authority of the country. It is also the Monetary authority of the country.

Central banks have been created by the developed countries in world at the beginning of the 20th century. This has been necessitated due to starting of many commercial banks and also that the banking business has become very prominent in the economies. Banks have become economic hubs accepting deposits and giving loans, they are conducting financial transactions through its cheque clearance system. Gradually cheques have replaced cash from trade and business. Some Banking laws like the Negotiable Instruments Acts were enacted by many countries of the world in the last quarter of 19th century. The Indian Negotiable Instruments Act was enacted in the year 1881. Negotiable Instruments Acts legalised the usage cheques, promissory notes and bill of exchanges in trade and commerce and by the citizens of the country.

In view increasing importance of the banking system in the economy and the proliferation of banks, it became necessary to have some regulations in place and to have an authority to oversee the functions and managements of the banks. This is the genesis of Central Banks in the countries.

Creation of Reserve Bank of India

Creation of Reserve Bank of India was recommended by the Hilton-Young Commission report submitted in the year 1926. The Govt. of India (British Government) enacted the Reserve

Bank of India Act 1934, and RBI came in to existence in the year 1935. It was created as a joint stock company with government holding some shares.

The Preamble of the Reserve Bank of India Act describes the basic functions of the Reserve Bank as:

> to regulate the issue of bank notes, to keep reserves with a view to securing monetary stability in India and generally to operate the currency and credit system in the best interests of the country.

The Central Office of the Reserve Bank was initially established in Kolkata, but later it was permanently moved to Mumbai in 1937. The Reserve Bank continued to act as the Central Bank for Myanmar till Japanese occupation of Burma and later up to April 1947, though Burma seceded from the Indian Union in 1937. After partition, the Reserve Bank served as the Central Bank for Pakistan until June 1948, when the State Bank of Pakistan commenced operations. After independence of the country (1947), Government of India nationalized RBI in 1949 and made it an autonomous authority as Central Bank of the country. It is now fully owned by Govt. of India.

The role and objectives of RBI is mentioned in the preamble of RBI Act 1934 which is mentioned above. But the role of the RBI kept on increasing over the years.

In the beginning RBI had no mandatory authority over banks. In the same year 1949 when RBI was nationalized, the Government of India enacted The Banking Companies Act, 1949 which was later changed to Banking Regulation Act, 1949 as per amending Act of 1965 (Act No. 23 of 1965). The Banking Companies' Act, 1949 was for the purpose to streamline the functioning and activities of commercial banks and this Act gave RBI authority over the commercial banks and the mandate to control them.

Hence the authority of RBI as the Central Bank of the country stem from the RBI Act of 1934 and the Banking Regulation Act of 1949. Both these acts have been later amended many times to widen the authority of RBI.

Besides these two Acts, RBI also derive many further authorities to control and monitor the foreign exchange business, payment systems in the country, etc., through many other Acts passed by the Govt. of India.

Main Functions of RBI are:

- RBI is the Monetary Authority of the country, which formulates implements and monitors the monetary policy (interest rates, credit policies, money supply) with the objective for maintaining price stability and ensuring adequate flow of credit to productive sectors.
- Banker to banks and the banker of last resort: RBI maintains banking accounts of all scheduled banks. Also acts as the banker of last resort. In this role, RBI injects funds into the system to help banks tide over temporary mismatches of funds. Later RBI moved to an auction system of repos and reverse repos to suck-out or inject liquidity to the market.
- Regulator and supervisor of the financial system (banking system and other financial system and NBFCs): Prescribes broad parameters of banking operations within which the country's banking and financial system functions with the objective to maintain public confidence in the system, protect depositors' interest and provide cost-effective banking services to the public.
- RBI is the Manager of Foreign Exchange Reserves of the country and is the regulator of the Foreign Exchange Management Act, 1999, with objective to facilitate external trade and payment and promote orderly development and maintenance of foreign exchange market in India.
- RBI is the Issuer of currency notes and coins with objective to give the public adequate quantity of supplies of currency notes and coins in good quality.
- Banker to the government performs merchant banking function for the central and the state governments and acts as their banker.

- RBI manages public debt office (central and state government borrowings).
- Under the Payment and Settlement Systems Act, 2007 RBI is the authority to operate or authorise others to operate payment settlement systems.
- Provides settlement platform for cheque clearing, NEFT, RTGS, and ECS.
- RBI provides deposit insurance to bank depositors through its wholly owned subsidiary DICGC.

RBI as the Regulator and Controller of Banking Activities

RBI has control over banking activities in the country and also all related financial activities similar to banking activity. This authority extends to all areas like bank licencing, branch licensing, activities that can be undertaken by banks. RBI also has power to control the management of banks to ensure that they work within the set guidelines. RBI also has supervisory and controlling authority on non-banking businesses like NBFCs of all nature, and financial institutions of all kinds.

From the year 1960, Reserve Bank of India was vested with extensive powers for the supervision of banking in India as the Central Banking Authority and was given powers to compulsorily merge weak banks with other banks to safeguard the public interest. This authority was given to RBI as the country experienced periodic bank failures during the past two decades.

Co-operative banks with paid-up share capital and reserves of ₹ 1 lakh and above were brought under the purview of the Banking Regulation Act, 1949 with effect from 1st March 1966 and within the ambit of the Reserve Bank's supervision. With this, banking related functions (viz. licensing, area of operations, interest rates, etc.) for coop banks are now governed by RBI. However, registration, management, audit, and liquidation, etc. of coop banks are governed by State Governments as per the provisions of respective State Acts.

RBI has largely succeeded in streamlining and consolidating banking sector in the country. It became proactive to safeguard interests of the depositors and managed to enforce mergers to save the weak banks from closing down.

From period 1949 to 1991, it monitored banking operations by framing rules and guidelines for every aspect of banking and involved itself in micro management of banks. From the year 1991, financial sector reforms were introduced and RBI played a stellar role in transforming Indian banking to global banking standards. In the process, it distanced itself from the micro management of banks and moved to the macro management of the banks.

In case of commercial banks, RBI authority is almost complete and in case of banks in cooperative sector, RBI authority on them is on banking related areas. Coop banks are also governed by respective state govt.'s cooperative laws.

The rate of interest both on bank deposits and bank loans are now can be decided by the banks themselves. However, in earlier years (before October 1997) even the interest rates were prescribed by RBI. The rate of interest on deposits and loans are now fixed by individual banks and is generally market determined.

The following table gives the key interest rates in banking business:

Table 3.1: Structure of Interest Rates

(Per cent per annum)

Year (as at end March)	Call/ Notice Money Rates	Deposit Rates*				Lending Rates*	MCLR (1-year)
		Savings #	Term Deposits				
			1-3 yrs	3-5 yrs	Above 5 yrs		
1	2	3	4	5	6	7	8
2004-05	4.65	3.5	5.25-5.75	5.75-6.25	6.25	10.25-11.00	--
2005-06	5.60	3.5	6.00-6.75	6.25-7.00	6.50-7.00	10.25-12.75	--
2006-07	7.22	3.5	6.75-8.50	7.75-9.50	7.75-8.50	12.25-14.75	--
2007-08	6.07	3.5	8.00-8.75	8.00-8.75	8.50-9.00	12.25-15.75	--
2008-09	7.26	3.5	8.00-8.75	8.00-8.50	7.75-8.50	11.50-16.75	--

2009-10	3.29	3.5	6.00-7.00	6.50-7.50	7.00-7.75	11.00-15.75	--
2010-11	5.89	3.5	8.25-9.00	8.25-8.75	8.50-8.75	8.25-9.50	--
2011-12	8.22	4	9.00-9.25	9.00-9.25	8.50-9.25	10.00-10.75	--
2012-13	8.09	4	8.75-9.00	8.75-9.00	8.50-9.00	9.70-10.25	--
2013-14	8.28	4	8.75-9.25	8.75-9.10	8.50-9.10	10.00-10.25	--
2014-15	7.97	4	8.50-8.75	8.50-8.75	8.25-8.50	10.00-10.25	--
2015-16	6.98	4	7.25-7.50	7.00-7.50	7.00-7.30	9.30-9.70	--
2016-17	6.25	4	6.75-7.00	6.50-6.90	6.50-6.75	7.75-8.20	8.00-8.50
2017-18	5.94	3.50-4.00	6.40-6.75	6.25-6.70	6.25-6.75	7.80-7.95	8.15-8.30
2018-19	6.27	3.50-4.00	6.25-7.25	6.25-7.25	6.25-7.25	8.05-8.55	8.45-8.80
2019-20	5.43	3.00-3.50	5.00-6.20	5.70-6.40	5.70-6.40	7.45-7.90	7.75-8.20
2020-21	3.44	2.70-3.00	4.90-5.30	5.25-5.35	5.25-5.50	6.55-7.05	7.00-7.40
2021-22	3.26	2.70-3.00	5.00-5.20	5..05-5.45	5.05-5.60	6.45-7.00	7.00-7.30
2022-23	4.38	2.70-3.00	5.30-5.60	5.35-6.10	5.35-.5.90	6.80-7.65	7.60-7.90

: Savings deposit rate from 2011-12 onwards relates to balance up to ₹ 1 lakh. Savings deposit rate was deregulated with effect from October 25, 2011.

* : Data on deposit and lending rates relate to five major Public Sector Banks up to 2003-04. While for the subsequent years, they relate to five major banks.

Notes: 1. Data on lending rates relate to either Prime Lending Rate (PLR) or Benchmark Prime Lending Rate (BPLR), Base Rate or Marginal Cost of Funds Based Lending Rate (MCLR) (overnight and 1-Year) as the case may be for the relevant year.

2. BPLR system effective November 2003 was replaced by the Base Rate System effective from July 1, 2010.

3. Base Rate System effective from July 1, 2010 was replaced by the MCLR System effective from April 1, 2016.

4. Call/Notice money rates are weighted average rates for the year.

Source: Scheduled Commercial Banks (excluding RRBs and SFBs) and the Reserve Bank of India.

Call/notice money rates are the rates at which banks lend or borrow from other banks. Bank deposit rates are given for savings and term deposits. Term deposit rates are given as a maximum range as each bank may have its own rate which may be slightly different from other banks.

Similarly, the lending rates are also shown as a maximum range of rates as individual bank's lending rates may be different.

MCLR rate is Marginal Cost of funds-based Lending Rate, a benchmark lending rate now fixed by individual banks.

None of the above interest rates are controlled by RBI and are fixed by the banks themselves. We can observe that interest rates both for deposits and bank loans have come down over the years to the present levels. Bank deposit rates were over 10% and loan interest was about 20% in 1970s and 1980s.

It is interesting to learn about the reduction in interest rates over the years and the reasons for it. It is also important to visualise the future trend in these rates—whether it will fall further or it can go up?

As RBI has no role in fixing the interest rates, it is called as market determined. But how the market moves and what are the factors that influence the changes in interest rates?

In some way RBI is a player in this. There is one basic benchmark rate of interest in the economy. This benchmark rate is the interest rate at which RBI lends to commercial banks in its role as bankers' bank. This rate is known as 'bank rate' fixed by RBI. Now RBI is not using bank rate as the reference benchmark rate. RBI now uses 'repo rate' as the benchmark rate. Repo rate is the rate of interest at which RBI lends to commercial banks against govt. securities as collateral for the borrowing.

How RBI fixes its repo rate? Repo rate is very important benchmark rate in the financial markets and all banks and FIs will consider the repo rate as the base rate and fix their own lending rates or deposit rates generally with a margin over the repo rate.

Further RBI as the monetary authority of the country has the onus to fix the repo rate keeping in mind the inflation level in the country and the money supply in the economy. RBI needs to encourage markets, either to borrow or lend keeping in mind the desired progress and direction of the economic activities.

The chapter on interest rate structure in this book gives more information on this aspect.

RBI as the Monetary Authority of the Country

The preamble of the RBI Act, 1934 says that "to constitute a Reserve Bank for India to regulate the issue of bank notes and the keeping of reserves with a view to securing monetary stability in India and generally to operate the currency any credit system of the country to its advantage;".....

RBI is constituted with a view to securing monetary stability in the country and to operate currency and credit system to the advantage of the country. Though owned by Govt. of India, RBI is made an autonomous body and RBI acts independently as the monetary authority of the country.

RBI formulates its monetary policy well in advance to support the govt.'s fiscal policies for the development of various sectors of the country. RBI's areas of controls in this are mainly,

- The currency management,
- Money supply and bank credit to provide liquidity,
- Price rise and inflation control.

This RBI tries to do using many monetary tools available to it. RBI conducts reviews regularly and brings in necessary changes to achieve its objectives.

The role of monetary authority is to formulate, implement and monitors the monetary policies. Main objective of formulation of monetary policy is to maintain price stability, exercise control on inflation by suitable policy measures, and to ensure the credit flow to the productive sectors of the economy.

It is thus interesting to learn about RBIs role in containing inflation. One measure generally followed by RBI is by controlling the money supply in the economy. Money supply is not merely the cash held by public. It also includes bank deposits as money at bank is equal to cash for the account holders. RBI tries to have money supply just enough to meet all genuine and development related activities. Excess money supply may lead to price rise and inflation. A Short money supply will inhibit business activity and prices may fall.

In May 2016, RBI Act, 1934 was amended and made certain changes in the monetary policy framing system by RBI as under:

Prior to the amendments in 2016, 'the flexible inflation targeting framework' was governed by an Agreement on Monetary Policy Framework between the Government and the Reserve Bank of India. In May 2016, the Reserve Bank of India (RBI) Act, 1934 was amended to provide a statutory basis for the implementation of the flexible inflation targeting framework. The amended RBI Act provides for the inflation target to be set by the Government of India, in consultation with the Reserve Bank, once in every five years. Accordingly, the Central Government has notified in the Official Gazette, 4 per cent Consumer Price Index (CPI) inflation as the target for the period from August 5, 2016 to March 31, 2021 with the upper tolerance limit of 6 per cent and the lower tolerance limit of 2 per cent.

Prior to the year 2016, a Technical Advisory Committee (TAC) on monetary policy with experts from monetary economics, central banking, financial markets and public finance advised the Reserve Bank on the stance of monetary policy. However, its role was only advisory in nature. RBI took the final decisions.

In year 2016, RBI Act was amended and the Section 45ZB of the amended RBI Act, 1934 provided for an empowered six-member monetary policy committee (MPC) to be constituted by the Central Government by notification in the Official Gazette. Accordingly, the Central Government in September 2016 constituted the MPC as under:

1. Governor of the Reserve Bank of India—Chairperson, ex officio;
2. Deputy Governor of the Reserve Bank of India, in charge of Monetary Policy—Member, ex officio;
3. One officer of the Reserve Bank of India to be nominated by the Central Board—Member, ex officio;

4. Shri Chetan Ghate, Professor, Indian Statistical Institute (ISI)—Member;
5. Professor Pami Dua, Director, Delhi School of Economics—Member; and
6. Dr. Ravindra H. Dholakia, Professor, Indian Institute of Management, Ahmedabad—Member.

(Members referred to at 4 to 6 above, will hold office for a period of four years or until further orders, whichever is earlier.)

Now the MPC determines the policy interest rate required to achieve the inflation target. With the formation of MPC, the TAC on Monetary Policy ceased to exist.

At present (April 2023), the monetary policy committee has following members:

1. Shri Shaktikanta Das, RBI Governor.
2. Dr. Michael Debabrata Patra, RBI Deputy Governor in charge of monetary policy.
3. Dr. Rajiv Ranjan, RBI Executive Director (the officer of the Reserve Bank nominated by the Central Board under Section 45ZB(2)(c) of the Reserve Bank of India Act, 1934).
4. Dr. Shashanka Bhide, Honorary Senior Advisor, National Council of Applied Economic Research, Delhi.
5. Dr. Ashima Goyal, Emeritus Professor, Indira Gandhi Institute of Development Research, Mumbai.
6. Prof. Jayanth R. Varma, Professor, Indian Institute of Management, Ahmedabad.

The Monetary Policy Framework

The Reserve Bank of India (RBI) is vested with the responsibility of conducting monetary policy. Monetary policy refers to the policy of the central bank with regard to the use of monetary instruments under its control to achieve the goals specified in the Act.

Under the amended RBI Act, the monetary policy making operates as under:

- The MPC is required to meet at least four times in a year.
- The quorum for the meeting of the MPC is four members.
- Each member of the MPC has one vote, and in the event of an equality of votes, the Governor has a second or casting vote.
- On the 14th day, the minutes of the proceedings of the MPC are published which include:
  (a) the resolution adopted by the MPC;
  (b) the vote of each member on the resolution, ascribed to such member; and
  (c) the statement of each member on the resolution adopted.
- Once in every six months, the Reserve Bank is required to publish a document called the Monetary Policy Report to explain:
  (a) the sources of inflation; and
  (b) the forecast of inflation for 6-18 months ahead.

At present Reserve Bank operates the monetary policy framework of the country under the amended RBI Act. Monetary policy framework works as under:

- The framework aims at setting the policy (repo) rate based on an assessment of the current and evolving macroeconomic situation; and modulation of liquidity conditions to anchor money market rates at or around the repo rate. Repo rate changes transmit through the money market to the entire the financial system, which, in turn, influences aggregate demand—a key determinant of inflation and growth.
- Once the repo rate is announced, the operating framework designed by the Reserve Bank envisages liquidity management on a day-to-day basis through appropriate actions, which aim at anchoring the operating target—the weighted average call rate (WACR)—around the repo rate.

- The operating framework is fine-tuned and revised depending on the evolving financial market and monetary conditions, while ensuring consistency with the monetary policy stance.

Thus, the aim of monetary policy is to ensure that the inflation rate in the country is kept within the accepted band agreed upon by GOI. RBI has to fix the repo rate in such a way that the interest rate structure in the economy is in line with the benchmark repo rate. Then RBI shall manage the money supply and bank credit to be conducive for growth of the various sectors of economy as planned by the GOI. RBI is required to keep watch on the economy and make changes in repo rate, money supply and availability of bank credit for all productive purposes.

There are several direct and indirect instruments that are used by RBI for implementing monetary policy which is as under:

- *Repo Rate*: The (fixed) interest rate at which the Reserve Bank provides overnight liquidity to banks against the collateral of government and other approved securities under the liquidity adjustment facility (LAF).
- *Reverse Repo Rate*: The (fixed) interest rate at which the Reserve Bank absorbs liquidity, on an overnight basis, from banks against the collateral of eligible government securities under the LAF.
- *Liquidity Adjustment Facility (LAF)*: The LAF consists of overnight as well as term repo auctions. The Reserve Bank also conducts variable interest rate reverse repo auctions, as necessitated under the market conditions. Progressively, the Reserve Bank has increased the proportion of liquidity injected under fine-tuning variable rate repo auctions of range of tenors. The aim of term repo is to help develop the inter-bank term money market, which in turn can set market-based benchmarks for pricing of loans and deposits, and hence improve transmission of monetary policy.
- *Marginal Standing Facility (MSF)*: A facility under which scheduled commercial banks can borrow additional

amount of overnight money from the Reserve Bank by dipping into their Statutory Liquidity Ratio (SLR) portfolio up to a limit at a penal rate of interest. This provides a safety valve against unanticipated liquidity shocks to the banking system.

- *Corridor*: The MSF rate and reverse repo rate determine the corridor for the daily movement in the weighted average call money rate.
- *Bank Rate*: It is the rate at which the Reserve Bank is ready to buy or rediscount bills of exchange or other commercial papers. The Bank Rate is published under Section 49 of the Reserve Bank of India Act, 1934. This rate has been aligned to the MSF rate and, therefore, changes automatically as and when the MSF rate changes alongside the policy repo rate changes.
- *Cash Reserve Ratio (CRR)*: The average daily balance that a bank is required to maintain with the Reserve Bank as a share of such per cent of its Net Demand and Time Liabilities (NDTL) that the Reserve Bank may notify from time to time in the Gazette of India.
- *Statutory Liquidity Ratio (SLR)*: The share of NDTL that a bank is required to maintain in safe and liquid assets, such as, unencumbered government securities, cash and gold. Changes in SLR often influence the availability of resources in the banking system for lending to the private sector.
- *Open Market Operations (OMOs)*: These include both, outright purchase and sale of government securities, for injection and absorption of durable liquidity, respectively.
- *Market Stabilisation Scheme (MSS)*: This instrument for monetary management was introduced in 2004. Surplus liquidity of a more enduring nature arising from large capital inflows is absorbed through sale of short-dated government securities and treasury bills. The cash so mobilised is held in a separate government account with the Reserve Bank.

Source: RBI on monetary policy-overview.

Prior to banking sector reforms introduced in the year 1991, RBI was using CRR and SLR regularly as monetary tools to control bank credit. After banking sector reforms RBI has accepted the prescribed maximum of 5% and 25% for CRR and SLR respectively. But the changes in CRR and SLR within the band also have their effects on banks' lending.

LAF facilities consisting of repo and reverse repo auctions are now used as monetary tools. Repo rate has now become very important policy rate by RBI which sets the movement of interest rates in financial sectors of the country. Change in repo rate is also accompanied with changes in other policy rates like reverse repo, MSF rate and Bank Rate. Repo, reverse repo and MSF facilities are also aimed to help banks in their day-to-day liquidity management. Reverse repo, open market operations and market stabilisation scheme is aiming at mainly to remove excess liquidity with banks.

Changes in repo rate by RBI now get transmitted to banks deposit rates and lending rates. Increase or decrease in lending rates by banks will impact the credit demand from the borrowers. Higher loan interest will discourage borrowers to borrow from banks and lower loan interest may increase the demand for bank loans.

The movement of interest rates fixed in terms of monetary policy by RBI and the reserve requirements for banks fixed by RBI are shown in the following table:

Major monetary policy rates and reserve requirements—Bank Rate, LAF (Repo, Reverse Repo & MSF) rates, CRR & SLR

Effective Date		Fix Range LAF Rates				
	Bank Rate	Repo	Reverse	Cash Reserve Ratio	Marginal Standing Facility	Statutory Liquidity Ratio
08-02-2023	6.75	6.50	-	-	6.75	-
07-12-2022	6.50	6.25	-	-	6.50	-
30-09-2022	6.15	5.90	-	-	6.15	-
05-08-2022	5.65	5.40	-	-	5.65	-
08-06-2022	5.15	4.90	-	-	5.15	-
21-05-2022	-	-	-	4.50	-	-
04-05-2022	4.65	4.40	-	-	4.65	-

22-05-2021	-	-	-	4.00	-	-
27-03-2021	-	-	-	3.50	-	-
22-05-2020	4.25	4.00	3.35	-	4.25	-
17-04-2020	-	4.40	3.75	-	-	-
11-04-2020	-	-	-	-	-	18.00
28-03-2020	-	-	-	3.00	-	-
27-03-2020	4.65	4.40	4.00	-	4.65	-
04-01-2020	-	-	-	-	-	18.25
12-10-2019	-	-	-	-	-	18.50
04-10-2019	5.40	5.15	4.90	-	5.40	-
07-08-2019	5.65	5.40	5.15	-	5.65	-
06-07-2019	-	-	-	-	-	18.75
06-06-2019	6.00	5.75	5.50	-	6.00	-
13-04-2019	-	-	-	-	-	19.00
04-04-2019	6.25	6.00	5.75	-	6.25	-
07-02-2019	6.50	6.25	6.00	-	6.5	-
05-01-2019	-	-	-	-	-	19.25
01-08-2018	6.75	6.50	6.25	-	6.75	-
06-06-2018	6.50	6.25	6.00	-	6.50	-
14-10-2017	-	-	-	-	-	19.5
02-08-2017	6.25	6.00	5.75	-	6.25	-
24-06-2017	-	-	-	-	-	20.00
06-04-2017	6.50	-	6.00	-	6.50	-
07-01-2017	-	-	-	-	-	20.50
04-10-2016	6.75	6.25	5.75	-	6.75	-
01-10-2016	-	-	-	-	-	20.75
09-07-2016	-	-	-	-	-	21.00
05-04-2016	7.00	6.50	6.00	-	7.00	-
02-04-2016	-	-	-	-	-	21.25
29-09-2015	7.75	6.75	5.75	-	7.75	-
27-06-2015	-	-	-	4.00	-	-
02-06-2015	8.25	7.25	6.25	-	8.25	-
04-03-2015	8.50	7.50	6.50	-	8.50	-
07-02-2015	-	-	-	-	-	21.50
15-01-2015	8.75	7.75	6.75	-	8.75	-
09-08-2014	-	-	-	-	-	22.00
14-06-2014	-	-	-	-	-	22.50
28-01-2014	9.00	8.00	7.00	-	9.00	-

Source: RBI.

We can observe from the above table the movement of policy rates by RBI. The repo rate which was 8% in the year 2014 has come down over a period and it is 4% in 2020. Repo rate is the benchmark rate as it is the rate at which banks can borrow funds from RBI by offering securities. In view of this, repo rate is taken into account by all others in the financial market segments, including banks, to fix their own rates for deposits or for loans. As we observe that repo rate has come down by 4% from 2014 to 2020 we can understand the downward movement of bank deposit rates and bank loan rates over these years.

However, from the year 2022 repo rate started going up and by December 2022 it was 6.25% and in February 2023 it was 6.50%. We can understand the impact on banking sector as banks have hiked their deposit interest rates and loan interest rates in the year 2022 and 2023.

RBI policy rate is generally guided by the expected inflation rate in the economy based on RBI survey on it. RBI presents its monetary policy reports twice in a year in April and October.

Monetary policy report of April 2023 stated as under:

THE MONETARY POLICY REPORT OF APRIL 2023—EXCERPTS

Date: Apr 20, 2023

Minutes of the Monetary Policy Committee Meeting, April 3, 5 and 6, 2023

[Under Section 45ZL of the Reserve Bank of India Act, 1934]

The forty second meeting of the Monetary Policy Committee (MPC), constituted under Section 45ZB of the Reserve Bank of India Act, 1934, was held during April 3, 5 and 6, 2023.

2. The meeting was attended by all the members—Dr. Shashanka Bhide, Honorary Senior Advisor, National Council of Applied Economic Research, Delhi; Dr. Ashima Goyal, Emeritus Professor, Indira Gandhi Institute of Development Research, Mumbai; Prof. Jayanth R. Varma, Professor, Indian Institute of Management, Ahmedabad; Dr. Rajiv Ranjan,

Executive Director (the officer of the Reserve Bank nominated by the Central Board under Section 45ZB(2)(c) of the Reserve Bank of India Act, 1934); Dr. Michael Debabrata Patra, Deputy Governor in charge of monetary policy—and was chaired by Shri Shaktikanta Das, Governor.

3. According to Section 45ZL of the Reserve Bank of India Act, 1934, the Reserve Bank shall publish, on the fourteenth day after every meeting of the Monetary Policy Committee, the minutes of the proceedings of the meeting which shall include the following, namely:

(a) the resolution adopted at the meeting of the Monetary Policy Committee;

(b) the vote of each member of the Monetary Policy Committee, ascribed to such member, on the resolution adopted in the said meeting; and

(c) the statement of each member of the Monetary Policy Committee under sub-section (11) of section 45ZI on the resolution adopted in the said meeting.

4. The MPC reviewed the surveys conducted by the Reserve Bank to gauge consumer confidence, households' inflation expectations, corporate sector performance, credit conditions, the outlook for the industrial, services and infrastructure sectors, and the projections of professional forecasters. The MPC also reviewed in detail the staff's macroeconomic projections, and alternative scenarios around various risks to the outlook. Drawing on the above and after extensive discussions on the stance of monetary policy, the MPC adopted the resolution that is set out below.

Resolution

5. On the basis of an assessment of the current and evolving macroeconomic situation, the Monetary Policy Committee (MPC) at its meeting today (April 6, 2023) decided to:

- Keep the policy repo rate under the liquidity adjustment facility (LAF) unchanged at 6.50 per cent.

The standing deposit facility (SDF) rate remains unchanged at 6.25 per cent and the marginal standing facility (MSF) rate and the Bank Rate at 6.75 per cent.

- The MPC also decided to remain focused on withdrawal of accommodation to ensure that inflation progressively aligns with the target, while supporting growth.

These decisions are in consonance with the objective of achieving the medium-term target for consumer price index (CPI) inflation of 4 per cent within a band of +/- 2 per cent, while supporting growth.

The main considerations underlying the decision are set out in the statement below.

Assessment

Global Economy

6. Global economic activity remains resilient amidst the persistence of inflation at elevated levels, turmoil in the banking system in some advanced economies (AEs), tight financial conditions and lingering geopolitical hostilities. Recent financial stability concerns have triggered risk aversion, flights to safety and heightened financial market volatility. Sovereign bond yields fell steeply in March on safe haven demand, reversing the sharp increase in February over aggressive monetary stances and communication. Equity markets have declined since the last MPC meeting and the US dollar has pared its gains. Weakening external demand, spillovers from the banking crisis in some AEs, volatile capital flows and debt distress in certain vulnerable economies weigh on growth prospects.

Domestic Economy

7. The second advance estimates (SAE) released by the National Statistical Office (NSO) on February 28, 2023 placed India's real gross domestic product (GDP) growth at 7.0 per cent in 2022-23. Private consumption and public investment were the major drivers of growth.

8. Economic activity remained resilient in Q4. Rabi foodgrains production is expected to increase by 6.2 per cent in 2022-23. The index of industrial production (IIP) expanded by 5.2 per cent in January while the output of eight core industries rose even faster by 8.9 per cent in January and 6.0 per cent

in February, indicative of the strength of industrial activity. In the services sector, domestic air passenger traffic, port freight traffic, e-way bills and toll collections posted healthy growth in Q4, while railway freight traffic registered a modest growth. Purchasing managers' indices (PMIs) pointed towards sustained expansion in both manufacturing and services in March.

9. Amongst urban demand indicators, passenger vehicle sales recorded strong growth in February while consumer durables contracted in January. Among rural demand indicators, tractor and two-wheeler sales were robust in February. As regards investment activity, growth in steel consumption and cement output accelerated in February. Merchandise exports and non-oil non-gold imports contracted in February while the strong growth in services exports continued.

10. CPI headline inflation rose from 5.7 per cent in December 2022 to 6.4 per cent in February 2023 on the back of higher inflation in cereals, milk and fruits and slower deflation in vegetables prices. Fuel inflation remained elevated, though some softening was witnessed in February due to a fall in kerosene (PDS) prices and favourable base effects. Core inflation (i.e., CPI excluding food and fuel) remained elevated and was above 6 per cent in January-February. The moderation observed in inflation in clothing and footwear, and transportation and communication was largely offset by a pick-up in inflation in personal care and effects and housing.

11. The average daily absorption under the LAF moderated to ₹1.4 lakh crore during February-March from an average of ₹1.6 lakh crore in December-January. During 2022-23, money supply (M3) expanded by 9.0 per cent and non-food bank credit rose by 15.4 per cent. India's foreign exchange reserves were placed at US$ 578.4 billion as on March 31, 2023.

Outlook

12. The inflation trajectory for 2023-24 would be shaped by both domestic and global factors. The expectation of a record rabi foodgrains production bodes well for the food prices outlook. The impact of recent unseasonal rains and hailstorms, however, needs to be watched. Milk prices could remain firm due

to high input costs and seasonal factors. Crude oil prices outlook is subject to high uncertainty. Global financial market volatility has surged, with potential upsides for imported inflation risks. Easing cost conditions are leading to some moderation in the pace of output price increases in manufacturing and services, as indicated by the Reserve Bank's enterprise surveys. The lagged pass-through of input costs could, however, keep core inflation elevated. Taking into account these factors and assuming an annual average crude oil price (Indian basket) of US$ 85 per barrel and a normal monsoon, CPI inflation is projected at 5.2 per cent for 2023-24, with Q1 at 5.1 per cent, Q2 at 5.4 per cent, Q3 at 5.4 per cent and Q4 at 5.2 per cent, and risks evenly balanced.

13. A good rabi crop should strengthen rural demand, while the sustained buoyancy in contact-intensive services should support urban demand. The government's thrust on capital expenditure, above trend capacity utilisation in manufacturing, double digit credit growth and the moderation in commodity prices are expected to bolster manufacturing and investment activity. According to the RBI's surveys, businesses and consumers are optimistic about the future outlook. The external demand drag could accentuate, given slowing global trade and output. Protracted geopolitical tensions, tight global financial conditions and global financial market volatility pose risks to the outlook. Taking all these factors into consideration, real GDP growth for 2023-24 is projected at 6.5 per cent with Q1:2023-24 at 7.8 per cent; Q2 at 6.2 per cent; Q3 at 6.1 per cent; and Q4 at 5.9 per cent, with risks evenly balanced.

14. With CPI headline inflation ruling persistently above the tolerance band, the MPC decided to remain resolutely focused on aligning inflation with the target. It is essential to rein in the generalisation of price pressures and anchor inflation expectations. An environment of low and stable prices is necessary for the resilience in domestic economic activity to be sustained. While the policy rate has been increased by a cumulative 250 basis points since May 2022, which is still working through the system, there can be no room for letting down the guard

on price stability. Taking these factors into account, the MPC decided to keep the policy repo rate unchanged at 6.50 per cent in this meeting, with readiness to act, should the situation so warrant. The MPC will continue to keep a strong vigil on the evolving inflation and growth outlook and will not hesitate to take further action as may be required in its future meetings. The MPC also decided to remain focused on withdrawal of accommodation to ensure that inflation progressively aligns with the target, while supporting growth.

15. All members of the MPC—Dr. Shashanka Bhide, Dr. Ashima Goyal, Prof. Jayanth R. Varma, Dr. Rajiv Ranjan, Dr. Michael Debabrata Patra and Shri Shaktikanta Das—unanimously voted to keep the policy repo rate unchanged at 6.50 per cent.

16. Dr. Shashanka Bhide, Dr. Ashima Goyal, Dr. Rajiv Ranjan, Dr. Michael Debabrata Patra and Shri Shaktikanta Das voted to remain focused on withdrawal of accommodation to ensure that inflation progressively aligns with the target, while supporting growth. Prof. Jayanth R. Varma expressed reservations on this part of the resolution.

Source: RBI.

The monetary policy report includes the forecast of CPI inflation. CPI inflation is projected at 5.2 per cent for 2023-24, with Q1 at 5.1 per cent, Q2 at 5.4 per cent, Q3 at 5.4 per cent and Q4 at 5.2 per cent, and risks evenly balanced.

It also says that the real GDP growth for 2023-24 is projected at 6.5 per cent with Q1:2023-24 at 7.8 per cent; Q2 at 6.2 per cent; Q3 at 6.1 per cent; and Q4 at 5.9 per cent, with risks evenly balanced.

Taking these factors into account, the MPC decided to keep the policy repo rate unchanged at 6.50 per cent in this meeting, with readiness to act, should the situation so warrant.

Repo rate was 4% in 22-5-2020 and the repo rate has been increased by a cumulative 250 basis points since May 2022. MPC in its observation stated that it is still working through the system, and there can be no room for letting down the guard on price stability. Taking these factors into account, the

MPC decided to keep the policy repo rate unchanged at 6.50 per cent in this meeting.

We can also observe that the repo rate is near or higher than the inflation rate predicted. This is because the interest rates for deposits shall be more than inflation rate or else there is no incentive to the depositors to save. The interest rate on deposits after adjusting it to inflation is the real interest earning to the depositor. Under normal circumstances the 'real interest rate' for deposit should always be positive.

At the same time the bank loan interest rates are also crucial as unless the loans are given at reasonable interest rates, borrowers will be discouraged to borrow from banks which in turn will affect production and growth in the economy.

Thus, while fixing the repo rate RBI aims to check inflation and promote production and growth. This calls for a balancing act by RBI. Govt is always interested to boost agriculture, industry, and trade to increase employment and GDP. This has led many times to divergent views by Govt and RBI. RBI has the primary responsibility to check inflation and price rise. As RBI is the monetary authority independent from govt., monetary policy rates can be changed by RBI only.

Functions of RBI—Currency Management

The preamble to the RBI Act, 1934 describes its main functions as "...to regulate the issue of Bank Notes and keeping of reserves with a view to securing monetary stability in India and generally to operate the currency and credit system of the country to its advantage."

Sections 33 and 34 of the RBI Act prescribes rules for assets and liabilities of the Issue Dept. of RBI which is entrusted with the issue and management of currency notes as under:

Sec. 33. Assets of the Issue Department.

(1) The assets of the Issue Department shall consist of gold coin, gold bullion, [foreign securities], rupee coin and rupee securities to such aggregate amount as is not less than the total of the liabilities of the Issue Department as hereinafter defined.

[(2) The aggregate value of the gold coin, gold bullion and foreign securities held as assets and the aggregate value of the gold coin and gold bullion so held shall not at any time be less than two hundred crores of rupees and one hundred and fifteen crores of rupees, respectively.]

[(3) The remainder of the assets shall be held in rupee coin, Government of India rupee securities of any maturity, promissory notes drawn by the National Bank for any loans or advances under clause (4E) of Section 17 and such bills of exchange and promissory notes payable in India as are eligible for purchase by the bank under sub-clause (a) or sub-clause (b) or sub-clause (bb) of clause (2) of Section 17 or under clause (1) of Section 18.]

(4) For the purposes of this section, gold coin and gold bullion shall be valued at [a price not exceeding the international market price for the time being obtaining], rupee coin shall be valued at its face value, and securities shall be valued [at rates not exceeding the market rates] for the time being obtaining.

(5) Of the gold coin and gold bullion held as assets, not less than seventeen-twentieths shall be held in [India], and all gold coin and gold bullion held as assets shall be held in the custody of the bank or its agencies; Provided that gold belonging to the bank which is in any other bank or in any mint or treasury or in transit may be reckoned as part of the assets.

(6) For the purposes of this section, the foreign securities which may be held as part of the assets shall be—

(i) Securities of the following kinds payable in the currency of any foreign country which is a member of the International Monetary Fund, namely:

(a) balances with the bank which is the principal currency authority of that foreign country and any other balances or securities in foreign currency maintained with or issued by the International Monetary Fund, the International Bank for Reconstruction and Development, the International Development Association or the International Finance Corporation [or Asian Development Bank] or the Bank for

International Settlements or [any banking or financial institution [approved] by the Central Government] in this behalf, provided that they are repayable within a [period of ten years];

(b) bills of exchange bearing two or more good signatures and drawn on and payable at any place in that foreign country and having a maturity not exceeding ninety days; and

(c) Government securities of that foreign country maturing [within ten years];

(ii) any drawing rights representing a liability of the International Monetary Fund.

Sec. 34. Liabilities of the Issue Department.

(1) The liabilities of the Issue Department shall be an amount equal to the total of the amount of the currency notes of the Government of India and bank notes for the time being in circulation.

Prior to the year 1956, RBI was following 'proportional reserve system' for note issue. Under this system the Issue Dept. of RBI shall have assets of minimum 40% in the shape of gold bullion and foreign securities. Within this 40%, minimum gold value shall be ₹ 40 crores. Remaining 60% assets can be rupee coins rupee securities. In the year 1956 in view of demand for currency notes by the system, RBI moved to 'minimum reserve system' of maintaining assets. Under this system, issue dept. is obliged to maintain minimum of gold bullion and foreign securities of ₹ 200 crores and ₹ 115 crores respectively. Rest of the assets can be in rupee securities.

Though minimum reserve system allowed flexibility for issue of notes it was felt that this system may lead to inflationary trend in the economy due to expansion in currency note issue. This is mainly due to the fact that Govt. of India can borrow from RBI any amount, by issuing securities in the form of promissory notes. In fact, the deficit in yearly govt. budgets is met this way. These borrowings from Govt. of India have the effect of increasing money supply in the economy and resultant increase in currency notes with the public.

This was a serious issue leading to inflation and price rise. As the Govt. of India is the supreme authority in the matter, only self-restraint by Govt. of India can keep the economy in good condition. This will require self-imposed budgetary deficits ratios to be observed by Govt. of India. Govt. of India is aware of the situation and generally works out this aspect in consultation and on the advice of RBI as the monetary authority of the country.

In recent years RBI has achieved some success in this. At present RBI is holding assets in its issue dept. against the liability of currency notes issued by it in the form gold bullion and foreign securities alone. It is not holding rupee securities as assets of the issue dept. We can observe this in the latest balance sheet of RBI for its year ending with March 2021.

Excerpt from RBI balance sheet dated 31-3-2021 is as under:

Reserve Bank of India Balance Sheet as on March 31, 2021

(Amount in ₹ crore)

Liabilities	Schedule	2019-20	2020-21	Assets	Schedule	2019-20	2020-21
Liabilities of Issue Department				Assets of Issue Department (ID) (As backing for Notes Issued)			
Notes Issued	5	26,35,574.66	28,26,862.67	Gold - ID	7	1,13,145.92	1,04,140.13
				Rupee Coin		784.83	743.40
				Investments-Foreign-ID	8	25,21,643.91	27,21,979.14
				Investments-Domestic-ID	9	0.00	0.00
				Domestic Bills of Exchange and other Commercial Papers		0.00	0.00
						26,35,574.66	28,26,862.67

Source: RBI.

RBI is now managing to have assets against the notes issued by it, in the form of gold bullion, rupee coins and foreign investments. This reserve system is aimed to provide stability to the Indian rupee. RBI has reduced the rupee assets of issue dept.

which was 60.94% in 1998 to nil in the year 2017. Reduction of rupee assets over the years is shown in the table below.

RBI issue dept. assets held against currency issued

Year ending June	Total assets of issue dept. ₹ billion	Out of which rupee assets ₹ billion	% of rupee assets to total assets %
1998	1568.62	956.05	60.94
2000	2015.01	1039.24	51.57
2001	2263.90	1088.22	48.06
2002	2590.83	765.67	29.55
2003	2925.38	232.72	7.95
2005	3784.80	15.17	0.40
2010	8420.40	10.46	0.12
2017	15063.31	0	0
2018	19119.60	0	0
2019	21687.97	0	0
2020	26355.74	0	0
2020-21	28268.62	0	0

Source: Assets of issue dept. from annual reports of RBI.

The total assets of Issue Dept. are equal to the currency notes issued by it.

*RBI, from the year 2020-21, changed its the accounting year to April-March (earlier July-June). Hence 2020-21 figures are as at 31st March 2021.

@ Assets of the Issue dept. also includes the rupee coins held by RBI as stated earlier. This represents just a small and insignificant holding compared to total assets. The share of rupee coins in total assets was as under:

Assets of Issue Department 'Rs. In billions'	30-6-2018	30-6-2019	30-6-2020	31-3-2021
Gold Coin and Bullion (as backing for Note issue)	743.49	792.04	1,131.46	1,041.40
Rupee Coin	9.26	8.28	7.85	7.43
Investments-Foreign	18,366.85	20,887.65	25,216.44	27,219.79
Investments-Domestic	0.00	0.00	0.00	0.00

Assets of Issue Department 'Rs. In billions'	30-6-2018	30-6-2019	30-6-2020	31-3-2021
Domestic Bills of Exchange and other Commercial Papers	0.00	0.00	0.00	0.00
Total Assets	19,119.60	21,687.97	26,355.75	28,268.62

Source: RBI balance sheets

Money and Money Supply in the Economy

The economic definition of money is that it is a unit of value, medium of exchange and store of value.

Value of anything is expressed in terms of the currency of the country. So, money serves the purpose as unit of value. We can buy goods and services by paying the price in money, so it serves as a medium of exchange. When we store the money with us it represents the storage of value as we can use it any time in future to buy things.

Money is issued by the govt. or by RBI on behalf of the govt. How much money is there in the country is important to know. But in modern economy it has different meaning. Money being a medium of exchange it represents the total purchasing power. In modern economy an individual deposits his money in a bank account either in SB or current account or in term deposit. So, the physical money goes to bank. In view of this the balance of individuals or entities in bank accounts are also part of money as they are free to use it for purchases whenever they like. Hence while counting the total money this new money equivalent is also to be counted to know the actual purchasing power with the public. This total is called the money supply in the economy.

RBI publishes the position of money supply on fortnightly basis for information. There are many terminologies used to denote the money supply as under:

1. Reserve money (MO)—This has three components in it as under

(a) Currency with the public
(b) Bankers deposits with RBI
(c) Other deposits with RBI

Reserve money is the total of (a), (b), and (c) shown as above.

2. (M1) Narrow money—

(a) Currency with the public
(b) Demand deposit in all banks (e.g. current account, savings account)
(c) Other deposits with RBI

Narrow money also has three components mentioned. This is higher than the reserve money as in place of banker's deposit with RBI, it takes demand deposits of all banks in to account.

3. (M2)—M2 = M1 + Post office bank savings

M2 is similar to M1 with addition of post office savings. Post office savings accounts are also demand deposits in the same category as deposits in all other banks.

4. (M3) Broad money—

(a) Currency with the public
(b) Demand deposits with the banks
(c) Term deposits with the banks
(d) Other deposits with RBI

M3 has four components as mentioned above. M3 is also called as 'broad money' or 'money aggregate'. Term deposits of banks are added as bank term deposits are also repayable on demand by customer, as per practice and convention in our country. Hence M3 represents the total liquidity with the public and it represents purchasing power in the hands of public. RBI considers M3 as an important indicator in its monetary control policy. RBI regularly publishes the position of reserve money and M3.

M4—M4 = M3 + total post office deposits.

In this, total deposits held by post offices in savings, term deposit and recurring deposits are added but other deposit schemes operated by post office like the NSC, IVP, KVP, and PPF, etc. are not included.

Money supply thus expresses the total purchasing power with the public represented by money and money equivalents.

RBI periodically publishes the information of money supply in the economy as under:

The following table shows money stock as per different categories of money stock like M1, M2, M3, and M4. However, money stock M3 is considered as very relevant by RBI for many purposes like monitoring and taking policy decisions. RBI publishes regularly 'statement on money supply' which gives much information on the money supply and how the money supply is finding its uses in the economy.

The table below gives us the glimpse as to how RBI monitors money supply in the economy and how the money supply is put to use.

We can understand that M3 is also called as broad money, actually shows the total money at the disposal of the citizens. Besides the physical cash one may be having, one has bank accounts where he has deposited his money. These bank accounts are also equivalent to cash as balance in bank deposit accounts including the term deposit accounts are payable on demand. Hence M3 shows the total money at the disposal of country's citizens.

Though the bank deposits are payable on demand, in practice the money remains with the bank as all the depositors does not demand for payment all at once. Only exception is when there is a run on any bank. Hence, we may be curious to know as to what happens to all these monies lying with banks. We may also be interested to know how these monies are used and for what purposes?

The following table titled statement of money supply which is periodically published by RBI shows us the components of money supply (M3-broad money) and how it is utilised in the economy.

RBI—Money Stock Measures—Date: Nov. 11, 2019

Money (₹ Crore)

Item	Outstanding as on March 31/last reporting Fridays of the month/reporting Fridays				
	2018-19	2018	2019		
		Sep. 28	Aug. 30	Sep. 13	Sep. 27
	1	2	3	4	5
1. Currency with the Public (1.1 + 1.2 + 1.3 – 1.4)	2052234	1842936	2082639	2108161	2089198
1.1 Notes in Circulation	2110883	1899547	2150382	2176744	2160124
1.2 Circulation of Rupee Coin	25144	24954	25258	25281	25281
1.3 Circulation of Small Coins	743	743	743	743	743
1.4 Cash on Hand with Banks	84536	82308	93744	94607	96950
2. Deposit Money of the Public	1658051	1448770	1511661	1458949	1557208
2.1 Demand Deposits with Banks	1626309	1423190	1480679	1428385	1525227
2.2 'Other' Deposits with Reserve Bank	31742	25580	30982	30564	31981
3. M1 (1 + 2)	3710285	3291706	3594300	3567109	3646406
4. Post Office Saving Bank Deposits	140599	125873	140599	140599	140599
5. M2 (3 + 4)	3850884	3417579	3734899	3707708	3787005
6. Time Deposits with Banks	11720589	11131202	12082792	12081296	12167762
7. M3 (3 + 6)	15430874	14422908	15677092	15648406	15814168
8. Total Post Office Deposits	367287	333620	367287	367287	367287
9. M4 (7 + 8)	15798161	14756528	16044379	16015693	16181455

Note: For scheduled banks, March-end data pertain to the last reporting Friday.
2.2: Exclude balances held in IMF Account No. 1, RBI employees' provident fund, pension fund, gratuity and superannuation fund.

2021

The above table shows the components of money supply and how the total money supply is used in the economy. The data is for 31.3.2021 and 27.8.2021. The table also gives the variations over the fortnight, variations during the year and also the 'year on year' variations. These figures show the trends in the changes over the periods.

While M3 represents the money supply, sources: i, ii, iii, iv and v are the deployment of money supply. The sources and its categories mentioned in the table are explained below for understanding them.

Five categories of money supply deployments:

(i) Net bank credit to government: It includes:

- RBI's credit to government: RBI lends to government for short-term expenditure management.
- Other banks' credit to government: This represents the total of commercial and cooperative banks investments in government securities, including treasury bills.

(ii) Bank credit to commercial sector: It is also includes:

- RBI's credit to commercial sector: This is the aggregate of RBI investments in shares, bonds of financial institutions and also its subsidiaries (like ARDC, DICGC), debentures of land mortgage banks, loans and advances to financial institutions like, IFCI and state financial corporations, and internal bills purchased and discounted.
- Other banks' credit to commercial sector: Loans given by commercial and cooperative banks to commercial sector. Also includes investments by banks in securities (shares, bonds, etc.) issued by commercial sector.

(iii) Net foreign exchange assets of banking sector: It is total of RBI's foreign exchange assets and the foreign assets held by commercial and cooperative banks. RBI holds majority of the foreign assets as part of its forex reserve. The percentage of foreign assets held by banks is small.

Statement on Money Supply

(₹ crore)

Item	Outstanding as on		Variations over									
	2021	2021	Financial year so far						Year-on-year			
			Fortnight		2020-21		2021-22		August 28, 2020		August 27, 2021	
	Mar. 31	Aug. 27	Amount	%	Amount	%	Amount	%	Amount	%	Amount	%
1	2	3	4	5	6	7	8	9	10	11	12	13
M3	18844578	19328505	-77617	-0.4	848008	5.0	483927	2.6	1970881	12.6	1680533	9.5
Components (i+ii+iii+iv)												
i) Currency with the Public	2751828	2830920	-23653	-0.8	233363	9.9	79092	2.9	500477	24.0	247809	9.6
ii) Demand Deposits with Banks	1995120	1926054	-6090	-0.3	-78486	-4.5	-69066	-3.5	178527	12.1	266847	16.1
iii) Time Deposits with Banks	14050278	14525375	-48131	-0.3	691675	5.5	475097	3.4	1282896	10.6	1159684	8.7
iv) 'Other' Deposits with Reserve Bank	47351	46156	257	0.6	1456	3.8	-1195	-2.5	8982	29.0	6192	15.5
Sources (i+ii+iii+iv-v)												
i) Net Bank Credit to Government Sector (a+b)	5850374	6075960	-17417	-0.3	653377	13.2	225586	3.9	893089	18.9	462221	8.2
a) Reserve Bank	1099686	1191232	2805	-	22954	-	91547	-	80224	-	176086	
b) Other Banks	4750689	4884728	-20222	-0.4	630423	15.9	134039	2.8	812865	21.5	286135	6.2

Item	Outstanding as on		Variations over									
	2021	2021	Financial year so far						Year-on-year			
			Fortnight		2020-21		2021-22		August 28, 2020		August 27, 2021	
	Mar. 31	Aug. 27	Amount	%	Amount	%	Amount	%	Amount	%	Amount	%
ii) Bank Credit to Commercial Sector (a+b)	11668466	11608342	7985	0.1	-162407	-1.5	-60124	-0.5	587078	5.7	732105	6.7
a) Reserve Bank	8709	8616	-82		-1601		-93		3968		-2949	
b) Other Banks	11659757	11599726	8067	0.1	-160806	-1.5	-60031	-0.5	583110	5.7	735054	6.8
iii) Net Foreign Exchange Assets of Banking Sector	4578846	4893905	-63442	-1.3	401340	10.6	315059	6.9	940186	28.8	691529	16.5
iv) Government's Currency Liabilities to the Public	26913	27124	0	0.0	103	0.4	211	0.8	450	1.7	673	2.5
v) Banking Sector's Net Non-Monetary Liabilities	3280021	3276826	4743	0.1	44405	1.5	-3195	-0.1	449922	17.2	205995	6.7
of which: Net Non-Monetary Liabilities of R.B.I.	1356660	1316710	-32341	-2.4	43607	3.2	-39950	-2.9	315843	28.6	-105239	-7.4

Note: 1. Data are provisional.

2. Since July 11, 2014, monetary data reflect the impact of revised accounting framework in respect of transactions related to repo/reverse repo, term repo/reverse repo, overnight variable rate repo/reverse repo and MSF.

(iv) Government's currency liabilities to the public: These comprise the holdings of one rupee notes, rupee coins and small coins with the public.

(v) Banking sectors' net non-monetary liabilities: This includes capital and reserves, branch adjustments, and bills payables. The liabilities are net of investments in fixed assets, and branch adjustments. This also includes RBI net non-monetary liability.

Item five is subtracted from the total of the first four items i.e. (i + ii + iii + iv) – v, to arrive at total deployment which is equal to M3. These figures are analysed by us as under:

2021

₹ in crores	Mar 31, 2021	% to M3	Aug 27, 2021	% to M3
Components of money supply—M3				
i) Currency with the Public	2751828	14.6	2830920	14.6
ii) Demand Deposits with Banks	1995120	10.6	1926054	10.0
iii) Time Deposits with Banks	14050278	74.6	14525375	75.2
iv) 'Other' Deposits with Reserve Bank	47351	0.2	46156	0.2
M3 total	18844578		19328505	
Deployment of money supply				
i) Net Bank Credit to Government Sector (a + b)	5850374	31.0	6075960	31.4
ii) Bank Credit to Commercial Sector (a + b)	11668466	61.9	11608342	60.1
iii) Net Foreign Exchange Assets of Banking Sector	4578846	24.3	4893905	25.3
iv) Government's Currency Liabilities to the Public	26913	0.1	27124	0.1
v) Banking Sector's Net Non-Monetary Liabilities	3280021	-17.3	3276826	-16.9
Sources (i + ii + iii + iv - v)	18844578		19328505	

The table above shows the analysis based on RBI table. We can observe that as at 27 August 2021, 31.4% of M3 has been taken by govt., as borrowings from banking sector. 60.1% has been deployed by banks as loans to commercial sector. 25.3% is held as foreign securities.

As at March 2021, govt. borrowing from banking sector was 31% of money supply which has gone up by 0.4% in August this year. As regards bank credit to commercial sector we may observe that in August 2019, banks demand and term deposits formed 75.2% of money supply. Banks other than RBI can extend bank credit only after providing for CRR and SLR requirements. CRR is to be placed with RBI as cash balance and SLR are to be invested in approved govt. securities. The applicable rates in August 2021 were 4% CRR and 18% SLR—total 22% of total demand and time deposits of the banks. This means that banks can lend up to 78% of their deposits. But banks will require maintaining extra liquidity with them to absorb day to day fluctuations in their deposits in the shape of cash and balance with RBI in current account. Under the present dispensing, banks can borrow from RBI in case they are in need of funds urgently, on repo basis by giving govt. or approved securities to RBI. For this purpose, banks generally hold more govt. or other approved securities besides the SLR requirements. Thus, banks can lend only after providing for CRR & SLR and also after providing for their liquidity needs.

Bank credit to commercial sector was 61.9% of M3 in March 2021 and it has come down to 60.1% of M3 in August 2021 showing decline in bank credit during the year 2021. The CRR and SLR requirements were same in March 2021 also.

The other major category of uses of money supply is in the form of foreign exchange securities held by Indian banking sector. It formed 25.3% of M3 as at August 2021. Major chunk in this is held by RBI as forex reserve. Forex reserve is very important and crucial for the country and its level reflects the solvency of the country in its foreign trade. High forex reserves improve the credit rating of the country in international markets. It also gives stability to the Indian currency in the international forex market. For this reason, RBI has moved from its earlier practice of holding rupee assets of issue dept, and now the assets of issue dept. are held only in bullion and foreign securities. Coins issued by Govt. of India also form a small fraction in total assets of issue dept. along with bullion and foreign assets.

Hence if RBI desires to control money supply in the economy it has to control the availability of bank credit. RBI cannot control the physical cash lying with public and also the deposits of the public with the bank. The effective control will be by restricting the bank credit. If banks are restricted in their giving loans to borrowers either by reducing the capacity of banks to lend or by making the credit expensive, then it can control flow of money for business activities. This RBI does by different measures as under:

1. By increasing the interest rates on borrowing. This is achieved by increasing the Bank Rate and repo rate by RBI. The increase in these rates by RBI signals its intention which is then acted upon by banks and others by increasing the loan interest rates. Bank loans will become costlier for the borrowers and this will discourage them to borrow. This control is now the main tool that RBI uses now.
2. By increasing CRR and SLR which are required to be maintained by banks compulsorily. Cash reserve ratio is cash reserve banks are required to maintain with RBI or other approved banks as a percentage to its total deposits. RBI has power to increase it to maximum 15%. Statutory liquidity ratio is the required investment by banks to provide a cushion and buffer. These investments are to be in securities issued by the central and state govts. which bears the guarantee of central govt. this is also calculated on the total deposits of the bank. RBI has power to increase it to maximum 40% of total deposit of the bank.

   At present CRR is 4% and SLR is 18% (10-9-2021). This means banks will be left with 78% of their deposits which they can lend to borrowers. By increasing these ratios individually or both together RBI can effectively curtail the credit expansion of banks.

   However, RBI is not using this tool to control bank credit now as it affects the banks adversely.

3. Selective or restrictive credit policies: RBI can also curtail credit to any particular segment of borrowers, by issuing guidelines to banks to restrict credit to particular industry/activity. This selective and restrictive credit controls are used mainly to discourage bank credit for undesirable activities like hoarding and black marketing leading to price rice in the commodities or services.

Prior to introducing banking reforms in the country, RBI was controlling the interest rates on bank deposits and bank loans. RBI was prescribing the interest rate category wise and maturity wise for loans and deposits. All banks were offering the same rates. Then RBI had full control on interest rates on deposits and loans. RBI could increase or decrease the rates as per its assessment on money supply and bank credit.

Banking reforms introduced in 1991, decided to do away with RBI prescriptions of interest rates and allow the banks to determine the same keeping in mind the market conditions and priorities. RBI has since freed the interest rates on deposits including interest on savings bank deposits. As regards the loan interest rates practically the prescriptions were withdrawn allowing banks to decide on interest rates on loans based on its policies for loans. Very few prescribed interest rates now exist in export finance and in some areas of social lending.

At present RBI is influencing interest rates movements through its benchmark rates like the 'Bank Rate' and 'repo'/'reverse repo rate'. Increasing or decreasing these rates indicate and give signal to banks and financial system of the country, the expected/desired direction for financial markets. RBI benchmark rates are usually taken as base by banks and financial institutions to work out their own deposit or loan rate. Thus, the trend in increase or decrease of benchmark rates by RBI gets transmitted to the interest rates of financial system of the country.

Historically RBI used CRR and SLR requirements of banks as tool to control money supply in the economy. By increasing these ratios for banks, RBI can impound excess liquidity in the system. Banks will be unable give loan due to impounding of their funds in these ratios. Similarly, by reducing the CRR and SLR requirements for banks RBI can make more funds available to banks for lending.

After the banking sector reforms were taken up from the year 1991, RBI has accepted the recommendations of Narasimham committee report to keep the CRR and SLR within the band of 5% for CRR and 25% for SLR. In earlier years it used to be very high and RBI was generally using the ratios to curtail the bank credit. In the year 1990-91, CRR was as high as 15% and SLR was at 38.5%. Now the CRR is 4% and SLR is 18% (August 2021). RBI is not using CRR and SLR ratios as monetary tools to control bank credit expansion.

Repo and Reverse Repo Operations by RBI

RBI introduced in the year 2000, the Liquidity Adjustment Facility (LAF) and subsequent revisions were made in 2001 and 2004. This was in terms of the recommendations of Narasimham Committee on Banking Sector Reforms (1998). It was suggested by the committee report that RBI may not use CRR and SLR as monetary tools to control money supply in future and in its place Liquidity Adjustment Facility (LAF) may be started and be used as monetary tool to control money supply.

Sub-section (12AB) of Section 17 of the RBI Act, 1934, defines repo and reverse repo as under:

- "repo" means "an instrument for borrowing funds by selling securities of the Central Government or a State Government or of such securities of a local authority as may be specified in this behalf by the Central Government or foreign securities, with an agreement to repurchase the said securities on a mutually agreed future date at an agreed price which includes interest for the funds borrowed".
- "reverse repo" means "an instrument for lending funds by purchasing securities of the Central Government or a State Government or of such securities of a local authority as may be specified in this behalf by the

> Central Government or foreign securities, with an agreement to resell the said securities on a mutually agreed future date at an agreed price which includes interest for the funds lent."

Repos are for a minimum period of one day and a maximum period of one year.

Earlier to the introducing of LAF system, banks were borrowing from RBI to meet their urgent and temporary needs for funds at 'Bank Rate'. Bank Rate is the policy benchmark rate announced by RBI for this lending to banks. Generally, it was on unsecured basis and RBI was fixing the borrowing limits to each eligible bank.

Under LAF system, banks can borrow from RBI under repo but banks need to provide collaterals in the form eligible govt. or other securities to secure the loan from RBI. This is a short-term loan and the repo instrument has a repurchase agreement whereby when the bank repays the loan it will get back the securities it has handed over to RBI at a predetermined price. In practice banks can use excess SLR securities held by them, over and above the SLR ratio, to borrow on short-term basis from RBI. RBI declares its repo rate which rate also is a benchmark rate now similar to Bank Rate. As the borrowing by banks from RBI has mainly now shifted to repo system, repo rate has become an active benchmark rate now considered in financial circles.

Reverse repo is the new instrument now used by RBI to borrow from banks by offering securities. This is now used by RBI to absorb money from banks for the purpose of absorbing surplus liquidity in banking sector. Banks having surplus funds will be happy to give loan to RBI on secured basis.

RBI announces the interest rate for reverse repo along with its repo rate. Reverse repo rate is lower from the repo rates. From 22-5-2020, repo rate is 4% and reverse repo rate is 3.35%. Bank rate is 4.25%. These rates are continuing now (12-02-2022).

Now LAF system of repo and reverse repo are the main tools of RBI to inject money to banking system when needed, through repo, and also to absorb the surplus liquidity with banking system through reverse repo. Thus, RBI tries to maintain the money supply in the system to control price rise or inflationary trend in the economy.

From Feb. 2020, RBI has also started long-term repo operations (LTROs) auctions for one year and three years.

RBI Functions—Credit Policy

RBI as the monetary authority has control on the bank credit. While the availability of bank credit is based on funds available with banks for lending, RBI has the authority to prescribe rules for bank lending. Earlier RBI use to prescribe the loan interest rates also. But now the interest rates on loans are decided by the banks themselves. Banks can frame their interest rates for loans as a policy of the bank based on guidelines issued by RBI. RBI has prescribed the broad guidelines to be followed to form the policy for interest rates on loans by the banks.

RBI has the authority to frame rules for lending by banks. RBI has issued guidelines to the banks on the following subjects relating to bank credit.

1. Restrictions for bank lending to particular sector or individual.
2. Selective credit control guidelines against some essential commodities.
3. Guidelines for the eligible purposes for which loan can be sanctioned.
4. Guidelines for the assessments of loan requirement of the borrowers by bank.
5. Guidelines for obtaining security for the loan sanctioned.
6. Guidelines for sanctioning unsecured loans and their limit.
7. Guidelines for margin to be maintained in case of each type of securities.

8. Guidelines on prudential norms for income recognition, asset classification and provisioning to be followed by banks.
9. Guidelines for capital requirements for banks.
10. Guidelines for priority sector lending and social lending to poor.
11. Guidelines for preferential lending to export sector.
12. Guidelines for consortium arrangement, multiple banking arrangement and loan syndication for large borrowers.
13. Guidelines for lending against shares and other paper securities.
14. Guidelines related to interest rates for certain borrowers.
15. Guidelines for declaring the benchmark lending rates by banks.
16. Prompt corrective action under which RBI put a bank under watch and may restrict sanction of fresh loans.

Extract from Master Circular—Loans and Advances—Statutory and Other Restrictions

RBI/2015-16/95 DBR.No.Dir.BC.10/13.03.00/2015-16 July 1, 2015

2.1	Statutory Restrictions	
2.1.1	Advances against bank's own shares	In terms of Section 20(1) of the Banking Regulation Act, 1949, a bank cannot grant any loans and advances on the security of its own shares.
2.1.2	Advances to bank's Directors	Section 20(1) of the Banking Regulation Act, 1949 also lays down the restrictions on loans and advances to the directors and the firms in which they hold substantial interest.
2.1.3	Restrictions on Holding Shares in Companies	While granting loans and advances against shares, statutory provisions contained in Sections 19(2) and 19(3) of the Banking Regulation Act, 1949 should be strictly observed.

2.1.4	Restrictions on Credit to Companies for buy-back of their Securities	In terms of provisions of the Companies Act, 2013, companies are permitted to purchase their own shares or other specified securities out of their • free reserves, or • securities premium account, or • the proceeds of any shares or other specified securities, • subject to compliance of various conditions specified therein. Therefore, banks should not provide loans to companies for buy-back of shares/securities.
2.2	Regulatory Restrictions	
2.2.1	Granting loans and advances to relatives of Directors	Without prior approval of the Board or without the knowledge of the Board, no loans and advances should be granted to relatives of the bank's Chairman/Managing Director or other Directors, Directors (including Chairman/Managing Director) of other banks and their relatives, Directors of Scheduled Co-operative Banks and their relatives, Directors of Subsidiaries/Trustees of Mutual Funds/Venture Capital Funds set up by the financing banks or other banks, as per details given below.
2.2.2	Restrictions on Grant of Loans & Advances to Officers and Relatives of Senior Officers of Banks	The statutory regulations and/or the rules and conditions of service applicable to officers or employees of public sector banks indicate, to a certain extent, the precautions to be observed while sanctioning credit facilities to such officers and employees and their relatives.
2.2.3	Restrictions on Grant of Financial Assistance to Industries Producing/ Consuming Ozone Depleting Substances (ODS)	2.2.3.1 Banks should not extend finance for setting up of new units consuming/producing the Ozone Depleting Substances (ODS). No financial assistance should be extended to small/medium scale units engaged in the manufacture of the aerosol units using chlorofluorocarbons (CFC) and no refinance would be extended to any project assisted in this sector.

2.2.4	Restrictions on Advances against Sensitive Commodities under Selective Credit Control (SCC)	With a view to preventing speculative holding of essential commodities with the help of bank credit and the resultant rise in their prices, in exercise of powers conferred by Section 21 & 35A of the Banking Regulation Act, 1949, the Reserve Bank of India, being satisfied that it is necessary and expedient in the public interest to do so, issues, from time to time, directives to all commercial banks, stipulating specific restrictions on bank advances against specified sensitive commodities. The commodities, generally treated as sensitive commodities are the following: (a) food grains i.e. cereals and pulses, (b) selected major oil seeds indigenously grown, viz. groundnut, rapeseed/mustard, cottonseed, linseed and castor seed, oils thereof, vanaspati and all imported oils and vegetable oils, (c) raw cotton and kapas, (d) sugar/gur/khandsari, (e) Cotton textiles which include cotton yarn, man-made fibres and yarn and fabrics made out of man-made fibres and partly out of cotton yarn and partly out of man-made fibres. Banks are free to fix prudential margins on advances against these sensitive commodities. However, in case of advance against Levy Sugar, a minimum margin of 10% will apply. (ii) Valuation of sugar stocks (a) The unreleased stocks of the levy sugar charged to banks as security by the sugar mills shall be valued at levy price fixed by government. (b) The unreleased stocks of free sale sugar including buffer stocks of sugar charged to the bank as security by sugar mills, shall be valued at the average of the price realised in the preceding three months (moving average) or the current market price, whichever is lower; the prices for this purpose shall be exclusive of excise duty.
2.3	Restrictions on other loans and advances	

2.3.1	Loans and Advances against Shares, Debentures and Bonds	**Advances to individuals** Banks may grant advances against the security of shares, debentures or bonds to individuals subject to the following conditions: Amount of advance: Loans against the security of shares, debentures and bonds should not exceed the limit of Rupees ten lakhs per individual if the securities are held in physical form and Rupees twenty lakhs per individual if the securities are held in dematerialised form. Banks should maintain a minimum margin of 50 per cent of the market value of equity shares/convertible debentures held in physical form. In the case of shares/convertible debentures held in dematerialised form, a minimum margin of 25 per cent should be maintained. **2.3.1.2 Advances to Share and Stock Brokers/Commodity Brokers** (i) Banks and their subsidiaries should not undertake financing of 'Badla' transactions. (ii) Share and stock brokers/commodity brokers may be provided need based overdraft facilities/line of credit against shares and debentures held by them as stock-in-trade. (iii) The ceiling of Rupees ten lakhs/Rupees twenty lakhs for advances against shares/debentures to individuals will not be applicable in the case of share and stock brokers/commodity brokers and the advances would be need based. (iv) RBI has issued detailed guidelines applicable to share brokers registered with SEBI. (v) A uniform margin of 50 per cent shall be applied on all advances/financing of IPOs/issue of guarantees on behalf of share and stockbrokers.
2.3.2	Advances against Fixed Deposit Receipts (FDRs) Issued by Other Banks	The banks should desist from sanctioning advances against FDRs, or other term deposits of other banks.

2.3.4	Loans against Certificate of Deposits (CDs)	Banks may lend against CDs and buy back their own CDs, until further notice, only in respect of CDs held by mutual funds, subject to the provisions of paragraph 44(2) of the SEBI (Mutual Funds) Regulations, 1996.
2.3.5	Finance for and Loans/Advances against Indian Depository Receipts (IDRs)	No bank should grant any loan/advance for subscription to Indian Depository Receipts (IDRs). Further, no bank should grant any loan/advance against security/collateral of IDRs issued in India.
2.3.6	Bank Finance to Non-Banking Financial Companies (NBFCs)	5. Activities not Eligible for Bank Credit 5.1 The following activities undertaken by NBFCs, are not eligible for bank credit: (i) Bills discounted/rediscounted by NBFCs, except for rediscounting of bills discounted by NBFCs arising from sale of— (a) commercial vehicles (including light commercial vehicles), and (b) two wheeler and three wheeler vehicles, subject to the following conditions: • the bills should have been drawn by the manufacturer on dealers only; • the bills should represent genuine sale transactions as may be ascertained from the chassis/engine number; and • before rediscounting the bills, banks should satisfy themselves about the bona fides and track record of NBFCs which have discounted the bills. (ii) Investments of NBFCs both of current and long-term nature, in any company/ entity by way of shares, debentures, etc. However, Stock Broking Companies may be provided need-based credit against shares and debentures held by them as stock-in-trade. (iii) Unsecured loans/inter-corporate deposits by NBFCs to/in any company. (iv) All types of loans and advances by NBFCs to their subsidiaries, group companies/ entities. (v) Finance to NBFCs for further lending to individuals for subscribing to Initial Public Offerings (IPOs) and for purchase of shares from secondary market.

		5.2 Leased and Sub-Leased Assets As banks can extend financial assistance to equipment leasing companies, they should not enter into lease agreements departmentally with such companies as well as other Non-Banking Financial Companies engaged in equipment leasing.
		7. Other Prohibitions on Bank Finance to NBFCs 7.1 Bridge loans/interim finance Banks should not grant bridge loans of any nature, or interim finance against capital/ debenture issues and/or in the form of loans of a bridging nature pending raising of long-term funds from the market by way of capital, deposits, etc. to all categories of Non-Banking Financial Companies and also RNBCs. Banks should strictly follow these instructions and ensure that they are not circumvented in any manner whatsoever by purport and/or intent by sanction of credit under a different nomenclature like unsecured negotiable notes, floating rate interest bonds, etc., as also short-term loans, the repayment of which is proposed/ expected to be made out of funds to be or likely to be mobilised from external/other sources and not out of the surplus generated by the use of the asset(s). 7.2 Advances against collateral security of shares to NBFCs Shares and debentures cannot be accepted as collateral securities for secured loans granted to NBFC borrowers for any purpose. 7.3 Restriction on guarantees for placement of funds with NBFCs Banks should not execute guarantees covering inter-company deposits/loans thereby guaranteeing refund of deposits/ loans accepted by NBFCs/firms from other NBFCs/firms. The restriction would cover all types of deposits/loans irrespective of their source, including deposits/loans received by NBFCs from trusts and other institutions. Guarantees should not be issued for the purpose of indirectly enabling the placement of deposits with NBFCs.

2.3.7	Financing Infrastructure/ Housing Projects	In order to harmonise the definition of 'infrastructure lending for the purpose of financing of infrastructure by the banks and Financial Institutions' with that of the Master List of Infrastructure sub-sectors' notified by the Government of India on October 7, 2013, the definition of 'infrastructure lending' has been revised as below: (As amended from time to time)
2.3.10	Advances for purchase of gold and lending against gold Bullion/coins/ Primary gold	Accordingly, it is advised that with effect from November 19, 2012 no advances should be granted by banks for purchase of gold in any form including primary gold, gold bullion, gold jewellery, gold coins, units of Gold Exchange Traded Funds (ETF) and units of gold Mutual Funds. However, banks can provide finance for genuine working capital requirements of jewellers. The scheme of Gold (Metal) Loan detailed vide our circular DBOD. No. IBS. BC. 1519/23.67.001/1998-99 dated December 31, 1998 as amended from time to time, will continue to be in force.
2.3.19	Grant of Loans for acquisition of Kisan Vikas Patras (KVPs)	Banks should, therefore, ensure that no loans are sanctioned for acquisition of/investing in Small Savings Instruments including Kisan Vikas Patras.
2.3.23	Bridge Loans against receivables from government	(i) Banks should not extend bridge loans against amounts receivable from Central/State Governments by way of subsidies, refunds, reimbursements, capital contributions, etc. The following exemptions are, however, made: fertilizer industry and exporters.

Source: RBI

The above are the restrictions or conditions placed on certain types of advances or lending to certain category of borrowers.

Besides, Credit policy of RBI encompasses all the areas of bank credit. Banks are obliged to follow the rules and guidelines issued by RBI from time to time. These guidelines include:

1. Purpose for which loan can be sanctioned.
2. Eligibility of borrowers to avail loans.
3. Margins and security requirements.

4. Loan interest rates for which banks are authorised to declare their loan interest rates based on the broad guidelines issued by RBI for the basis of fixing rates.
5. Banks are mandated to lend 40% of loans to priority sector which is identified by govt. and RBI.
6. Banks are mandated to lend to export sector.
7. Banks are mandated to lend to weaker sections of the society and self-help groups of weaker sections.
8. Banks are mandated to lend to Food Corporation of India for its food procurement programme.

In fact, every aspect of bank credit falls under the jurisdiction of RBI to frame guidelines. Over the years as the economy has progressed and banks are having surplus funds to lend, RBI has been removing and relaxing the guidelines to enable banks to gainfully employ their funds. During years 1950 to 1990, bank credits for productive purposes were only encouraged and personal loans were discouraged as a policy. But now this distinction is removed and banks are allowed to extend bank credit to individuals for all eligible activities like housing, vehicle, education, consumer durables. At present RBI is generally laying down broad guidelines for the eligibility for loans and encourages banks to frame their own policies for lending to each type of borrowers or activities.

In fact, now the position is that banks will have to find out whether the intended bank credit falls under any of the statutory or supervisory restrictions which is given in the table above. For other loans, banks shall be guided by RBI guidelines applicable, if there is any. For remaining cases banks can have their own board approved credit policies which shall be based on the credit policy guidelines issued by RBI from time to time.

We can understand that as the banks have now large resources and are capable of giving bank credit to all segments of the society, the guiding principle now is that the bank credit shall be for productive purposes (to industries, trade, MSME, small business, agriculture and allied activities, exports, housing, education, infrastructure, etc.) and also to individuals as personal loans for all legal and desirable purposes. Bank credit for disrupting the economy like hoarding, black-marketing or speculating shall not be allowed. Similarly bank credit for illegal activities is not allowed. Under personal loan categories, extending bank credit for investments in equities or other securities are generally not to be allowed.

RBI functions—International accounting standards and capital requirements—Prudential norms for banks and FIs

RBI introduced prudential norms for banks in the year 1992.

Prudential norms for banks and other financial entities are also prescribed by RBI as part of its bank credit policies. The accounting norms and asset classification norms prescribed by the central bank in the country are known as the prudential norms. These norms are as per the international standards accepted by the Basel committee set up by Bank for International Settlements. International norms are prescribed but the actual norms are to be adopted by the central banks of the countries as suitable to its country.

Following are the prudential norms:

- Income recognition norms
- Asset classification norms
- Provisioning norms

Important features of these norms are:

- Recognising income in the books only when it is recovered.
- Classifying the assets; standard and substandard category based on conduct of the loan account.
- Making provisions for NPAs out of the current year's income and keeping the provisions to set off future loss in those NPAs.

RBI has advised banks on the prudential norms which has also undergone some changes in the past. The latest and applicable guidelines of RBI are given in its circular mentioned below.

RBI Master Circular—Prudential norms on Income Recognition, Asset Classification and Provisioning pertaining to Advances—RBI/2015-16/101—DBR.No.BP.BC.2/21.04.048/ 2015-16 July 1, 2015.

Following table gives the relevant extract from the above circular.

	Subject	Relevant guidelines
1	Non-performing Assets	1. An asset, including a leased asset, becomes non-performing when it ceases to generate income for the bank. 2. A non-performing asset (NPA) is a loan or an advance where; (i) interest and/or instalment of principal remain overdue for a period of more than 90 days in respect of a term loan, (ii) the account remains 'out of order' as indicated at paragraph 2.2 below, in respect of an Overdraft/Cash Credit (OD/CC), (iii) the bill remains overdue for a period of more than 90 days in the case of bills purchased and discounted, (iv) the instalment of principal or interest thereon remains overdue for two crop seasons for short duration crops, (v) the instalment of principal or interest thereon remains overdue for one crop season for long duration crops, (vi) the amount of liquidity facility remains outstanding for more than 90 days, in respect of a securitisation transaction undertaken in terms of guidelines on securitisation dated February 1, 2006. (vii) in respect of derivative transactions, the overdue receivables representing positive mark-to-market value of a derivative contract, if these remain unpaid for a period of 90 days from the specified due date for payment.
2	Income Recognition Norms	1. The policy of income recognition has to be objective and based on the record of recovery. Internationally income from non-performing assets (NPA) is not recognised on accrual basis but is booked as income only when it is actually received. Therefore, the banks should not charge and take to income account interest on any NPA. This will apply to government guaranteed accounts also. 2. However, interest on advances against Term Deposits, National Savings Certificates (NSCs), Indira Vikas Patras (IVPs), Kisan Vikas Patras (KVPs) and Life policies may be taken to income account on the due date, provided adequate margin is available in the accounts. 3. Fees and commissions earned by the banks as a result of renegotiations or rescheduling of outstanding debts should be recognised on an accrual basis over the period of time covered by the renegotiated or rescheduled extension of credit.

3	Asset Classification Norms	Categories of NPAs Banks are required to classify non-performing assets further into the following three categories based on the period for which the asset has remained non-performing and the realisability of the dues: 1. Substandard Assets 2. Doubtful Assets 3. Loss Assets
	1. Substandard Assets	With effect from March 31, 2005, a substandard asset would be one, which has remained NPA for a period less than or equal to 12 months. Such an asset will have well defined credit weaknesses that jeopardise the liquidation of the debt and are characterised by the distinct possibility that the banks will sustain some loss, if deficiencies are not corrected.
	2. Doubtful Assets	With effect from March 31, 2005, an asset would be classified as doubtful if it has remained in the substandard category for a period of 12 months. A loan classified as doubtful has all the weaknesses inherent in assets that were classified as substandard, with the added characteristic that the weaknesses make collection or liquidation in full—on the basis of currently known facts, conditions and values—highly questionable and improbable.
	3. Loss Assets	A loss asset is one where loss has been identified by the bank or internal or external auditors or the RBI inspection but the amount has not been written off wholly. In other words, such an asset is considered uncollectible and of such little value that its continuance as a bankable asset is not warranted although there may be some salvage or recovery value.
4	Provisioning Norms	
	Provision for Loss assets	Loss assets should be written off. If loss assets are permitted to remain in the books for any reason, 100 per cent of the outstanding should be provided for.

<table>
<tr>
<td></td>
<td>Provision for Doubtful assets</td>
<td>(i) 100 per cent of the extent to which the advance is not covered by the realisable value of the security to which the bank has a valid recourse and the realisable value is estimated on a realistic basis.
(ii) In regard to the secured portion, provision may be made on the following basis, at the rates ranging from 25 per cent to 100 per cent of the secured portion depending upon the period for which the asset has remained doubtful:
<table>
<tr><th>Period for which the advance has remained in 'doubtful' category</th><th>Provision requirement (%)</th></tr>
<tr><td>Up to one year</td><td>25</td></tr>
<tr><td>One to three years</td><td>40</td></tr>
<tr><td>More than three years</td><td>100</td></tr>
<tr><td colspan="2">Note: Valuation of Security for provisioning purposes</td></tr>
</table>
With a view to bringing down divergence arising out of difference in assessment of the value of security, in cases of NPAs with balance of ₹ 5 crore and above stock audit at annual intervals by external agencies appointed as per the guidelines approved by the board would be mandatory in order to enhance the reliability on stock valuation. Collaterals such as immovable properties charged in favour of the bank should be got valued once in three years by valuers appointed as per the guidelines approved by the Board of Directors.</td>
</tr>
<tr>
<td></td>
<td>Provision for Substandard assets</td>
<td>(i) A general provision of 15 per cent on total outstanding should be made without making any allowance for ECGC guarantee cover and securities available.
(ii) The 'unsecured exposures' which are identified as 'substandard' would attract additional provision of 10 per cent, i.e., a total of 25 per cent on the outstanding balance.</td>
</tr>
<tr>
<td>5</td>
<td>Provision for Standard assets</td>
<td>(i) The provisioning requirements for all types of standard assets stands as below. Banks should make general provision for standard assets at the following rates for the funded outstanding on global loan portfolio basis:
(a) farm credit to agricultural activities and Small and Micro Enterprises (SMEs) sectors at 0.25 per cent;
(b) advances to Commercial Real Estate (CRE) Sector at 1.00 per cent;
(c) advances to Commercial Real Estate – Residential Housing Sector (CRE - RH) at 0.75 per cent;
(d) housing loans extended at teaser rates and restructured advances as indicated in Para 5.9.13 and 12.4 respectively;
(e) all other loans and advances not included in (a), (b), and (c) above at 0.40 per cent.</td>
</tr>
</table>

6	Prudential norms on creation of floating provisions by banks	The bank's board of directors should lay down approved policy regarding the level to which the floating provisions can be created. The bank should hold floating provisions for 'advances' and 'investments' separately and the guidelines prescribed will be applicable to floating provisions held for both 'advances' & 'investment' portfolios.
7	Provisioning Coverage Ratio (PCR)	(i) Provisioning Coverage Ratio (PCR) is essentially the ratio of provisioning to gross non-performing assets and indicates the extent of funds a bank has kept aside to cover loan losses. (ii) From a macro-prudential perspective, banks should build up provisioning and capital buffers in good times i.e. when the profits are good, which can be used for absorbing losses in a downturn. This will enhance the soundness of individual banks, as also the stability of the financial sector. It was, therefore, decided that banks should augment their provisioning cushions consisting of specific provisions against NPAs as well as floating provisions, and ensure that their total provisioning coverage ratio, including floating provisions, is not less than 70 per cent. Accordingly, banks were advised to achieve this norm not later than end-September 2010. (iii) Majority of the banks had achieved PCR of 70 per cent and had represented to RBI whether the prescribed PCR is required to be maintained on an ongoing basis. The matter was examined and till such time RBI introduces a more comprehensive methodology of countercyclical provisioning taking into account the international standards as are being currently developed by Basel Committee on Banking Supervision (BCBS) and other provisioning norms, banks were advised that: (a) the PCR of 70 per cent may be with reference to the gross NPA position in banks as on September 30, 2010; (b) the surplus of the provision under PCR vis-a-vis as required as per prudential norms should be segregated into an account styled as "countercyclical provisioning buffer", computation of which may be undertaken as per the format given in Annex - 3; and (c) this buffer will be allowed to be used by banks for making specific provisions for NPAs during periods of system wide downturn, with the prior approval of RBI.

We may observe from the prudential norms fixed for banks are aiming at making the financial status of the bank sound and transparent. Banks are required to identify non-performing assets strictly as per norms and classify them appropriately. Banks are required to make provisions for the substandard assets from the current year's profits before arriving at their net profit. Banks cannot book interest income from NPA accounts. This gives the true picture about the financial health of the bank.

Further the provisioning norms also require banks to provide for their standards assets though it is in fraction of one per cent. Banks are also required to create floating provision for NPAs both in loans and investments. Banks were also advised to hold total provision of 70% against their NPA position as on September 2010. Thus, banks are required to hold minimum prescribed provisions for NPAs and also hold some buffer provision to take care of future losses.

The Application of Basel Norms to the Indian Banking Sector

There has been a time gap in adoption of the Basel norms in our country—Basel I norms (1988) were adopted in 1996, Basel II norms (2004) were adopted in 2008 and the transition to Basel III norms (2010) commenced in September 2013 and is expected to be complete by 31 March 2019. The RBI norms have, however, been more stringent than the Basel norms. As against the Basel norms of minimum CRAR of eight per cent, RBI prescribed a CRAR of nine per cent for Indian banks. At present, the minimum CRAR prescribed by RBI under Basel III norm is 9 per cent plus 2.5 per cent Capital Conservation Buffer (CCB).

Capital Adequacy Ratios for Banks—Basel III Norms

Basel committee has prescribed the minimum capital standard for banks active in international trade and our country being a member has accepted the recommendations. Under the minimum capital standards prescribed by Basel committee, central banks are advised to prescribe their own standard for capital requirement for banks keeping in view of the minimum 8% prescribed. Central banks are also advised to decide and make applicable the minimum capital standard also for all other categories of banks in the country besides the internationally active banks.

RBI has prescribed minimum 9% capital standards to all the banks in the country as against 8% minimum prescribed by Basel committee.

Further, under Basel III norms the requirement of capital has been increased by 2.5% as Capital Conservation Buffer (CCB). For Indian banks, RBI has prescribed the minimum capital requirement at 11.5% inclusive of this new additional requirement. Basel III norms are made applicable for Indian banks from the year 2012 and by the year 2019 banks are required to comply with the capital level minimum at 11.5%.

Following tables give the position of CAR of private sector and public sector banks in the country as at 31-3-2019.

Table 3.2: Bank-wise Capital Adequacy Ratio (Private Banks)

	CAR %	31 Mar. 2017		31 Mar. 2018		31 Mar. 2019	
		CAR	Tier I	CAR	Tier I	CAR	Tier I
1	AU Small Finance Bank Ltd.*	23.04	-	19.31	18.40	19.31	16.00
2	Axis Bank Ltd.	14.95	11.87	16.57	13.04	15.84	12.54
3	Bandhan Bank Ltd.	26.36	24.76	31.48	30.28	29.20	27.90
4	City Union	15.83	15.36	16.22	15.79	15.55	15.03
5	DCB Bank Ltd.	13.76	11.87	16.47	12.72	16.81	13.10
6	Dhanlaxmi Bank Ltd.	10.26	9.01	13.87	10.60	13.90	10.57
7	HDFC Bank Ltd.	14.60	12.80	14.80	13.20	17.10	15.80
8	ICICI Bank Ltd.	17.39	14.35	18.42	15.92	16.89	15.09
9	IDFC First Bank Ltd.	18.90	18.50	18.00	17.50	15.47	15.27
10	IndusInd Bank	15.31	14.72	15.03	14.58	14.16	13.70
11	Karur Vysya Bank Ltd.	12.54	11.85	14.43	13.92	16.00	-
12	Kotak Mahindra Bank Ltd.	16.77	15.90	18.22	17.80	17.45	16.90
13	RBL Bank Ltd.	13.72	11.40	15.33	13.61	13.46	11.84
14	The Federal Bank Ltd.	12.39	11.81	14.70	14.18	14.14	13.38
15	The Jammu & Kashmir Bank Ltd.	10.80	8.70	11.42	9.24	12.46	10.60
16	The Karnataka Bank Ltd.	13.30	12.21	12.04	11.29	13.17	11.17
17	The South Indian Bank Ltd.	12.37	10.90	12.70	10.40	12.61	10.00
18	Yes Bank Ltd.	17.00	13.30	18.40	13.20	16.50	11.30

*CAR as per Basel II Norms

Source: AceEquityCARE

Public Sector Banks

Table 3.3: Bank-wise Capital Adequacy Ratio
(Public Sector Banks—PSBs)

	CAR %	Q4 FY17		Q4 FY18		Q4 FY19	
		CAR	Tier I	CAR	Tier I	CAR	Tier I
1	Allahabad Bank	11.45	8.49	8.69	6.69	12.51	9.68
2	Andhra Bank	12.38	9.17	11.00	7.44	13.68	10.38
3	Bank of Baroda	12.24	9.94	12.13	10.46	13.42	11.55
4	Bank of India	12.14	8.90	12.94	9.73	14.19	11.07
5	Bank of Maharashtra	11.18	9.01	11.00	9.00	11.86	9.91
6	Canara Bank	12.86	9.77	13.22	10.30	11.90	9.03
7	Central Bank of India	10.95	8.62	9.04	7.01	9.61	7.49
8	Corporation Bank	13.64	12.20	12.55	11.33	12.30	10.52
9	Indian Bank	10.50	8.21	9.25	7.17	13.21	11.29
10	Indian Overseas Bank	11.64	8.88	10.50	7.61	10.20	7.85
11	Oriental Bank of Commerce	13.11	10.35	12.60	10.36	12.73	9.98
12	State Bank of India	12.03	9.26	12.24	9.41	12.72	10.65
13	Syndicate Bank	10.93	8.27	10.94	8.96	14.23	11.36
14	UCO Bank	11.79	9.02	11.46	9.03	10.70	8.64
15	Union Bank of India	11.14	8.94	12.62	9.87	11.78	9.48
16	United Bank of India	11.32	8.90	12.30	10.52	13.00	10.14

Source: AceEquityCARE Ratings Limited (Formerly known as Credit Analysis & Research Ltd.) Website: www.careratings.com Follow us on/ company/CARE

We may observe that the banks in private sector banks have complied with the CAR of 11.5%, many of the public sector banks fell short of capital requirement as 31-3-2019. GOI has provided capital support for few more banks in the FY 2020-21.

RBI Functions—Inspection of Banks

RBI has the authority to inspect banks and also call for information as and when required from the banks. The inspection of the banks is either on site or off site. However, RBI conducts inspection of all commercial banks once in a year.

RBI inspection of the banks more particularly identifies the deviations in observing prudential norms and correct classification of assets. Provisioning requirements are also gone into. RBI observations in all these matters are final and binding on banks and banks shall have to carry out the necessary changes in their accounts. RBI also has authority to impose penalty or take appropriate action against the bank for deviations observed. If the deviations, particularly in observing prudential norms, are of serious nature then RBI may initiate actions as it deems fit to correct the situation.

RBI Functions—Prompt Corrective Action Framework

RBI is the banking supervisor in the country. As its duty as monetary authority of the country it is pursuing financial stability by keeping watch over money supply and bank credit. Flow of bank credit to support development is dependent on the financial wellbeing of the banks. Besides prescribing many policy guidelines for banks to ensure that the NPAs are contained to the minimum by the banks, RBI keeps a close watch on the credit portfolios and NPAs of commercial banks. It also keeps a watch on the capital levels of the banks to ensure that the minimum capital CRAR prescribed under Basel norms are maintained by the banks.

RBI has put in place a system to check deterioration of financial strength of a bank and avoid the situation wherein the bank slips into serious trouble. This pre-emptive action by RBI is named as prompt corrective action (PCA).

This is introduced with a view to take immediate corrective actions in case a bank is heading to trouble situation which may seriously impact its financial position, particularly if the NPAs are on the rise.

RBI has introduced PCA in December 2002 as a structured early intervention mechanism along the lines of other central banks in the developed countries. The Revised PCA Framework was issued by the Reserve Bank on April 13, 2017 and implemented with respect to the bank financials as on March 31, 2017.

Under PCA framework RBI evaluates the bank on the areas of its capital structure, asset quality, profitability and leverage and analyses indications for risk in these areas of banks working. Based on the study banks may be identified as falling under three categories of risk perception known as risk threshold 1, 2 or 3 categories. The banks falling under these categories are put under PCA mechanism which will include mandatory actions and also discretionary actions to be initiated by RBI against these banks.

On 02-11-2021, RBI issued revised guidelines and the parameters of PCA framework and made it applicable from January 1, 2022.

The broad parameters of the revised PCA framework are given in the two tables given below.

PCA matrix—Parameters, Indicators and Risk Thresholds

Parameter	Indicator	Risk Threshold 1	Risk Threshold 2	Risk Threshold 3
(1)	(2)	(3)	(4)	(5)
Capital (Breach of either CRAR or CET 1 ratio)	CRAR - Minimum regulatory prescription for Capital to Risk Assets Ratio + applicable Capital Conservation Buffer (CCB) and/or Regulatory Pre-Specified Trigger of Common Equity Tier 1 Ratio (CET 1 PST) + applicable Capital Conservation Buffer (CCB)	Upto 250 bps below the Indicator prescribed at column (2) Upto 162.50 bps below the Indicator prescribed at column (2)	More than 250 bps but not exceeding 400 bps below the Indicator prescribed at column (2) More than 162.50 bps below but not exceeding 312.50 bps below the Indicator prescribed at column (2)	In excess of 400 bps below the Indicator prescribed at column (2) In excess of 312.50 bps below the Indicator prescribed at column (2)
	Breach of either CRAR or CET 1 ratio to trigger PCA			
Asset Quality	Net Non-Performing Advances (NNPA) ratio	>=6.0% but <9.0%	>=9.0% but < 12.0%	>=12.0%
Leverage	Regulatory minimum Tier 1 Leverage Ratio	Upto 50 bps below the regulatory minimum	More than 50 bps but not exceeding 100 bps below the regulatory minimum	More than 100 bps below the regulatory minimum

When a bank is listed under PCA framework as above then bank will be put under corrective mode immediately on the following basis.

Mandatory and Discretionary Actions

<table>
<tr><th>Specifications</th><th>Mandatory actions</th><th>Discretionary actions</th></tr>
<tr><td>Risk Threshold 1</td><td>(i) Restriction on dividend distribution/remittance of profits
(ii) Promoters/Owners/Parent (in the case of foreign banks) to bring in capital</td><td rowspan="3">Common menu
(i) Special Supervisory Actions
(ii) Strategy related
(iii) Governance related
(iv) Capital related
(v) Credit risk related
(vi) Market risk related
(vii) HR related
(viii) Profitability related
(ix) Operations/ Business related
(x) Any other</td></tr>
<tr><td>Risk Threshold 2</td><td>In addition to mandatory actions of Threshold 1,
(i) Restriction on branch expansion; domestic and/or overseas</td></tr>
<tr><td>Risk Threshold 3</td><td>In addition to mandatory actions of Threshold 1 & 2,
(i) Appropriate restrictions on capital expenditure, other than for technological upgradation within Board approved limits</td></tr>
</table>

Source: RBI

We may observe that depending on the nature of weakness detected RBI will put the bank concerned under PCA and this will place restrictions on the banks in some areas of its operation. Generally, this will not hinder the routine banking business of the bank concerned. The restrictions may require the bank to enhance capital, speed up the recovery of NPAs. There can be some specific restrictions imposed on the bank as under:

- Restrictions on sanction of loans
- Restrictions for new lines of business
- Restrictions for taking or renewing costly deposits
- Restrictions for paying dividend
- Restriction on borrowing form interbank market
- Reduction in stake in subsidiaries
- Reducing exposure to sensitive sector like capital market, Real estate sector, non-SLR securities

The purpose of PCA is to bring back the bank to health and normalcy at the earliest. But if the financials of the bank do not improve despite all efforts, then RBI may take the final decision as to the future of the bank concerned. This may involve;

- bring in new management/board
- appoint consultants for business
- organisational restructuring
- change of ownership
- impose moratorium on bank
- merge/amalgamate or liquidate bank

Indian banks have faced sharp rise in NPAs from the year 2014 which peaked in the year 2017-18. There has been steep increase in NPAs of banks. The public sector banks are badly affected and they also lacked adequate capital funds.

In the year 2018, RBI placed 11 state owned banks under PCA framework on the basis of increased NPAs and inadequate capital. In the year 2019, six public sector banks were removed from this PCA framework as their workings and capital have improved. Remaining five public sector banks continued under PCA framework. By the end of September 2021, further four public sector banks were removed from PCA framework as their position improved. Now there is one public sector bank—Central Bank of India, in the list.

PCA framework has become a contentious issue between Govt. and RBI. Govt. was unhappy as this framework has placed restrictions on public sector banks for fresh loans, which is hampering loan sanctions by these banks. In view of listing the public sector banks under PCA framework and also the capital requirement under Basel Accord III framework which was to be completed by March 2019, govt. was, in a way, forced to recapitalise the public sector banks.

4

RBI and GOI Relations

RBI is the creation of GOI in the year 1935 as the Central Bank of the country. When RBI was formed it was a company and it was nationalised in the year 1949. After nationalisation RBI is fully owned by Govt. of India. Under the RBI Act 1934, RBI is created as a Central Bank mainly for the purpose of currency issues and as a bank for the GOI. RBI is also made the supervisor of banking system in the country and is entrusted with the responsibility for financial stability in the country. This responsibility made RBI as the monetary authority of country.

Like in all the developed economies of the world, the currency management and monetary policy management was bifurcated from the functions of the government and given to the Central Bank of the country. The purpose to allow the management of monetary policy by the professionally managed central bank of the country is to maintain it separately from the government which generally is an elected one in democratic countries. Government is the fiscal authority of the country and its decisions on fiscal matter are final. Experiences all over the world have been that the both monetary and fiscal authorities should not vest with government and rather it shall be managed by government as the fiscal authority and the Central Bank as the monetary authority. Probably this is based on the experiences that sometimes these two policies may clash and it will become necessary to strike a balance between these two policies in the larger interest of the country's economy. In a way, it is a check on the government to ensure economic well-being of the country.

Another important development is the worldwide migration from cash transactions to banking habits from 20th century onwards. Banking activity has become very important in the economy as banks acts as conduits for transfer of money from depositors to business and trade. This financial intermediation is now the backbone of economic growth. In view of this change in modern economy, the role of central bank became very crucial to oversee the banking business in the country and to ensure that the banking business is providing for the growth and prosperity of the country.

Though banking business has started just like any other type of business, it now occupies the central stage as in fact it is facilitating all other economic activities in the country. Banking business has become indispensable. In today's world we cannot imagine the status of the economy if banking system fails. It will be like a catastrophe and the economy will be doomed. Today we cannot think of an economy without banks. Though it is possible that some new arrangement may evolve over the period to replace the traditional banking business under some different system, till such time such new arrangements are created and tested, the banks will continue to lead the economy. This being the case the central bank's role also assumes greater importance as controller of banking system.

Governments will decide on all fiscal matters like taxation, creation and distribution of wealth, income generation, government spending, welfare measures, development of industry and trade, development of infrastructure in country, etc. However, government is not expected to manage the monetary matters like quantum of currency printing and distribution of it, managing bank credit which is an important source for investment, understanding the economic principles in operation for controlling inflation, price rise, and financial stability and such like matters. Management of bank credit expansion, controlling inflation and checking price rise are very critical for the economy. These matters will require a different type of skills to take decisions. These also shall be based on long-term perspectives. It is also experienced by countries that many a time the fiscal policy and the monetary policy are at loggerheads and have different views.

Hence, we find that central banks of the countries are generally created as separate entities outside the direct control of governments. Underlying principle is that central banks shall be autonomous bodies headed by professionals whose only concern shall be financial wellbeing of the economy. Ideally central banks should not be under the influence or control of governments to enable them to take independent views and decisions on monetary matters.

These are the background for the evolvement of central banks in the countries. But as stated earlier the RBI is the creation of GOI and GOI is the sole owner of RBI. GOI as the owner of RBI is responsible for the organisational set up of RBI. Under the present system, RBI is headed by Governor and assisted by four deputy governors beside other supporting staff. RBI is managed by a central board of directors; all directors being appointed by GOI. RBI also has few local boards. Governor and deputy governors are appointed by the GOI for fixed tenures. Presently two deputy governors are taken from the cadre of serving RBI officers and two deputy governors are taken from outside. Governor is always appointed from outside.

Role of RBI with Regard to Monetary Policies of the Country

While the Govt. of India is fiscal authority of the country and in this role GOI decides on the various tax collections from the citizens. This tax collection is the source of funds to the GOI. GOI spends on its administrative expenses by paying salaries and other expenses related to its employees and establishments. GOI also required spending on its armed forces for maintaining it and all other related defence expenses.

GOI, under the federal system, will also give a predetermined share in the tax collections of the country, to all the states of the country.

GOI is also committed to the development of the economy by creating infrastructure necessary for the growth of agriculture, trade and commerce, and industries. GOI is also spending large funds for the welfare of the citizens in the fields of education, health and some direct economic assistance to citizens in the form of subsidies and grants.

GOI prepares its annual budgets in advance every year and places its budget estimates to Parliament for approval. The income and expenditures of GOI is bifurcated into revenue and capital heads. Revenue budget of GOI is important as it reveals the income of the GOI from various taxes and other income receipts. If the expenses of the GOI in its revenue budget are in excess of its total revenues then the budget is known as a deficit budget.

Deficit budget means GOI is spending more than its annual revenues as expenses during the year. It's important to understand how GOI can spend more than its income.

In the crudest form, GOI can print new currencies to the extent of deficit and use this additional currency. This will have the effect of increasing currency with the public. But the currency is now printed at RBI on the directions of GOI. RBI is supposed to have equal assets with it to issue additional currency notes. For this purpose, GOI may issue bonds and give it to RBI. RBI may hold these bonds with it till maturity or it can sell it to public in the secondary market for GOI bonds.

Thus, the deficit budget of GOI will have the effect of increasing GOI debt. It is also said that the issue of additional currency may have impact on inflation rate in the economy. GOI and RBI are both concerned about inflation rate in the economy as it will impact the interest rates. Further the impact of additional currency released to the system due to deficit financing of the annual budget of GOI will disturb the money supply in the economy.

RBI is the monetary authority and it is its duty to keep watch on inflation, interest rates and bank credit expansion in the country. It becomes necessary for RBI and GOI to synchronise their efforts to achieve the desired stability in the economy and provide impetus for growth of the economy.

Till recently, the monetary policy decisions are taken by the governor though he is assisted by a committee in its advisory capacity. The central board also works as advisory body to the governor on monetary policy matters.

Over the years, RBI was given more responsibilities and many new Acts have been enacted through which RBI derives additional duties and powers. RBI authority on banks mainly stems from RBI Act, 1934 and The Banking Regulation Act, 1949. RBI is made the authority to manage foreign exchange business and act as custodian of foreign exchange reserves under The Foreign Exchange Management Act, 1999. RBI is also made the controlling authority under the Payment and Settlement Systems Act, 2007.

RBI has been associated with GOI in its development programmes. After nationalisation of banks in 1969 and in 1980, GOI wanted the banks to support development programmes of the GOI. RBI created the priority sector concept and made it mandatory to Indian banks to lend 40% of their bank credit to priority sector comprising of agriculture, SSI and service sectors (now known as Micro, Small and Medium Enterprises—MSME). RBI initiated the Lead Bank scheme as a system to plan for all-round development of each district in the country. RBI initiated loan schemes for various GOI sponsored schemes under poverty alleviation programmes. RBI was proactive in directing bank credit to the development of the economy based on GOI plans. RBI is supporting export sector and has prescribed separate targets for banks to lend to exporters.

The credit policy of RBI has been always responsive to all GOI programmes for development of the economy.

There have been no problems between RBI and GOI on latter's development agenda and the requirement for bank credit for segments of borrowers and for the activities identified as growth areas. However, there were some differences between RBI and GOI on many monetary policy related matters. Most of the time, mutual consultations have solved the issues between them.

But it appears that some issues between GOI and RBI are now getting more debated and straining the relations. This is now more visible from the year 2014 when the BJP led govt.

came into power in the centre. There were some areas of disagreements.

One such area has been the management of monetary policy rates like repo and reverse repo rates. As this rate is crucial and affects the bank credit expansion or contraction, the timing of changes in the policy rates and the quantum of increase or decrease in the rates is generally argued. GOI feels that the changes shall be made at appropriate times to boost the credit off take and production.

When BJP Govt. came in power in the year 2014, Shri Raghuram Rajan (from 4 September 2013 to 4 September 2016) was the governor who was appointed by the previous government.

Some of the issues that arose since the year 2014 onwards between GOI and RBI which highlighted the difference in opinions between them are discussed below.

1. GOI views on the functions of RBI

In the year 2015, when Shri Raghuram Rajan was the governor, GOI wanted to make some changes in the role of RBI. GOI wanted to create an independent public debt office to take care of GOI borrowings. This function is hitherto managed by RBI. GOI also wanted to take away RBI functions as payment system authority and designate Securities Exchange Board of India (SEBI) as the payment system authority. In fact, GOI made references of its intentions in the annual financial bill (budget proposal) of the GOI.

It was understood that RBI was not in favour of shifting public debt office from RBI. RBI advised GOI that it may not be advisable to create separate public debt office directly under the control of GOI as the expertise to handle public debt office is not available outside of RBI at the present. It may take long time for GOI to build expertise in the proposed public debt office and may not prove as a good move by GOI.

RBI also argued against removing RBI authority on payment system of the country. The main reason given was that the payment settlement system will require and is possible only through banks and the final settlements between banks shall have to be controlled by RBI only. Removing the payment system from RBI will create dual authorities (RBI and SEBI) and will weaken the system. It is better that the central bank of the country manages the payment systems.

RBI also pointed out that creating a public debt office for managing GOI securities and SEBI becoming the payment system authority, the repo and reverse repo rate which is based on selling and buying of GOI securities will move away from RBI. With this RBI will lose its main monetary tool of repo and reverse repo for controlling the liquidity in the market.

As the things turned out, GOI must have had second thoughts on the above two issues and retraced its steps proposing these changes.

2. GOI views on formation of Monetary Policy Committee

Further GOI was also interested to set up Monetary Policy Committee to decide on the monetary policy and policy rates. This is the major issue that have cropped up between GOI and RBI.

As regards the issue of setting up of monetary policy committee for deciding monetary policy rates, it appears that RBI had conceded and agreed to refer the matter to an expert committee to make suitable recommendations in 2013 itself. A committee headed by Shri Urjit Patel—deputy governor of RBI, was appointed and this committee submitted its report in January 2014 recommending setting up of Monetary Policy Committee.

In September 2016, based on committee recommendations, GOI created a six-member Monetary Policy Committee (MPC). Shri Urjit Patel's was the new governor of RBI at the time. MPC had its first meeting for two days on October 3 and October 4, 2016.

This committee is headed by the governor and there are other members appointed by the GOI. With this change, the authority of governor to decide on the policy rates independently, came to an end and the authority is now vested with the Monetary Policy Committee.

3. Appointment of Governor of RBI

The term of Shri Raghuram Rajan as governor was ending on 4 September 2016. There were speculations whether he will be given a second term by GOI. It was said that the governor and GOI did not had good rapport, as they had differences in their views, and that GOI may not consider second term for Raghuram Rajan. Shri Raghuram Rajan in the meantime made it public that he is not looking for extension and that he is planning to go back after completing his term.

BJP Government then elevated Shri Urjit Patel who was then deputy governor, as the new RBI governor. Shri Urjit Patel took over as governor from 4 September 2016 (till 10.12.2018). He supported the GOI's move to demonetise ₹ 500 and 1000 rupee notes which took place in November 2017.

It appears that even after the appointment of Shri Urjit Patel as Governor of RBI, the differences between GOI and RBI continued for some other matters.

4. Matter Regarding RBI Supervision over Banks

The year 2017 was bad for banking in India and the banks were burdened with huge NPAs. The loans disbursed prior to the 2014 were the main NPAs added. At this stage, GOI and the finance minister blamed RBI for its lack of supervision over banks leading to huge NPAs. Countering this allegation against RBI, Governor Shri Urjit Patel gave public statements that the NPAs are mainly in public sector banks and that the working of the public sector banks is not ownership neutral. He said that RBI's control on public sector banks is not effective as the GOI is the owner of these banks and RBI has no control or RBI cannot take any action against public sector bank managements. His stand was that while RBI has control over private sector banks, its control on public sector banks is not very effective due to GOI ownership.

Sh. Viral Acharya a deputy governor of RBI also made some statement warning the GOI against diluting RBI's authority to manage monetary policy.

Probably for the first time in the history, GOI and RBI voiced their differences in public and blamed each other.

5. Transfer of RBI Surplus to GOI

There was also an issue of transfer of RBI surplus to GOI. RBI was transferring its surplus to GOI every year after providing for some reserve accounts maintained by it. These reserves are kept as hedge for future exigencies and also to make RBI financially sound. RBI's view had merit in it as the financial strength of central bank of the country is very important. However, GOI felt that RBI is having more than necessary reserves and that such excess amount should be transferred to GOI. This issue appears to be the bone of contention during Shri Urjit Patel's tenure as Governor. This issue is discussed in detail later in this chapter.

In way the differences between GOI and RBI came to open, clearly showing that there are differences of opinions and views between them.

6. RBI action against public sector banks under Prompt Corrective Action (PCA) framework

Further, in the year 2018 RBI placed 11 public sector banks under the Prompt Corrective Action (PCA) framework as their NPAs have gone up steeply and their capital base was weakened. These 11 banks under (PCA) are:

1. Dena Bank,
2. Allahabad Bank,
3. United Bank of India,
4. Corporation Bank,
5. IDBI Bank,
6. UCO Bank,
7. Bank of India,
8. Central Bank of India,
9. Indian Overseas Bank,
10. Oriental Bank of Commerce,
11. Bank of Maharashtra.

These banks were restricted on their credit expansion and this action put pressure on GOI. GOI was forced to recapitalise these banks in view of Basel Accord III which had recommended additional capital buffer for the banks. Banks were required to maintain capital level of minimum 11.5% on their risk weighted assets under Basel Accord prescription.

Prompt Corrective Action or PCA is a framework under which banks with weak financial metrics are put under watch by the RBI. The PCA framework deems banks as risky if they slip below certain norms on three parameters—capital ratios, asset quality and profitability.

GOI was unhappy about PCA framework of RBI which resulted in some restrictions on public sector banks on their credit sanctioning. GOI wanted the PCA framework to be in line with international standards. GOI was concerned with the restrictions on banks for fresh advances particularly to MSME sector.

RBI took the stand that PCA does not really limit the normal lending operations of banks as RBI has placed restrictions on credit by banks only to unrated borrowers or those with high risks. There is no complete ban on banks on their lending.

RBI did not budge from its stand on these banks and these banks continued under PCA list. This then forced the GOI to provide capital to these banks at the earliest in order to improve their CAR ratios.

In order to understand the seriousness of the issue and the reason why RBI had to invoke PCA framework and restrict banks on lending, we shall have to look at the NPA positions of banks particularly the public sector banks.

The following table shows the NPA position of commercial banks as a group and also that of public sector banks from the year 2006-07 to 2018-19.

For the scheduled commercial banks as a group, we can observe that gross NPA crossed 3% in 2012-13 and rose to 7.5% 2015-16, 9.3% in 2016-17 and 11.2% in 2017-18. However, it came down to 9.1% in 2018-19.

In case of public sector banks, the position was worse. Gross NPAs of public sector banks rose to 9.3% in 2015-16, to 11.7% in 2016-17 and peaked to 14.6% in 2017-18. Then it came

(Amount in ₹ crore)

Year (end-March)	Advances		Non-Performing Assets (NPAs)					
	Gross	Net	Gross			Net		
			Amount	As Percentage of Gross Advances	As Percentage of Total Assets	Amount	As Percentage of Net Advances	As Percentage of Total Assets
1	2	3	4	5	6	7	8	9
Scheduled Commercial Banks								
2006-07	2007413	1981237	50517	2.5	1.5	20280	1.0	0.6
2007-08	2503431	2476936	56606	2.2	1.3	24730	1.0	0.6
2008-09	3024652	2999924	69954	2.3	1.3	31564	1.1	0.6
2009-10	3262079	3496720	81718	2.5	1.4	39127	1.1	0.6
2010-11	3995982	4297487	93997	2.4	1.3	41799	1.0	0.6
2011-12	4648808	5073559	136968	2.9	1.6	65205	1.3	0.8
2012-13	5971820	5879773	192769	3.2	2.0	98693	1.7	1.0
2013-14	6875748	6735213	263015	3.8	2.4	142656	2.1	1.3
2014-15	7560666	7388160	322916	4.3	2.7	175841	2.4	1.5
2015-16	8171114	7896467	611607	7.5	4.7	349814	4.4	2.7
2016-17	8476705	8116109	791791	9.3	5.6	433121	5.3	3.1
2017-18	9266210	8745978	1039679	11.2	6.8	520679	6.0	3.4
2018-19	10287085	9709829	936474	9.1	5.6	355076	3.7	2.1

Year (end-March)	Advances		Non-Performing Assets (NPAs)					
	Gross	Net	Gross			Net		
			Amount	As Percentage of Gross Advances	As Percentage of Total Assets	Amount	As Percentage of Net Advances	As Percentage of Total Assets
1	2	3	4	5	6	7	8	9
Public Sector Banks								
2006-07	1464493	1440146	38968	2.7	1.6	15325	1.1	0.6
2007-08	1819074	1797401	40600	2.2	1.3	17836	1.0	0.6
2008-09	2283473	2259212	45918	2.0	1.2	21155	0.9	0.6
2009-10	2519331	2701300	57301	2.3	1.3	29643	1.1	0.7
2010-11	3079804	3304433	71042	2.3	1.3	36055	1.1	0.7
2011-12	3550389	3877308	112488	3.2	1.9	59391	1.5	1.0
2012-13	4560169	4472845	164461	3.6	2.4	90037	2.0	1.3
2013-14	5215920	5101137	227264	4.4	2.9	130635	2.6	1.6
2014-15	5616718	5476250	278468	5.0	3.2	159951	2.9	1.8
2015-16	5821952	5593577	539956	9.3	5.9	320376	5.7	3.5
2016-17	5866373	5557232	684732	11.7	7.0	383089	6.9	3.9
2017-18	6141698	5697350	895601	14.6	8.9	454473	8.0	4.5
2018-19	6382461	5926286	739541	11.6	7.3	285123	4.8	2.8

Source: RBI.

down to 11.6% in 2018-19. Net NPA of public sector banks were very high at 8% in 2017-18. It came down to 4.8% in 2018-19.

In the financial year 2018-19, the NPA levels of the banks came down and have shown encouraging progress. This was mainly facilitated by GOI recapitalising banks and also due to GOI's support by creating new recovery law in the form of The Insolvency and Bankruptcy Code, 2016 (IBC) for speedy recovery of dues mainly from corporate borrowers.

The Insolvency and Bankruptcy Code, 2016 (IBC) has been enacted, which has provided for the taking over management of the affairs of the corporate debtor at the outset of the corporate insolvency resolution process. Coupled with debarment of wilful defaulters and persons associated with NPA accounts from the resolution process, this has effected a fundamental change in the creditor-debtor relationship. Further, the Banking Regulation Act, 1949 has been amended to provide for authorisation to RBI to issue directions to banks to initiate the insolvency resolution process under IBC. As per RBI's directions under the aforesaid amended provision in the Banking Regulation Act, 1949, banks have filed cases under IBC before the National Company Law Tribunal in respect of RBI-specified borrowers.

In the year 2019, RBI removed following five banks from the PCA framework in two phases after these banks received capital support from the government that resulted in improvement in their financial parameters.

1. Allahabad bank
2. Corporation bank
3. Bank of India (BoI)
4. Bank of Maharashtra (BoM)
5. Oriental Bank of Commerce (OBC)

Further, out of 11 banks put under the PCA framework in 2018, Dena Bank ceased to exist as a separate entity after its merger with Bank of Baroda in April 2019.

IDBI Bank has been acquired by LIC of India in January 2019. LIC took up 51% stake in this bank. This is also known as a bail out operation as IDBI bank is saddled with huge NPAs due to which RBI placed it under PCA framework. With LIC takeover, IDBI bank is not considered as public sector bank now. IDBI bank is hopeful that it will come out of PCA framework in this year (2019). However, it took longer time and only in March 2021 IDBI bank was taken out of PCA framework.

In Sept. 2019, four banks; Indian Overseas Bank (IOB), Central Bank of India, UCO Bank and United Bank of India were still continuing under PCA framework. GOI has taken steps to infuse capital to these banks and expects that they will be out of PCA framework soon.

Finance ministry announced capital infusion to these banks in 2019 as under:

	Public sector bank	Capital infusion (₹ in crore)
1	Indian Overseas Bank	3800
2	Central Bank of India	3300
3	UCO Bank	2100
4	United Bank of India	1600

United Bank of India is merged with Punjab National Bank and no longer exists after 31.3.2021. UCO Bank was taken out of PCA list on 9 September 2021 and Indian Overseas Bank was taken out of the list on 29 September 2021.

Now only Central Bank of India continues to be in PAC framework.

With hind sight, we can realise that the RBI has controlled the situation of public sector banks and forced them to take immediate corrective steps to regain healthy status. GOI appears to have yielded to RBI's views on this and did not insist for dilution of norms of PAC framework.

7. GOI views on NBFCs

Infrastructure Leasing & Financial Services (IL&FS) is a major non-banking financial company (NBFC) and it defaulted in repayments in September 2018. Banking industry had nearly ₹ 60000/- crores exposure in it. Total debt of the company is said to be about ₹ 99000 crores. IL&FS had major institutional shareholders as under:

	Name	% holding
1	LIC of India	25.34
2	Orix Corporation of Japan	23.54
3	The Abu Dhabi Investment Authority	12.56
4	HDFC	9.02
5	Central Bank of India	7.67
6	SBI	6.42
	Total	84.55

This affected the banks and also other NBFCs as they were required to show the loans to IL&FS as NPA. It is said that GOI wanted to bail-out IL&FS and also to allow banks to postpone declaring the account as NPA under the existing strict prudential norms prescribed by RBI.

Economic affairs secretary of GOI Shri S.C. Garg said that the government is monitoring the situation of debt-ridden IL&FS and would take appropriate action to ensure that there is no undue impact on the financial system. In October 2018, the government constituted a new board headed by Kotak Mahindra Bank Executive Vice-Chairman and Managing Director Uday Kotak and replaced the old Board of the company.

There was another big NBFC, Dewan Housing Finance Corporation Ltd (DHFL) which also defaulted in its payments in the year 2019.

But RBI did not agree to relax prudential norms to accommodate banks and NBFCs. It is believed that RBI also did not agree to the proposal to bail-out IL&FS. RBI felt that there is no liquidity crisis in the economy warranting any such action from RBI.

Here also RBI's stand not to relax prudential norms has prevailed and GOI has accepted it. GOI also did not press for bail-out or any liquidity support to NBFCs.

8. RBI's directives to banks on 12 February 2018 prohibiting banks from treating restructured loans as standard loans

The guidelines issued by RBI on asset classification and provisioning norms on 12 February 2018 are as under:

A. Asset Classification

In case of restructuring, the accounts classified as 'standard' shall be immediately downgraded as non-performing assets (NPAs), i.e., 'sub-standard' to begin with. The non-performing assets, upon restructuring, would continue to have the same asset classification as prior to restructuring. In both cases, the asset classification shall continue to be governed by the ageing criteria as per extant asset classification norms.

B. Provisioning Norms

Accounts restructured under the revised framework shall attract provisioning as per the asset classification category as laid out in the Master Circular on Prudential Norms on Income Recognition, Asset Classification and Provisioning pertaining to Advances dated July 1, 2015, as amended from time to time.

RBI instructions on prudential norms for restructured loans were strict and banks were finding it difficult as these norms are affecting their workings (capital requirement and profitability). At this juncture banks were burdened with high level of NPAs and restructuring of loans in many cases is desired.

GOI was also of the view that RBI instructions are rigid and hurting public sector banks. GOI felt that the rules are too tight, and may compound bad loan problem of banks. GOI also felt that the Basel norms shall be adopted for the capital requirements of banks in the country. As per Basel Committee recommendations the capital adequacy ratio was fixed originally at 8% on risk weighted assets. Subsequently additional 2.5% was prescribed under Basel III norms. However, RBI had prescribed 9% minimum capital for Indian banks which is higher. With the additional capital requirement under Basel III norms RBI has prescribed 9% + 2.5% = 11.5% capital requirements for Indian banks.

RBI stand was that any dilution in the prudential norms applicable to the banks shall weaken the banks in the long run.

All these developments showed that the relationship between RBI and GOI is not smooth. It was evident from the facts that Shri Urjit Patel resigned from his job as governor of RBI on 10 December 2018 and left RBI. GOI appointed Shri Shaktikanta

Das as the new governor in his place. Dy Governor Shri Viral Acharya, who was vocal on the issue of RBI's autonomy, also resigned in August 2019 and left RBI.

Thus, these were some of the issues between GOI and RBI that have cropped up after the year 2014. Some the issues have been amicably sorted out and they are:

1. Decision on the monetary policy rates is to be broad based decision by an appointed committee instead of discretion of the governor.—This matter was resolved with the constitution of Monetary Policy Committee in September 2016.
2. RBI should consider GOI's views on monetary policy. —this was also resolved by creating a system to fix inflation target by GOI in consultation with RBI and announce it. GOI has also created legal provision for inflation target fixing.
3. Transfer the RBI surplus to GOI every year after only reasonable reserves is kept for contingencies.—This matter is resolved and RBI capital framework was accepted as per the recommendations of Dr. Bimal Jalan committee. (Recommendations and the transfer of surplus to GOI is discussed below in this chapter)
4. GOI intention to create independent public debt office and making SEBI as the authority to control payment system in the country.—GOI has deferred these issues at present. There will be no changes in the existing functions of RBI.

   The following remaining matters pertaining to bank credit management and banking supervision falls under the authority of RBI. RBI has different views on these matters. Whether the views of the GOI is prudent and can prevail in these matters is debatable in view the autonomy of RBI.
5. GOI's views on PCA framework for inhibiting public sector banks on credit expansion.
6. GOI view on relaxing prudential norms for restructured loans.

7. GOI view on capital prescription for banks as per Basel norms i.e. basic 8% on RWA.

Legal Equation between GOI and RBI

We may have to understand that though RBI is owned by GOI, RBI is made an autonomous body to be capable of handling monetary policies for the betterment of the economy. This is for the purpose of having an independent monetary authority. But in case of differences between monetary authority (RBI) and fiscal authority (GOI) over any matter, then whose view shall prevail? This is an important issue to understand. Whether autonomy of RBI is absolute?

Here we may have to look at the section 7 of RBI Act, 1934 which is given below:

Sec. 7. *Management.*

(1) The Central Government may from time to time give such directions to the Bank as it may, after consultation with the Governor of the Bank, consider necessary in the public interest.

(2) Subject to any such directions, the general superintendence and direction of the affairs and business of the Bank shall be entrusted to a Central Board of Directors which may exercise all powers and do all acts and things which may be exercised or done by the Bank.

(3) Save as otherwise provided in regulations made by the Central Board, the Governor and in his absence the Deputy Governor nominated by him in this behalf, shall also have powers of general superintendence and direction of the affairs and the business of the Bank, and may exercise all powers and do all acts and things which may be exercised or done by the Bank.

Section 7(1) of the RBI act clearly says that GOI may give directions to RBI. It also says that such direction shall be issued after consultation with the governor of the bank. Section 7(2) informs that the subject to such directions to RBI, the general superintendence of the RBI shall be entrusted to central board of directors. This means that on issuing directions by the GOI, the powers of RBI governor will pass on to central board of directors.

This section makes it clear that GOI has the authority to issue directions to RBI which shall be followed. Though there have been differences in the perceptions on many matters between GOI and RBI in the past also, this provision to issue direction to RBI was not invoked by GOI so far, since the independence of country in 1947. This is a tribute to the relationship nurtured over the years between GOI and RBI.

However, GOI invoking this provision at any future time cannot be ruled out or argued against on the basis that it was not done in the past. The developing economy of our country may throw up new challenges and the fiscal authority and monetary authority may end up holding opposite views.

In fact, this is what has been transpired in the last few years.

It was reported that GOI has sent letters to the governor for his advice under Section 7(1) on at least on three occasions on the following issues:

1. Withdrawal of PCA from Public Sector Banks (PSB)—The government wanted the PCA framework be eased on PS banks so that MSMEs (micro, small and medium enterprises) could be given loans by those banks.

   The RBI is believed to have refused to oblige. RBI argued that such a step could be retrograde, and all efforts to clean up the bad loans of banks would go down the drain. This then necessitated GOI to recapitalise public sector banks.
2. GOI Concern for NBFC liquidity issue following the default of IL&FS in September 2018, and that Non-banking finance companies had urged the government to make the lending framework lenient. GOI wrote to the Governor for his views on deploying the central bank's capital reserves to infuse liquidity into the markets.

RBI's view was that there is no liquidity crisis in the financial markets and there is no need to create liquidity window to help NBFCs.

It is reported that the GOI wrote its first letter under section 7 of RBI Act to RBI after the Allahabad High Court suggested that the government consider giving directions to RBI under Section 7 of RBI Act. This was due to a case before the high court involving Independent Power Producers, who are aggrieved by the RBI's 12 February 2018 circular to banks which prohibited banks from deviating from NPA norms and provisioning norms.

Letters from GOI under Section 7(1) of RBI Act to the governor RBI seeking his views were sent for the first time in the history of the country. These letters in a way indicated that GOI may invoke the provisions of the RBI Act and issue directives to RBI. In such eventuality RBI Governor's authority shall be curtailed and the administrative powers will be vested with the central board of directors of RBI. This would have been a serious matter and because of this impasse Shri Urjit Patel, governor of RBI resigned from his post from 10th December 2018 as he did not agree with the views of GOI.

In a way this occurrence was a collision between GOI and RBI. The outcome was sad as the governor had to quit avoiding ignominy.

Since it took place, it is an indication for the future relationship between GOI and RBI. It is clear now that GOI is the final authority and its views shall prevail over for monetary policy also. This development may have greater implications as GOI appoints Governor as well as the directors to the central board of RBI. If the government in power ignores the professional views of RBI in the monetary policy matters, the economy may suffer in the long run.

So far GOI has not made RBI to relent on its stand on PCA framework and other prudential norms for banking and financial sectors. The impact of COVID-19 is now felt on the economy in the year 2020 and it may continue for next few years. There are indications that gross NPAs of banks and NBFCs are increasing. RBI in its financial report has indicated the same. This means it will be a stress period for banks. Health of banks will be vital for the economy during this crisis period. Close monitoring by RBI and timely effective actions to arrest the weakness in the banking system will be under test. GOI shall have to be very careful and take right decisions to safeguard the economy.

Monetary Policy Rates and Formation of Monetary Policy Committee

Prior to the year 2016, a Technical Advisory Committee (TAC) on monetary policy with experts from monetary economics, central banking, financial markets and public finance advised the Reserve Bank on the stance of monetary policy. However, its role was only advisory in nature. Governor RBI took the decisions.

GOI felt that the monetary policy and the rates shall be more responsive to the needs of the economy and the decision should be broad based. This called for creating an empowered monetary policy committee.

Earlier several committees have recommended formation of a full-fledged monetary policy committee (MPC) as under:

1. The Standing Committee on International Standards and Codes, 2002 (Chairman: Dr. Y.V. Reddy) recommended legislative changes in the RBI Act so as to facilitate a mechanism for effective monetary policy. It recommended setting up of a Monetary Policy Committee on the lines of the Board of Financial Supervision.
2. The Committee on Fuller Capital Account Convertibility, 2006 (Chairman: Shri S.S. Tarapore) recommended that there should be a formal Monetary Policy Committee. It also recommended that at some appropriate stage, a summary of the minutes of the Monetary Policy Committee should be put in the public domain with a suitable lag.
3. The Committee on Financial Sector Reforms, 2009 (Chairman: Dr. Raghuram G. Rajan) recommended that a Monetary Policy Committee should take a

more active role in guiding monetary policy actions. It should meet more regularly; its recommendations and policy judgments should be made public with minimal delays.

4. Financial Sector Legislative Reforms Commission (FSLRC-2013, Chairman: Shri B.N. Srikrishna) has recommended that an executive MPC should be constituted that would meet on a fixed schedule and vote to determine the course of monetary policy.
5. Finally, Urjit Patel Committee appointed in 2013 made the recommendations.

About the constitution of MPC, Urjit Patel Committee has recommended as under:

Report of the Expert Committee to Revise and Strengthen the Monetary Policy Framework

Urjit Patel Committee January 2014

> III.23. The Governor of the RBI will be the Chairman of the MPC, the Deputy Governor in charge of monetary policy will be the Vice Chairman, and the Executive Director in charge of monetary policy will be a member. Two other members will be external, to be decided by the Chairman and Vice Chairman on the basis of demonstrated expertise and experience in monetary economics, macroeconomics, central banking, financial markets, public finance and related areas.

Urjit Patel committee report recommended setting up of MPC with three RBI officers and two outside experts to be appointed by governor and deputy governor. However, GOI decided for six members MPC. Committee also recommended setting up of inflation target of 4% with +/- 2% permissible variation.

GOI amended the RBI Act, 1934 by inserting a new chapter, Chapter IIIF Monetary Policy by Finance Act of 2016. The amendment came to operation w.e.f. 27.6.2016. This amendment also introduced the concept of fixing inflation target by the GOI.

The relevant sections added in the RBI Act, 1934, for fixing inflation target and for constituting monetary policy committee are as under:

45ZA. Inflation target.

(1) The Central Government shall, in consultation with the Bank, determine the inflation target in terms of the Consumer Price Index, once in every five years.

(2) The Central Government shall, upon such determination, notify the inflation target in the Official Gazette.

45ZB. Constitution of Monetary Policy Committee.

(1) The Central Government may, by notification in the Official Gazette, constitute a Committee to be called the Monetary Policy Committee of the Bank.

(2) The Monetary Policy Committee shall consist of the following Members, namely:—

- (a) The Governor of the Bank—Chairperson, ex officio;
- (b) Deputy Governor of the Bank, in charge of Monetary Policy—Member, ex officio;
- (c) One officer of the Bank to be nominated by the Central Board—Member, ex officio; and
- (d) Three persons to be appointed by the Central Government—Members.

(3) The Monetary Policy Committee shall determine the Policy Rate required to achieve the inflation target.

(4) The decision of the Monetary Policy Committee shall be binding on the Bank.

Accordingly, GOI constituted six-member Monetary Policy Committee (MPC) in September 2016 as under:

1. Governor of the Reserve Bank of India—Chairperson, ex officio;
2. Deputy Governor of the Reserve Bank of India, in charge of Monetary Policy—Member, ex officio;
3. One officer of the Reserve Bank of India to be nominated by the Central Board—Member, ex officio;

4. Shri Chetan Ghate, Professor, Indian Statistical Institute (ISI)—Member;
5. Professor Pami Dua, Director, Delhi School of Economics—Member; and
6. Dr. Ravindra H. Dholakia, Professor, Indian Institute of Management, Ahmedabad—Member.

MPC had its first meeting for two days on October 3 and October 4, 2016.

Now the MPC determines the policy interest rate required to achieve the inflation target. The current mandate of the committee is to maintain 4% annual inflation until 31 March 2021 with an upper tolerance of 6% and a lower tolerance of 2%.

RBI surplus and transfer to GOI

This was a contentious issue between GOI and RBI. RBI is exempted from income tax as per the RBI Act. The Act provides that RBI shall transfer the surplus it generates every year to GOI after making all relevant provisions for reserves.

RBI generally makes huge earnings mainly coming from the interest earnings on the securities it is holding, its lending operations to GOI and banks, and other activities. However, the issue was that GOI felt that RBI is holding more reserves than is necessary and blocking funds. The transfer of surplus from RBI shall ease the budgetary shortfalls of the GOI.

This matter was then referred to Dr. Bimal Jalan (former Governor of RBI) committee constituted on 26-12-2018 to study and recommend the reserve requirement of RBI and the transfer of surplus to GOI. The committee submitted its recommendation which was accepted by RBI on 26th August 2019. As per recommendations, RBI agreed to transfer a sum of ₹ 1,76,051 crore to the Government of India (Government) comprising of ₹ 1,23,414 crore of surplus for the year 2018-19 and ₹ 52,637 crore of excess provisions identified as per the revised Economic Capital Framework (ECF) adopted. This was a huge transfer by RBI to GOI. This is discussed below.

RBI's annual report for the year ending 30 June 2019 contained the following statements:

> XII.2. There was an increase in the size of the Bank's balance sheet during 2018-19. The balance sheet increased by ₹ 4,853.11 billion, i.e. 13.42 per cent from ₹ 36,175.94 billion as on June 30, 2018 to ₹ 41,029.05 billion as on June 30, 2019. The increase on the asset side was due to increase in domestic and foreign investments by 57.19 per cent and 5.70 per cent, respectively and increase in gold by 16.30 per cent. On the liability side, the increase was due to increase in Notes issued, Other Liabilities and Provisions, and Deposits by 13.43 per cent, 11.10 per cent and 17.21 per cent, respectively. Domestic assets constituted 28.03 per cent while the foreign currency assets and gold (including gold held in India) constituted 71.97 per cent of total assets as on June 30, 2019 as against 23.18 per cent and 76.82 per cent, respectively as on June 30, 2018.
>
> XII.3. The Bank had developed the Economic Capital Framework (ECF) between 2014-15 and 2015-16 as an objective, rule-based, transparent methodology for determining the appropriate level of risk provisions to be made under the provisions of Section 47 of the RBI Act, 1934. Subsequent to the meeting of the Reserve Bank's Central Board held on November 19, 2018, the Reserve Bank, in consultation with the Government of India, constituted an Expert Committee to review the extant ECF of the Reserve Bank under the Chairmanship of Dr. Bimal Jalan, the former Governor. The Committee has since submitted its report to the Governor of the Reserve Bank. The Central Board in its meeting held on August 26, 2019, after deliberating on the report, accepted all the recommendations of the Committee and finalised the Reserve Bank's accounts for 2018-19 using the revised framework to determine risk provisioning and surplus transfer. As the Reserve Bank's financial resilience was within the desired range, the excess risk

provision amounting to ₹ 526.37 billion was written back from Contingency Fund (CF) to income.

XII.4. Further, provision was made towards Asset Development Fund (ADF) amounting to ₹ 0.64 billion on account of fresh investments by the Reserve Bank in National Centre for Financial Education (NCFE) and Indian Financial Technology and Allied Services (IFTAS).

XII.5. The surplus before the above adjustments amounted to ₹ 1,234.14 billion. Consequent to the said adjustments, the surplus transferable to Government of India was ₹ 1,759.87 billion (including ₹ 280 billion already transferred to the Government of India during the year).

Following table gives the Trends in Income, Expenditure and Net Disposable Income of RBI and also surplus transferred to GOI for last five years.

Table 4.1: Trends in Income, Expenditure and Net Disposable Income

(₹ billion)

Item	2014-15	2015-16	2016-17	2017-18	2018-19
1	2	3	4	5	6
(a) Income	792.56	808.70	618.18	782.81	1,930.36
(b) Total Expenditure[1]	133.56[2]	149.90[3]	311.55[4]	282.77[5]	170.45[6]
	10.00	10.00	0.50 131.40	141.90	0.64
	123.56	139.90	179.65	140.87	169.81
(c) Net Disposable Income (a-b)	659.00	658.80	306.63	500.04	1,759.91
(d) Transfer to funds[7]	0.04	0.04	0.04	0.04	0.04
(e) Surplus transferred to the Government (c-d)	658.96	658.76	306.59	500.00	1,759.87

Notes: 1. Since June 30, 2015, transfers to CF and ADF are being made through provisions head in Income Statement.

2. Includes a provision of ₹ 10 billion towards additional capital contribution in NHB.

3. Includes a provision of ₹ 10 billion towards additional capital contribution in BRBNMPL.

4. Includes a provision of ₹ 0.50 billion towards capital contribution in the Reserve Bank's subsidiary Reserve Bank Information

Technology (P) Ltd. (ReBIT) and a provision of ₹ 131.40 billion towards transfer to CF.

5. Includes a provision of ₹ 141.90 billion towards transfer to CF.
6. Includes a provision of ₹ 0.64 billion towards transfer to ADF.
7. An amount of ₹ 10 million each has been transferred to the National Industrial Credit (Long-term Operations) Fund, the National Rural Credit (Long-term Operations) Fund, the National Rural Credit (Stabilisation) Fund and the National Housing Credit (Long-term Operations) Fund during each of the five years.

Source: RBI

Relevant schedules giving details of income are given under:

Schedules	(Amount in ₹ billion)	2017-18	2018-19
Schedule 12:	Interest		
	(a) Domestic Sources		
	(i) Interest on holding of Rupee Securities	479.68	583.43
	(ii) Net Interest on LAF Operations	-95.41	10.46
	(iii) Interest on MSF Operations	1.25	1.35
	(iv) Interest on Loans and Advances	7.79	14.98
	Sub total	393.31	610.22
	(b) Foreign Sources		
	(i) Interest Income from Foreign Securities	234.28	278.11
	(ii) Net Interest on Repo/Reverse Repo transaction	0.00	-0.04
	(iii) Interest on Deposits	111.12	180.08
	Sub total	345.40	458.15
	Total	738.71	1,068.37
Schedule 13:	Other Income		
	(a) Domestic Sources		
	(i) Exchange	0.00	0.00
	(ii) Discount	0.00	0.00
	(iii) Commission	20.35	22.72
	(iv) Rent Realised	0.05	0.07
	(v) Profit/Loss on sale and redemption of Rupee Securities	60.36	0.40
	(vi) Depreciation on Rupee Securities inter portfolio transfer	-0.08	-0.27
	(vii) Amortisation of premium/discount of Rupee Securities	31.13	21.45
	(viii) Profit/Loss on sale of Bank's property	0.01	0.01

Schedules	(Amount in ₹ billion)	2017-18	2018-19
	(ix) Provision no longer required and Miscellaneous Income	3.67	526.18
	Sub total	115.49	570.56
	(b) Foreign Sources		
	(i) Amortisation of premium/discount of Foreign Securities	-36.08	-15.31
	(ii) Profit/Loss on sale and redemption of Foreign Securities	5.36	16.76
	(iii) Exchange gain/loss from Foreign Exchange transactions	-40.67	289.98
	Sub total	-71.39	291.43
	Total	44.10	861.99
	Total income	782.81	1930.06

For the year ending 30-6-2019 RBI earned interest income of ₹ 583.43 bn on domestic securities held by it (previous year ₹ 479.68 bn) and ₹ 458.15 bn income on foreign securities and deposits (previous year ₹ 345.40 bn) held by it. In the Year 2018-19 RBI earnings was high at ₹ 1068.37 bn, as compared to previous year 2017-18 which was ₹ 787.71 bn. During the year RBI earned ₹ 289.98 bn exchange gain in forex transactions (previous year loss of ₹ 40.67 bn). RBI has also reversed ₹ 526.18 bn as provision no longer required. In view of these, income for 2018-19 was quite high at ₹ 1930.06 bn. This has enabled RBI to transfer huge amount of ₹ 1,759.87 bn to GOI during the year. This is one time bonanza for the GOI.

The following table shows the income expenditure and surplus of RBI operations for the last ten years.

We can observe the trend in gross income over the years. In 2018-19 RBI has written back ₹ 526.18 bn as excess provision. However, the gross income of RBI in this year quite high compared to the previous years. We may also observe that RBI has not made provision for contingency fund in the year 2013-14, 2014-15, 2015-16. In 2018-19, it has written back the excess provision. Surplus transferred to GOI has increased from the year 2013-14 onwards.

As stated earlier huge amount of one-time transfer to GOI is worked out and based on Dr. Bimal Jalan (former Governor

Gross Income, Expenditure and Net Disposable Income

(₹ billion)

Item	2009-10	2010-11	2011-12	2012-13	2013-14	2014-15	2015-16	2016-17	2017-18	2018-19
	1	2	3	4	5	6	7	8	9	10
(a) Gross Income	328.84	370.70	531.76	743.58	646.17	792.56	808.70	618.18	782.81	1930.36
(b) Transfers to Internal Reserves (i+ii)	57.18	134.02	270.25	287.94	0	10.00	10.00	131.90	141.90	0.64
(i) Contingency Reserve	51.68	121.67	246.77	262.47	0	0	0	131.40	141.90	0
(ii) Asset Development Reserve	5.50	12.35	23.48	25.47	0	10.00	10.00	0.50	0	0.64
(c) Net Income (a-b)	271.66	236.68	261.51	455.63	646.17	782.56	798.70	486.28	640.91	1929.72
(d) Total Expenditure	84.03	86.55	101.37	125.49	119.34	123.56	139.90	179.65	140.87	169.81
(e) Net Disposable Income (c-d)	187.63	150.13	160.14	330.14	526.83	659.00	658.80	306.63	500.04	1759.91
(f) Transfer to funds*	0.04	0.04	0.04	0.04	0.04	0.04	0.04	0.04	0.04	0.04
(g) Surplus transferred to the Government (e-f)	187.59	150.09	160.10	330.10	526.79	658.96	658.76	306.59	500.00	1759.87

* : An amount of ₹ 10 million each has been transferred to the National Industrial Credit (Long-term Operations) Fund, the National Rural Credit (Long-term Operations) Fund, the National Rural Credit (Stabilisation) Fund and the National Housing Credit (Long-term Operations) Fund during each of the five years.

Source: Extracted from RBI annual reports

Reserve Bank of India Balance Sheet as on June 30, 2019

(Amount in ₹ billion)

Liabilities	Schedule	2017-18	2018-19	Assets	Schedule	2017-18	2018-19
Capital		0.05	0.05	Assets of Banking Department (BD)			
Reserve Fund		65.00	65.00	Notes, Rupee Coin, Small Coin	5	0.09	0.09
Other Reserves	1	2.28	2.30	Gold Coin and Bullion	6	696.74	882.98
Deposits	2	6,525.97	7,649.22	Investments-Foreign-BD	7	7,983.89	6,964.53
Other Liabilities and Provisions	3	10,463.04	11,624.51	Investments-Domestic-BD	8	6,297.45	9,898.77
				Bills Purchased and Discounted		0.00	0.00
				Loans and Advances	9	1,638.55	931.87
				Investment in Subsidiaries	10	33.70	19.64
				Other Assets	11	405.92	643.20
Liabilities of Issue Department				Assets of Issue Department (ID)			
Notes issued	4	19,119.60	21,687.97	Gold Coin and Bullion (as backing for Note issue)	6	743.49	792.04
				Rupee Coin		9.26	8.28
				Investments-Foreign-ID	7	18,366.85	20,887.65
				Investments-Domestic-ID	8	0.00	0.00
				Domestic Bills of Exchange and other Commercial Papers		0.00	0.00
Total Liabilities		36,175.94	41,029.05	Total Assets		36,175.94	41,029.05

of RBI) committee constituted on 26-12-2018 to study and recommend the reserve requirement of RBI and the transfer of surplus to GOI. The committee submitted its recommendation which was accepted by RBI on 26 August 2019. As per recommendations, RBI transferred a sum of ₹ 1,76,051 crore to the Government of India (Government) comprising of ₹ 1,23,414 crore of surplus for the year 2018-19 and ₹ 52,637 crore of excess provisions identified as per the revised Economic Capital Framework (ECF) adopted.

We may try to understand now the revised economic capital framework recommended by the committee and how it works for fixing the capital requirement of RBI.

Balance sheet of RBI as on June 30, 2019 is given below:

Liabilities of RBI include 'other liabilities and provisions' which is as per schedule 3 of the balance sheet. Same is given hereunder:

Schedule 3:	Other Liabilities and Provisions		
	(i) Contingency Fund (CF)	2,321.08	1,963.44
	(ii) Asset Development Fund (ADF)	228.11	228.75
	(iii) Currency and Gold Revaluation Account (CGRA)	6,916.41	6,644.80
	(iv) Investment Revaluation Account-Foreign Securities (IRA-FS)	0.00	157.35
	(v) Investment Revaluation Account-Rupee Securities (IRA-RS)	132.85	494.76
	(vi) Foreign Exchange Forward Contracts Valuation Account (FCVA)	32.62	13.04
	(vii) Provision for Forward Contracts Valuation Account (PFCVA)	0.00	0.00
	(viii) Provision for payables	27.88	22.81
	(ix) Gratuity and Superannuation Fund	175.13	206.10
	(x) Surplus Transferable to the Government of India	500.00	1,759.87
	(xi) Bills Payable	0.05	0.08
	(xii) Miscellaneous	128.91	133.51
	Total	10,463.04	11,624.51

While there are many accounts mentioned in the schedule, capital reserves of RBI and the nature of capital reserves is given hereunder:

Components of Capital Reserves of the RBI

Component	Amount in ₹ billion	
	30-6-2018	30-6-2019
Contingency Fund (CF)	2,321.08	1,963.44
Asset Development Fund (ADF)	228.11	228.75
Currency and Gold Revaluation Account (CGRA)	6,916.41	6,644.80
Investment Revaluation Account-Foreign Securities (IRA-FS)	0.00	157.35
Investment Revaluation Account (IRA)	132.85	494.76
Foreign Exchange Forward Contracts Valuation Account (FCVA).	32.62	13.04
Total	9631.07	9502.14

Source: Figures from RBI balance sheets of these years

Contingency Fund. The CF is a fund set apart for meeting the unforeseen contingencies, including depreciation in the value of securities, risks arising out of monetary/exchange rate policy operations, systemic risks and any risk arising on account of the special responsibilities enjoined upon the bank.

Asset Development Fund (ADF) is set aside for investment in subsidiaries and associates and for internal capital expenditure.

Currency and Gold Revaluation Account (CGRA) shows fund that is available to compensate RBI's loss in the value of gold and foreign exchange reserve holdings. Gains and losses of the values of Gold and Foreign Currency Assets decreases or increases the CGRA money. CGRA provides a buffer against exchange rate/gold price fluctuations.

The Investment Revaluation Account shows the buffer amount available with the RBI to compensate losses and to accommodate gains in (i) foreign securities and (ii) domestic securities. RBI holds significant portion of foreign securities and domestic securities (Government of India). Under IRA, the marked to market gains and losses are measured.

Foreign Exchange Forward Contracts Valuation Account (FCVA) measures marked to market (periodic) gains and losses for the RBI from foreign exchange forward contracts.

These capital reserve accounts are besides the capital, reserve fund and other reserves given in the balance sheet as under

₹ billion	30-6-2018	30-6-2019
Capital	0.05	0.05
Reserve fund	65.00	65.00
Other reserves	2.28	2.30
Total	67.33	67.35

Contingency Fund and Asset Development Funds are created from the gross income of RBI by making provisions for them before arriving at the surplus. Whereas the other reserve accounts are not created from gross income. These are created on the basis of revaluation of concerned assets and either increase or decrease in the value of assets like gold and foreign securities are taken to these reserve accounts. Increase in the value of these assets is not treated as income. Hence these reserves act as buffer to absorb the fluctuation in the values of these assets.

Dr. Bimal Jalan Committee recommendations were mainly in respect of reserves held in Contingency Fund and Asset Development Fund. Committee recommendations on the levels of reserves to be maintained are given under. The committee introduced two frameworks for arriving at the desired level of capital for RBI as under:

(i) *Realized Equity*: This is arrived by taking capital and the realised reserve funds available with RBI. In this only CF and ADF are added up with capital and reserve fund shown in the balance sheet. It will be as under:

₹ billion	30-6-2018	30-6-2019
Capital	0.05	0.05
Reserve fund	65.00	65.00
Other reserves	2.28	2.30
Total	67.33	67.35
Contingency fund (CF)	2,321.08	1,963.44

₹ billion	30-6-2018	30-6-2019
Asset development fund (ADF)	228.11	228.75
Total realized equity	2616.52	2259.54
Total assets (balance sheet)	36,175.94	41,029.05
% realised capital to assets	7.23%	5.59%

Committee recommended that the level of realised capital shall be within the band of 6.5% to 5.5% of the balance sheet. Central board of RBI approved to maintain 5.5% for June 2019 and the resultant excess risk provisions of ₹ 526.37 bn were written back.

(ii) *Economic capital levels*: The committee recommended revised framework for economic capital level to be within the range of 24.5 per cent to 20.0 per cent of balance sheet. Economic Capital is worked out by adding total capital reserves (both realised and revaluation reserves) to the capital plus reserve funds in the balance sheet. The figures are as under:

₹ billion	30-6-2018	30-6-2019
Capital	0.05	0.05
Reserve fund	65.00	65.00
Other reserves	2.28	2.30
Sub Total	67.33	67.35
Add total capital reserves (CF+ ADF+CGRA+IRA+FCVA)	9631.07	9502.14
Total (Economic Capital)	9698.40	9569.49
Total assets of RBI (balance sheet)	36,175.94	41,029.05
% Economic Capital to assets	26.81%	23.32%

As per the working shown in the table above, the economic capital as on June 30, 2019 stood at 23.32 per cent of balance sheet.

Based on these recommendations RBI central board has reversed the surplus from contingency fund and allowed it to be transferred to GOI. We may also observe that the capital reserves of RBI have come down from ₹ 9631.07 bn in June 2018 to ₹ 9502.14 bn in June 2019. The decline in capital reserve was ₹ 128.93 bn. RBI has claimed that the capital strength of RBI is highest in comparison to central banks of other countries.

5

Structure of Interest Rates in India

We are aware that interest rates play an important role in the economy. There are different interest rates applicable to bank deposits and bank loans, on-call money and notice money, interest rates on government bonds, on post office deposit schemes, on corporate bonds or debentures, etc. Actually, when we refer to the interest rate, it is basically on a lending transaction involved. When a bank or company receives deposits from the depositors it means that the banks or the companies are borrowing from the depositors. Similarly, govt. is borrowing from the individuals or others when it accepts money from them by issuing bonds or certificates. In all these cases the banks, companies and the govts. are the borrowers. They pay interest to the parties who have provided money to them in the name of deposits or investment in different types of securities offered.

Another type of borrowing is called loans. Banks or finance companies offer loans to the public or others as they have funds lying with them. They are giving loans so that they can make use of their funds and earn interest on the loans given. In this case, bank or finance company becomes the lenders and the parties' taking loans from them become the borrowers.

The word deposit, advance, loan, and investment is commonly used in financial world and all these financial terms indicate a debtor-creditor relationship being created between the parties who are involved in these types of financial transactions. It is interesting to know whether the words; deposit and loan have same meanings and whether they are same and whether these words can be used in the alternative to describe the same financial transaction.

For example, when public places its money with bank it is known as deposit and when one borrows from the bank it is known as loan. When an individual puts his money in the shares of the companies it is called investment. But when one puts his money in the debenture issues of the companies it is called loan. When the govt. accepts money from public by issuing bonds the transaction is known as govt. borrowing which means loan.

The term 'deposit' is defined in The Companies Act, 2013 and also in the RBI Act, 1934. But the term 'loan' is not defined specifically. Section 45-I(bb) of the RBI Act, 1934 defines deposit as:

'Deposit' includes and shall be deemed always to have included any receipt of money by way of deposit or loan or in any other form but does not include:

This section gives the list of receipts of money that does not fall under the definition of deposit.

The exclusions from the definition of deposit are as under:

- amount raised by way of share capital, or contributed as capital by partners of a firm;
- amount received from a scheduled bank, a co-operative bank, a banking company, Development bank, State Financial Corporation, IDBI or any other institution specified by RBI;
- amount received in ordinary course of business by way of security deposit, dealership deposit, earnest money, advance against orders for goods, properties or services;
- amount received by a registered money lender other than a body corporate;
- amount received by way of subscriptions in respect of a 'Chit'.
- amount received from the Central/State Government or any other source where repayment is guaranteed by Central/State Government or any amount received

from local authority or foreign government or any foreign citizen/authority/person;

- any amount received from financial institutions specified by RBI for this purpose;
- any amount received by a company from any other company;
- amount received by way of subscriptions to shares, stock, bonds or debentures pending allotment or by way of calls in advance if such amount is not repayable to the members under the articles of association of the company;
- amount received from directors of a company or from its shareholders by private company or by a private company which has become a public company;
- amount raised by issue of bonds or debentures secured by mortgage of any immovable property or other asset of the company subject to conditions;
- any amount raised by issuance of non-convertible debentures with a maturity more than one year and having the minimum subscription per investor at ₹ 1 crore and above, provided it is in accordance with the guidelines issued by the bank;
- the amount brought in by the promoters by way of unsecured loan;
- amount received from a mutual fund;
- any amount received as hybrid debt or subordinated debt;
- amount received from a relative of the director of an NBFC;
- any amount received by issuance of commercial paper;
- any amount received by a systemically important non-deposit taking non-banking financial company by issuance of 'perpetual debt instruments';
- any amount raised by the issue of infrastructure bonds by an Infrastructure Finance Company.

However, both these acts did not define the term 'loan'. Hence 'loan' is understood as the excluded items from the definition of 'deposit'. Hence the 'deposit' or 'loan' is not as per the common usage of the words in the financial world but will be decided by the provisions of the sections in the acts.

Broadly speaking we may understand that deposit is made at the instance and for the benefit of the person depositing the money. Deposit is payable on demand (as in the case of bank deposits) or after a fixed term.

Whereas loan is taken at the instance or for the benefit of the person requesting for the money (borrower) and in this transaction money is given with the intention to be returned, with or without interest. Loan is payable only when the obligation to repay the amount arises, as per the loan agreement.

In the modern economy, we observe that economic activities are growing and the economy of the country produces agriculture produces, and industrial products. There are other economic activities going on which produces different kinds of services. All these activities require labour to be employed to run the activities. These economic activities thus result in income generation for the labour and owners of such activities.

The income generated has to take care of the current consumption needs of the income earners. When the income generated exceeds, the consumption needs then a surplus is created. This surplus is also known as the savings. This surplus is held by individuals as cash and they hold on to the cash till they require it to spend at a future date. Generally, the surplus or the savings will be with some income earners from any category (wage earners, self-employed, professionals, salaried class, farmers, businessman, business firms, and business corporates). This surplus or savings will be lying idle as the persons having it may not spend it now and they are holding for future use. This aspect of the modern economy has given rise to financial intermediation. Banks have started it. Banks accepts the savings of individuals or firms as deposits and then offer loans to borrowers who want to use the money to develop/ expand business and earn from it. This financial intermediation of collecting the savings from people and making it available to other persons as loan is now a crucial function in the modern economy. It acts as a catalyst for faster development of the economy as a whole.

This financial intermediation is possible only when the savers are induced to part with their savings for some time. To induce them for parting their savings they are offered interest on their money as an incentive. Similarly, the borrowers from banks will be charged interest which is actually the cost borrowers will be paying for the borrowed money.

Now we have two interest rates; one interest rate for the deposits which are kept with banks and another loan interest rate that are charged to the borrowers. We can understand that the loan interest rate shall be higher as the banks will have to pay interest to depositors, meet their cost of operations and earn some profit.

Now the important question is how these two interest rates are decided and by whom. This is a very complicated issue. As the banking activities though present in the human societies since very long, modern banking has evolved in the twentieth century that also after the Second World War. Banking business has undergone lot of changes since then. Now Central banks are created in all countries to supervise the banking sector and also to act as the monetary authority.

Deposit interest rate and loan interest rate in the modern economy is a product of complex system followed. In today's world, as the economies are working to be free, it has to be market driven and the demand and supply will have its role to play on the interest rates. Govts. have role in providing stimulus to the markets for the purpose to sustain growth and prosperity of the country.

But the important economic factor that has bearing on the interest rates is the price stability and the inflation in the economy. Monetary authority of every country has its prime objective of controlling inflation and price stability. Price stability means that the prices of assets, commodities and services available in the country are maintained at the existing level or with a small change in it. If the prices are rising for any reason, then effectively the currency of the country gets depreciated. When the prices are rising, it means that inflation is taking place in the economy and the purchasing power of the currency is depreciating. This is the biggest concern of the government and the monetary authority of all countries in the world.

Further it is to be noted that the developed countries of the world are generally have achieved stable and minimum inflation rates. Countries like USA, UK, European countries, Japan and few others have low inflation rates in their economy which is less than 2% yearly. Some of them are near to zero inflation levels. However, the developing countries like India and others have higher inflation rates, between 4% to 10%. Other less developed countries may have more than 10% inflation and, in some cases, it can be very high also.

Now we may have to understand the connection between the interest rates and the inflation rate. We have to understand that the savings by the population of the country is very important as this savings which finds its way to banking system supports the bank credit expansion. Bank credit is needed to provide funds for investment in business and industry which in turn increases the production and earnings for the country. Savings can be attracted by giving reasonable rate of interest to the depositors. Here it is important to understand the deposit interest rate offered by banks and the actual interest earning to the depositor. For example, if the inflation rate in the country is 5% and then if bank pays less than 5% interest on deposits, the depositor will lose as there will be loss to him at the end of the year. His money has lost its value due to inflation; he will be a loser by keeping the deposit in the bank. Only if he is paid deposit interest which is more than 5% (inflation rate) his money will retain its value may be with a small return. Hence the interest rate allowed by bank to the depositor is the notional interest rate. When this rate is adjusted to the inflation, then the 'real interest rate' is arrived. So, the real interest earning to the depositor will have to be positive then only there will be incentive for him to save. Otherwise, he may spend his money now, instead of saving.

This is the basic logic of interest rate fixing and the first interest rate to be decided will the bank deposit interest rate as it is at the base of banking and financial system of the country. Other interest rates like loan interest rate, government security interest rate, bond or debenture interest rate and others will be linked to this basic rate.

In our country till 1997 the bank deposit rate and bank loan rates were fixed by RBI and banks were offering it to the public. Thereafter the RBI discontinued this practice and allowed banks to decide on their interest rates on deposits and advances. Now the banks are free to fix their rates for deposits and advances.

Though freedom is given to banks, banks shall be required to fix interest rates both on deposits and loans keeping in mind some benchmarks created by the monetary authority, i.e., RBI. Benchmark rates are discussed little later.

Deposit Rates and Lending Rates of Banks of G20 Countries

Inflation Rates in these Countries: The following table shows the bank deposit rates, bank lending rates and also the inflation rate in these countries. These figures have been collected from few sources named at the bottom of table. The figures may not be of a common date as these figures are pertaining to period from November 2019 to January 2020. These are collated for the purpose understanding the connection between inflation rate and banks deposit and loan rates. It is also for the purpose to compare the interest structure of these countries.

As earlier stated, the important interest rate in the financial system of a country is the commercial banks deposit rates that it offers to the depositors. The benchmark rate fixed by the central bank of the country is a policy rate and it is used by the central bank to cause changes in the movement of interest rates in the financial market to achieve the monetary goal of the country. This policy rate also causes changes in banks deposit and loan interest rates.

The G20 comprises 19 countries and the European Union. The 19 countries are Argentina, Australia, Brazil, Canada, China, Germany, France, India, Indonesia, Italy, Japan, Mexico,

Russia, Saudi Arabia, South Africa, South Korea, Turkey, the United Kingdom, and the United States.

The G20 (or Group of Twenty) is an international forum for the governments and central bank governors from 19 countries and the European Union (EU). This was Founded in 1999 with the aim to discuss policy pertaining to the promotion of international financial stability,

Countries	Bank fixed deposit range or average %	Bank lending rate	Inflation rate
Switzerland	-0.38	2.63	0.20
Japan	0.010-0.013	0.95	0.50
Euro Zone (19 countries including Germany, France & Italy)	0.30	1.91	1.30
UK	0.85-1.10	1.75	1.30
Australia	1.10-1.20	7.92	1.70
China	1.35-1.75	3.25	4.50
South Korea	1.63	3.18	0.70
USA	2.15-2.25	4.75	2.30
Canada	2.22-2.40	3.95	2.20
Saudi Arabia	2.25	8.3*	-0.20
Mexico	3.40	7.94	2.83
Malaysia	3.00-4.00	4.73	0.90
Indonesia	4.25	5.75	2.72
Russia	4.580	8.17	3.00
Brazil	5.09	50.16	4.31
India	3.50-7.00	9.40	7.35
South Africa	7.00-7.65	9.75	3.60
Turkey	9.75	12.75	11.84

*2018

Sources: 1. www.ceicdata.com 2. Trading economics

Data pertains to period Nov. 19 to Jan. 20.

There are 23 countries that use the euro as of 2018. The Eurozone consists of 19 members who are EU members and use the common currency Euro. They are Austria, Belgium, Cyprus, Estonia, Finland, France, Germany, Greece, Ireland, Italy, Latvia, Lithuania, Luxembourg, Malta, the Netherlands, Portugal, Slovakia, Slovenia, and Spain.

From the chart, we can observe the relationship between inflation rate and bank deposit rate.

Theoretically the bank deposit rate shall be more than the inflation rate so that the depositors get some real interest after adjusting for the inflation. But in many countries, we can observe that the bank deposit rate is less than the inflation rate. Also, in some cases we can observe that bank deposit rate is more than the inflation rate.

This is mainly for the reason that the monetary authorities of the countries decide on the benchmark rates, basing it on the expected inflation rate in the near future. Benchmark rates are not following the historical inflation rate but aiming to reduce inflation in the current year and making the changes in the benchmark rates to achieve the inflation target. This is an exercise by the monetary authority to direct and guide the inflation rate by undertaking suitable fiscal and monetary measures to bring down inflation. There can be other reasons and purposes also for the bank deposit rates to be lower than the inflation rate based on the policy of the country.

In our country the benchmark rate is the repo rate and it is fixed by the monetary policy committee. Prior to May 2020 the repo rate of 5.15% is fixed by it and it is said in the committee report that the present inflation target is fixed at 4% with +/– 2% margin. However, the inflation rate appears to have gone beyond this target. Present repo rate is 4% from 22 May 2020.

Bank deposit rates are generally fixed by the banks themselves. The practices of countries are different in many aspects. Banks in many countries offer some interest on savings accounts. But interest on savings account is generally low. Banks offer higher interest rates on term deposits and the rates are different for different maturities. In all the developed and developing countries generally bank deposit interest rates also vary amongst the local banks. Savings accounts and term deposit accounts of banks are also country specific and there are many variations in the features of these accounts.

Bank lending rates are also fixed by individual banks in maximum countries. Banks generally offer different loan interest rates to borrowers based on many factors. These factors may be the security cover available, purpose of loan, credit rating of the borrower, period of loan, etc. banks also have their internal benchmark rates for loans. Such internal benchmark lending rates are also known as the prime rates of the banks concerned. The prime rate is the interest rate that a commercial bank offers to its most creditworthy customers. Prime rate is lowest rate of interest a commercial bank charges to the customer.

Commercial banks' lending rates are very complex in nature and we cannot make any useful comparison or derive at any conclusions. Broadly we can find that bank lending rates will be higher than the bank deposit rates as banks have to earn and make the business profitable. Roughly we may presume that the loan interest rate will be higher by 3-4% than the deposit interest rate on an average basis.

Benchmark Rates

Monetary authorities in all countries have created some benchmark interest rates. There are many types of benchmark rates fixed by individual country which suit their system. These benchmark rates are not identical in their definitions. They have different meanings but they act as a reference rate for financial system in each country. It is important to note that whatever kind of benchmark rate has been prescribed by the central bank of any country, it will have a relationship with the expected inflation rate of the country. And by the operation of this system of fixing the benchmark rate, the central bank of the country gives direction to the financial system to arrange different interest rates in consonance with the benchmark rate. Benchmark rates of some important countries are given in the following table.

Worldwide Central Bank Rates

OECD & G20 Countries

38.00% (+ 2.00)	↑ Argentina I Benchmark Rate (Nov 12, 2020)	Central Bank
0.10% (- 0.15)	↓ Australia I Cash Rate (Nov 03, 2020)	Historical Rates
4.25% (+ 0.75)	↑ Brazil I Selic Rate (Jun 16, 2021)	Central Bank
0.25% (- 0.50)	↓ Canada I Target on Rate (Mar 27, 2020)	Historical Rates

0.75% (+ 0.25)	↑ Chile I Monetary Policy Rate (Jul 14, 2021)	Central Bank
3.85% (- 0.20)	↓ China I Loan Prime Rate, LPR (Apr 20, 2020)	Central Bank
1.75% (- 0.25)	↓ Colombia I Key Policy Rate (Sep 25, 2020)	Central Bank
0.50% (+ 0.25)	↑ Czech Republic I Repo Rate (Jun 23, 2021)	Central Bank
-0.35% (- 0.40)	↓ Denmark I Lending Rate (Mar 11, 2021)	Central Bank
0.00% (- 0.05)	↓ Eurozone I Key Interest Rate (Mar 10, 2016)	Historical Rates
1.20% (+ 0.30)	↑ Hungary I Base Rate (Jul 28, 2021)	Central Bank
1.00% (+ 0.25)	↑ Iceland I 7-d Deposit Rate (May 19, 2021)	Central Bank
4.00% (- 0.40)	↓ India I Policy Repo Rate (May 22, 2020)	Central Bank
3.50% (- 0.25)	↓ Indonesia I Repo Rate (Feb 18, 2021)	Central Bank
0.10% (- 0.15)	↓ Israel I Benchmark Rate (Apr 06, 2020)	Central Bank
-0.10% (- 0.10)	↓ Japan I Key Policy Rate (Jan 29, 2016)	Central Bank
4.25% (+ 0.25)	↑ Mexico I Benchmark Rate (Jun 24, 2021)	Central Bank
0.25% (- 0.75)	↓ New Zealand I Cash Rate (Mar 16, 2020)	Central Bank
0.00% (- 0.25)	↓ Norway I Key Policy Rate (May 07, 2020)	Central Bank
0.10% (- 0.40)	↓ Poland I Reference Rate (May 28, 2020)	Central Bank
6.50% (+ 1.00)	↑ Russia I Key Rate (Jun 11, 2021)	Central Bank
1.00% (- 0.75)	↓ Saudi Arabia I Repo Rate (Mar 16, 2020)	Central Bank
0.50% (- 0.25)	↓ South Korea I Base Rate (May 28, 2020)	Central Bank
3.50% (- 0.25)	↓ South Africa I Repurchase Rate (Jul 23, 2020)	Central Bank
0.00% (+ 0.25)	↑ Sweden I Repo Rate (Dec 19, 2019)	Central Bank
- 0.75% (- 0.50)	↓ Switzerland I SNB Policy Rate (Jan 15, 2015)	Central Bank
19.00% (+ 2.00)	↑ Turkey I 1 Week Repo Rate (Mar 18, 2021)	Central Bank
0.10% (- 0.15)	↓ United Kingdom I Bank Rate (Mar 19, 2020)	Historical Rates
0.00-0.25% (-1.00)	↓ USA I Funds Rate (Mar 15, 2020)	Historical Rates
38.00% (+ 2.00)	↑ Argentina I Benchmark Rate (Nov 12, 2020)	Central Bank
0.10% (- 0.15)	↓ Australia I Cash Rate (Nov 03, 2020)	Historical Rates
4.25% (+ 0.75)	↑ Brazil I Selic Rate (Jun 16, 2021)	Central Bank
0.25% (- 0.50)	↓ Canada I Target on Rate (Mar 27, 2020)	Historical Rates
0.75% (+ 0.25)	↑ Chile I Monetary Policy Rate (Jul 14, 2021)	Central Bank
3.85% (- 0.20)	↓ China I Loan Prime Rate, LPR (Apr 20, 2020)	Central Bank
1.75% (- 0.25)	↓ Colombia I Key Policy Rate (Sep 25, 2020)	Central Bank
0.50% (+ 0.25)	↑ Czech Republic I Repo Rate (Jun 23, 2021)	Central Bank
-0.35% (- 0.40)	↓ Denmark I Lending Rate (Mar 11, 2021)	Central Bank

0.00% (- 0.05)	↓ Eurozone I Key Interest Rate (Mar 10, 2016)	Historical Rates
1.20% (+ 0.30)	↑ Hungary I Base Rate (Jul 28, 2021)	Central Bank
1.00% (+ 0.25)	↑ Iceland I 7-d Deposit Rate (May 19, 2021)	Central Bank
4.00% (- 0.40)	↓ India I Policy Repo Rate (May 22, 2020)	Central Bank
3.50% (- 0.25)	↓ Indonesia I Repo Rate (Feb 18, 2021)	Central Bank
0.10% (- 0.15)	↓ Israel I Benchmark Rate (Apr 06, 2020)	Central Bank
-0.10% (- 0.10)	↓ Japan I Key Policy Rate (Jan 29, 2016)	Central Bank
4.25% (+ 0.25)	↑ Mexico I Benchmark Rate (Jun 24, 2021)	Central Bank
0.25% (- 0.75)	↓ New Zealand I Cash Rate (Mar 16, 2020)	Central Bank
0.00% (- 0.25)	↓ Norway I Key Policy Rate (May 07, 2020)	Central Bank
0.10% (- 0.40)	↓ Poland I Reference Rate (May 28, 2020)	Central Bank
6.50% (+ 1.00)	↑ Russia I Key Rate (Jun 11, 2021)	Central Bank
1.00% (- 0.75)	↓ Saudi Arabia I Repo Rate (Mar 16, 2020)	Central Bank
0.50% (- 0.25)	↓ South Korea I Base Rate (May 28, 2020)	Central Bank
3.50% (- 0.25)	↓ South Africa I Repurchase Rate (Jul 23, 2020)	Central Bank
0.00% (+ 0.25)	↑ Sweden I Repo Rate (Dec 19, 2019)	Central Bank
-0.75% (- 0.50)	↓ Switzerland I SNB Policy Rate (Jan 15, 2015)	Central Bank
19.00% (+ 2.00)	↑ Turkey I 1 Week Repo Rate (Mar 18, 2021)	Central Bank
0.10% (- 0.15)	↓ United Kingdom I Bank Rate (Mar 19, 2020)	Historical Rates
0.00-0.25% (-1.00)	↓ USA I Funds Rate (Mar 15, 2020)	Historical Rates

Source: Central Bank Rates (www.cbrates.com)

We may find that the benchmark rates have different nomenclatures. It may be noted that they are not same. Each country has fixed a rate and it is fixed for many different purposes. Some are interest rate that central bank is offering on deposits. Some are lending rates at which the central bank will lend to banks. Even the lending rates can be on different basis like secured and unsecured. But many of the central banks are using their lending rate on secured basis to commercial banks as the benchmark rate.

Interestingly these benchmark rates also reveal the status of the economy of the respective countries. The rates are the indicators to the level of inflation in these countries.

There are three countries Denmark Japan and Switzerland with negative benchmark rates at (-0.35%), (-0.10%), and

(-0.75%) respectively. It means that their inflation rates are nearer to zero. They are the developed countries. Their per capita GDP is quite high. Unemployment is quite low. In case of Japan, they are now facing the problem of dwindling population. Saudi Arabia has negative inflation rate at -0.20% which is the only country having this negative rate.

Eurozone (19 countries) and Sweden have zero benchmark rates. There are about 13 countries whose benchmark rates are below 2%. All these are developed countries.

About six countries (including India) have more than 5% benchmark rates. These are the developing economies.

China and India are the two major Asian countries developing fast. Benchmark rate of China is 3.85% and India is 4%. This means that though they are growing very fast and will become large economies in the near future, yet they have higher inflation rate. It is said that the growing economies will have higher inflation rates during the period of their growth but when they achieve the status of developed economy their inflation rate may come down nearer to zero.

This in a way explains why interest rates in India are falling. We can observe that in 1990s bank deposit rates have been nearly 13% p.a. and now (2019) it is down to the level of about 6-7% p.a. The reason is inflation rate was more than 10% then and now it is hovering around 5-6%. The aim of the govt. is bring down inflation to 3-3.5% level. When this happens the rate of interests will further fall and we may have similar interest structures as that of the present developed countries.

Though the benchmark rates in a way reflect the level of inflation in the countries, but there is no fixed formula or a direct link to inflation rate. Each country follows its own methodology for fixing the benchmark rate keeping in view the expected inflation and some other factors relevant to its country. Many times, the countries change the benchmark rates to trigger and induce the financial system to move in a desired direction either to control growth or to stop/reverse recessionary trend in the economy.

In our country the benchmark rate fixed by RBI is known as repo rate. RBI fixes repo rate and it is the rate at which banks can borrow from RBI by giving govt. securities as security for the loan. This means whenever a bank is in need of funds it can borrow from RBI at this interest rate.

Interest Rate and GDP Growth Rate

According to the views of economists in modern times the interest rates on deposits should be based on not only the inflation rate in the economy but also the GDP growth rate of the economy. It is argued that the inflation rate shall be considered for fixing the minimum interest rate whereas the GDP growth rate is the indicator for the maximum level for the interest rates.

Inflation in the economy has the effect of reducing the notional interest as the purchasing power of the money comes down. Actual interest earning will be less than what is the nominal interest rate mentioned. To find out the actual interest earned the *notional interest* has to be adjusted by deducting the percentage impact of inflation. This adjusted interest is called the *real rate of interest*.

Similarly, the potential rate of return on the capital shall be comparable to the real GDP growth rate in the economy. Thus, the real growth rate of the economy will determine the real interest rate in the economy. It is observed that the typical real interest rate on government paper in some of the advanced economies vary from 3 to 4 per cent, which is close to their growth rate of GDP. However, in the case of developing economies, the typical real interest rates are higher than those of the developed economies, and this is explained as due to the higher rates of growth in these economies.

This means two factors are important for determining the interest rates. First is the inflation rate to arrive at the *real interest rate*. Second is the real GDP growth rate or expected real GDP growth rate to determine the maximum *real interest rate* for benchmark interest rate.

The following table gives the real GDP growth rates and inflation rates of our country from the year 1980 to 2018.

Year	GDP (in bil. US$ PPP)	GDP per capita (in US$ PPP)	Share of world (GDP PPP in %)	GDP growth (real)	Inflation rate (in Percent)	Government debt (in % of GDP)
1980	382.0	557	2.89%	5.3%	11.3%	n/a
1981	442.7	632	3.01%	6.0%	12.7%	n/a
1982	486.5	680	3.11%	3.5%	7.7%	n/a
1983	542.6	742	3.25%	7.3%	12.6%	n/a
1984	583.3	781	3.23%	3.8%	6.5%	n/a
1985	633.6	830	3.29%	5.3%	6.3%	n/a
1986	677.3	869	3.33%	4.8%	8.9%	n/a
1987	722.1	907	3.33%	4.0%	9.1%	n/a
1988	819.3	1,007	3.49%	9.6%	7.2%	n/a
1989	901.8	1,086	3.57%	5.9%	4.6%	n/a
1990	986.9	1,164	3.62%	5.5%	11.2%	n/a
1991	1,030.6	1,193	3.57%	1.1%	13.5%	75.3%
1992	1,111.8	1,261	3.38%	5.5%	9.9%	77.4%
1993	1,192.4	1,323	3.48%	4.8%	7.3%	77.0%
1994	1,298.8	1,413	3.60%	6.7%	10.3%	73.5%
1995	1,426.3	1,522	3.74%	7.6%	10.0%	69.7%
1996	1,562.1	1,636	3.87%	7.6%	9.4%	66.0%
1997	1,653.1	1,698	3.87%	4.1%	6.8%	67.8%
1998	1,774.4	1,789	4.00%	6.2%	13.1%	68.1%
1999	1,954.0	1,935	4.19%	8.5%	5.7%	70.0%
2000	2,077.9	2,018	4.16%	4.0%	5.6%	73.6%
2001	2,230.4	2,130	4.26%	4.9%	4.3%	78.7%
2002	2,353.1	2,210	4.30%	3.9%	4.0%	82.9%
2003	2,590.7	2,395	4.46%	7.9%	3.9%	84.2%
2004	2,870.8	2,612	4.58%	7.8%	3.8%	83.3%
2005	3,238.3	2,901	4.77%	9.3%	4.4%	80.9%
2006	3,647.0	3,218	4.95%	9.3%	6.7%	77.1%
2007	4,111.1	3,574	5.16%	9.8%	6.2%	74.0%
2008	4,354.8	3,731	5.21%	3.9%	9.1%	74.5%
2009	4,759.9	4,020	5.68%	8.5%	11.0%	72.5%
2010	5,312.4	4,425	5.95%	10.3%	9.5%	67.5%
2011	5,782.0	4,750	6.09%	6.6%	9.5%	69.6%
2012	6,214.5	5,037	6.23%	5.5%	10.0%	69.1%
2013	6,727.3	5,383	6.41%	6.4%	9.4%	68.5%

Year	GDP (in bil. US$ PPP)	GDP per capita (in US$ PPP)	Share of world (GDP PPP in %)	GDP growth (real)	Inflation rate (in Percent)	Government debt (in % of GDP)
2014	7,362.5	5,814	6.65%	7.4%	5.8%	67.8%
2015	8,036.3	6,264	6.94%	8.0%	4.9%	69.9%
2016	8,787.9	6,761	7.27%	8.2%	4.5%	69.0%
2017	9,596.8	7,287	7.52%	7.2%	3.6%	69.8%
2018	10,505.2	7,874	7.77%	7.1%	3.5%	69.8%

Source: Wikipedia.

India's inflation rate was high and was in two digits for most of the past years. It came down to single digit inflation from the year 1991 and remained low till 2005. From 2006 to 2013 it was high and again crossed two-digit mark. From 2014 onwards inflation rate has come down to the low of 3.5% in 2018.

GDP growth rate was high since 2003 and the country was having one of the highest GDP growth rates next only to China. GDP growth rate remained high till 2018. But in 2019 GDP growth rate is expected to be lower at 5.6% as per some forecasts.

Higher than world average of GDP growth rate of our country is also a reason for interest rates to be higher than the other countries.

Structure of Interest Rates in India

We have studied the logics applicable for fixation of deposits rates in the economies. Now we can examine the interest rate structure prevailing in our country.

As discussed earlier the important rates that have bearing on all other interest rates are the bank deposit rates fixed by the commercial banks in the country. This is because bank deposits and bank accounts are in the centre of financial activities. Banks are the financial intermediaries who pool the savings of the public and then make it available to those who need the money to use it for many different purposes. Banks are generally considered as safe investments for the public. Banks also offer banking services which is essential for the public. Bank term deposits provide a relatively safe and with minimum risk investment for the public. Bank term deposits offer the unique facility to withdraw the deposit even before maturity with only some interest loss. This facility is not available in any other form of investments. For all these reasons even though bank deposits are not fully secured investments, it still occupies the prime place in the financial system of the country.

Total risk-free investment is the investment in govt. bonds or in any schemes operated by the govt. This investment is fully secured as the govt. is the borrower and such investments have sovereign guarantees which fully secure the money invested. Central and state govts., govt. corporations borrow from the public by issuing bonds containing sovereign guarantee, for relatively long maturities. Due to sovereign guarantee, technically these bonds must be the prime investment and shall carry an interest rate for risk free investments, i.e., the lowest rate in the system.

But due to blocking of money till maturity these bonds are not the first preference of the public to invest their savings. Though there is secondary market for disposing these bonds, they are still not considered as liquid and convenient as bank deposits.

However, we can observe that the rate of interest offered on these bonds or investments are very similar to bank deposit rates. Indian Govt. also accepts deposits through post offices under many schemes very similar to banks. Post offices are functioning as Savings Banks and accept term deposits similar to banks. Govt. decides the interest rates on these bonds and deposits with consultation with RBI and keeping in mind the commercial banks deposit rates and also the benchmark rate of RBI.

The following table gives the historical interest rates on bank term deposits, govt. securities, post office deposit schemes, and the benchmark rate of the RBI.

We can observe how the three important interest rates: bank deposit, govt. bond and post office deposits are converging to the same level. Whenever govt. has offered a better rate, it is mainly with a specific purpose. Even the benchmark rate of RBI is also at the same level.

Year	Interest rates on % p.a.					Bank rate/Repo rate from 2006
	Bank term deposits Maximum/range	Central Govt. securities range	Post office term deposit	National savings certificate	PPF	
Early 1970s	6.5-7					6
Mid 1970s	9					7-9
1977	10.00					9
1978	9.00					9
1979	9.00					9
1980	10.00					9
1981	10.00	5.98-7.50				9
1982	10.00	6.00-8.00				10
1983	11.00	6.25-9.00				10
1984	11.00	7.75-10.00				10
1985	11.00	7.75-10.50				10
1986	11.00	9.00-11.50				10
1987	11.00	10.00-11.50				10
1988	10.00	10.50-11.50				10
1989	10.00	10.00-11.50				10
1990	10.00	10.50-11.50				10
Mar-91	9.00-11.00	10.50-11.50	12.00-13.50		12	10.0
Mar-92	12.00-13.00	10.50-12.50	12.00-13.50		12	12.0
Mar-93	11.00-11.00	12.00-12.75	12.00-13.50	12	12	12.0

Year	Interest rates on % p.a.					Bank rate/Repo rate from 2006
	Bank term deposits Maximum/range	Central Govt. securities range	Post office term deposit	National savings certificate	PPF	
Mar-94	10.00-10.00	12.00-13.40	10.50-12.50	12	12	12.0
Mar-95	11.00-11.00	11.00-12.71	10.50-12.50	12	12	12.0
Mar-96	12.00-13.00	13.25-14.00	10.50-12.50	12	12	12.0
Mar-97	11.00-13.00	13.40-13.85	10.50-12.50	12	12	12.0
Mar-98	10.50-12.00	10.85-13.05	10.50-12.50	12	12	10.5
Mar-99	9.00-11.50	11.10-12.60	9.00-11.50	11.50	12	8.0
Mar-00	8.50-10.50	10.73-12.45	8.00-10.50	11	11	8.0
Mar-01	8.50-10.00	9.47-11.70	7.50-9.00	9.50	9	7.0
Mar-02	7.50-8.50	6.98-11.00	7.25-8.50	9	9	6.5
Mar-03	4.30-6.30	6.57-8.62	6.25-7.50	8	8	6.25
Mar-04	4.00-5.50	4.62-6.35	6.25-7.50	8	8	6
Mar-05	5.30-6.30	4.49-8.24	6.25-7.50	8	8	6
Mar-06	6.00-7.00	6.70-7.79	6.25-7.50	8	8	6.50
Mar-07	7.50-9.00	7.69-8.75	6.25-7.50	8	8	7.75
Mar-08	7.50-9.00	7.55-8.64	6.25-7.50	8	8	6.0
Mar-09	7.80-8.80	5.44-10.03	6.25-7.50	8	8	5.0
Mar-10	6.00-7.50	6.09-8.43	6.25-7.50	8	8	5.0

However, it is pertinent to note that the bank deposit rates are prescribed by RBI till the year 1996. Only from the year 1997 onwards banks are allowed freedom to fix their own rates. In view of this fact prior to 1997 the bank deposit interest rates were same for all banks without any variation.

Bank rate is the rate at which RBI lends short-term to commercial banks to tide over the liquidity problems of commercial banks. It is generally on unsecured basis. RBI moved to repo system from the year 2000. In a way repo replaced the bank rate functions but RBI is announcing both bank rate and repo rate. Under repo system banks can borrow from RBI for short-terms by giving securities with a condition to repurchase those securities from RBI.

Thus, in our country the fixing the bank deposit rates and also govt. bond rates are linked to the repo rate at present. Any change in repo rate announced by RBI is an indication to the banks and also to the govt. to align their interest rates to repo rate. In this way the policy repo rate of RBI influences the financial markets to move their interest rates as desired by RBI.

Interest rates over the historical period have shown divergent trends in keeping with the financial status of the country over these periods. As discussed earlier the interest rates reflect the phases of the economy when inflation was high or low and also the phases of GDP growth rates.

Our country which became independent in the year 1947 had undergone a long struggle to improve the economy. It started with many socialist economic views in the beginning and slowly achieved self-sufficiency in food production. Industrial developments took place and from 1990 onwards economy was opened up to participate in the globalisation. Country has travelled a long path from high inflation and low GDP to the present level of low inflation and high growth in GDP.

Interest Rate Structures from 2010 onwards

The table below gives interbank call money rate, bank savings rate, bank term deposit rates, banks' lending rates and the marginal cost-based lending rate (MCLR) of banks from the year 2010 to 2019.

Table 5.1: Structure of Interest Rates

(Per cent per annum)

Year (as at end March)	Call/ Notice Money Rates	Deposit Rates*				Lending Rates*	MCLR (1-year)
		Savings#	Term Deposits				
			1-3 yrs	3-5 yrs	Above 5 yrs		
1	2	3	4	5	6	7	8
2010-11	5.89	3.5	8.25-9.00	8.25-8.75	8.50-8.75	8.25-9.50	--
2011-12	8.22	4	9.00-9.25	9.00-9.25	8.50-9.25	10.00-10.75	--
2012-13	8.09	4	8.75-9.00	8.75-9.00	8.50-9.00	9.70-10.25	--
2013-14	8.28	4	8.75-9.25	8.75-9.10	8.50-9.10	10.00-10.25	--
2014-15	7.97	4	8.50-8.75	8.50-8.75	8.25-8.50	10.00-10.25	--
2015-16	6.98	4	7.25-7.50	7.00-7.50	7.00-7.30	9.30-9.70	--
2016-17	6.25	4	6.75-7.00	6.50-6.90	6.50-6.75	7.75-8.20	8.00-8.50
2017-18	5.94	3.50-4.00	6.40-6.75	6.25-6.70	6.25-6.75	7.80-7.95	8.15-8.30
2018-19	6.27	3.50-4.00	6.25-7.25	6.25-7.25	6.25-7.25	8.05-8.55	8.45-8.80
2019-20@		3.25-3.50	6.25-7.10	6.25-7.00	6.25-7.00	7.90-8.40	8.25-8.65

* : Data on deposit and lending rates relate to five major Public Sector Banks up to 2003-04. While for the subsequent years, they relate to five major banks.

: Savings deposit rate from 2011-12 onwards relates to balance up to ₹ 1 lakh. Savings deposit rate was deregulated with effect from October 25, 2011.

@ : As on September 5, 2019.

Notes:
1. Data on lending rates relate to either Prime Lending Rate (PLR) or Benchmark Prime Lending Rate (BPLR), Base Rate or Marginal Cost of Funds Based Lending Rate (MCLR) (overnight and 1-Year) as the case may be for the relevant year.
2. BPLR system effective November 2003 was replaced by the Base Rate System effective from July 1, 2010.
3. Base Rate System effective from July 1, 2010 was replaced by the MCLR System effective from April 1, 2016.
4. Call/Notice money rates are weighted average rates for the year.

Source: Scheduled Commercial Banks (excluding RRBs and SFBs) and the Reserve Bank of India, 15 Sept. 2019.

Call money rates are the interbank rates at which commercial banks borrow or lend between themselves for very short period like a day or couple of days. This is used by banks to manage their liquidity position on day-to-day basis.

Banks' lending rate and MCLR is discussed later under banks' lending rates below.

We can observe that bank savings rate has come down below 4% from the year 2017. Bank term deposits rate have come down from maximum rate of 9.25% to 7.10% in 2019. We see the trend of deposit interest rates coming down in this decade by 2%. This trend may continue in the coming years as well.

Bank lending rates are linked to bank deposit rates as deposit rates are the cost of funds to the banks. Bank lending rates shall always be more than deposit rates may be by a margin of 3-4% which are to take care of administrative costs; overheads and earnings for the banks. The lending rates shown in the table are the benchmark rates and the actual rates will be different for different categories of loans based on purpose, type of borrower and many other factors.

As we have observed earlier the important factors that affect the interest rates are the future inflation and GDP growth in our economy.

Interest rates on govt. securities for year 2011 to 2020 are given in the following table:

Table 5.2: Interest Rates on Central and State Government Dated Securities

(Per cent per annum)

Year	Central Government securities		State Government securities	
	Range	Weighted average	Range	Weighted average
1	2	3	4	5
2010-11	5.98-8.67	7.92	8.05-8.58	8.39
2011-12	7.80-10.01	8.52	8.36-9.49	8.79
2012-13	7.86-8.82	8.36	8.42-9.31	8.84
2013-14	7.16-9.40	8.45	7.57-9.94	9.18
2014-15	7.65-9.42	8.51	8.00-9.66	8.58

Year	Central Government securities		State Government securities	
	Range	Weighted average	Range	Weighted average
2015-16	7.54-8.27	7.89	7.95-8.88	8.28
2016-17	6.13-7.87	7.16	6.62-8.09	7.48
2017-18	6.42-7.67	6.97	6.81-8.45	7.67
2018-19	6.57-8.42	7.78	7.13-8.86	8.32
2019-20	5.57-7.78	6.85	5.78-8.23	7.24
2020-21	3.79-7.19	5.80	4.15-8.96	6.55

Source: Reserve Bank of India, 15 Sept. 2019.

Interest rates offered by Post Office are given in the following table:

Interest Rates on Post Office Deposit Schemes

Since	Post office SB %	Term deposit 1 to 5 years %	PPF %	NSC (viii) %	KVP %	Senior citizen saving scheme %	Sukanya samriddhi scheme %
Apr. 1, 2012	4	8.2-8.5	8.8	8.6	-	9.3	-
Apr. 1, 2013	4	8.2-8.4	8.7	8.5	-	9.2	-
Apr. 1, 2014	4	8.4-8.5	8.7	8.5	-	9.2	-
Apr. 1, 2015	4	8.4-8.5	8.7	8.5	8.7	9.3	9.2
Apr. 1, 2016	4	7.1-7.9	8.1	8.1	7.8	8.6	8.6
Apr. 1, 2017	4	6.9-7.7	7.9	7.9	7.6	8.4	8.4
Jan. 1, 2018	4	6.6-7.4	7.6	7.6	7.3	8.3	8.1
Oct. 1, 2018	4	6.9-7.8	8	8	7.7	8.7	8.5
Jan. 1, 2019	4	7.0-7.8	8	8	7.7	8.7	8.5
Jul. 1, 2019	4	6.9-7.7	7.9	7.9	7.6	8.6	8.4
Oct. 2020	4	5.5-6.7	7.1	6.8	6.9	7.4	7.6
Jul. 1, 2021	4	5.5-6.7	7.1	6.8	6.9	7.4	7.6

Interest rates on govt. securities and post office term deposits schemes have also come down in this decade. The trend is same as in bank term deposit rates.

Other Interest Rates in the Deposit Segment in the Country

We have studied the interest rate structure in cases of bank deposits, govt. bonds and post office deposits. We shall remember that govt. bonds are not deposits but they are borrowing by the govt. Post office deposit schemes are deposits as govt. has authorised post office to accept deposits from the public similar to a bank. Thus, post office is carrying out banking functions as an exception.

There are legal differences between deposit and loan. As per the present legal position and as per the Companies Act 2013, only banks and non-banking financial companies (NBFCs—who are registered with RBI) can accept deposits from public. Post office is an exception to this rule. Another category who can accept public deposit are the Housing Finance Companies, which are specifically authorized to collect deposits and companies authorized by Ministry of Corporate Affairs under the Companies Acceptance of Deposits Rules framed by Central Government under the Companies Act can also accept deposits also up to a certain limit.

In case of others like companies and firms, generally they are permitted to accept deposits only from their members subject to the provisions of the Companies Act, 2013.

As per guidelines issued by RBI to NBFCs on deposit interest rates, NBFCs can offer maximum of 12.5% interest on deposits. NBFCs who are authorised by RBI can accept deposits for one year to five years from the public. However, NBFCs cannot accept deposits that are payable on demand.

A category of NBFC known as Residuary Non-Banking Companies (RNBCs) who are authorised to accept deposits as their main business and are required to offer a minimum of 5% interest rate on the deposits received by them.

From the year 2017 RBI has stopped issuing registrations to new NBFCs and they will not be allowed to accept public deposits. Only the existing authorised NBFCs will continue under the new guidelines issued by RBI.

The following table shows the deposit interest rates offered by top 10 NBFCs in the country now (2021).

Top Company FD Rates

Company	CRISIL/ICRA Rating	Maximum FD rate (per annum)
ICICI Home Finance Ltd FD	CRISIL FAAA	5.70% p.a. - 6.65% p.a.
Mahindra Finance Ltd FD	CRISIL FAAA	5.70% p.a. - 6.45% p.a.
Shriram Transport Finance Ltd FD	ICRA MAA+	7.51% p.a. - 8.26% p.a.
PNB Housing Finance Ltd FD	CRISIL FAAA	5.90% p.a. - 6.70% p.a.
LIC Housing Finance Ltd FD	CRISIL FAAA	5.25% p.a. - 5.75% p.a.
HDFC Ltd FD	ICRA MAAA	Up to 6.55%
Housing and Urban Development Corporation (HUDCO) FD	ICRA AAA	7.25% p.a. - 7.50% p.a.
Sundaram Finance Company FD	CRISIL FAAA	5.72% p.a. - 6.22% p.a.
Muthoot Capital FD	CRISIL FAAA	7.75% p.a. - 8.00% p.a.

*The interest rates mentioned here tend to vary at the respective company's discretion. The rates mentioned here are for cumulative deposits as of May 2021.

Source: bankbazar.com

Bank Lending Rate Structure

Bank lending rates are also an important factor in the financial market. Basically, it is the cost of borrowing for those who borrow from the banks. Historically the bank lending rates were prescribed by RBI and banks were following it. RBI was fixing the borrower specific and activity specific rates of interest on loans.

After the financial sector reforms were introduced in the year 1991, RBI gradually stopped prescribing loan interest rates and gave the discretion to the banks to fix loan interest rates. For this purpose, RBI introduced a system of prime lending rate (PLR) in October 1994. This was the first creation of benchmark lending rates by the banks themselves. In April 2003, the system of benchmark PLR (BPLR) was introduced.

A new benchmark lending rate called the base rate system was introduced in July 2010 and banks were advised to fix their base rate as the new benchmark lending rate. Base rate became the minimum rate of interest for the bank loans. Banks were required to quote the rate of interest to their borrowers linking it to its base rate. Hence banks started quoting their interest rates on loans by adding the spread over the base rate.

This benchmark base rate system was again changed in April 2016 and banks were advised to create a new benchmark rate called Marginal Cost of Funds based Lending Rate (MCLR).

MCLR is lending rate calculated based on cost of raising new funds for the bank which include the cost of maintaining CRR/SLR, operating costs of banks and tenor premium. Banks will quote their lending rates to their borrowers linking it to MCLR. Thus, bank lending rates will move as per the movement in MCLR of the bank. Under the MCLR regime, banks shall adjust their interest rates as soon as the repo rate changes. Hence when RBI changes its repo rate the change will be transmitted to bank lending rates.

When MCLR was introduced in 2016, it was advised that the existing loans which were given based on the base rate system shall continue till its closure or renewal. Hence till the year 2018 banks are declaring both base rate and MCLR rate simultaneously.

Starting from April 2018, RBI has mandated that banks' base rates be linked to MCLR rates. Any increase or decrease in MCLR rates will now automatically be applicable to pre-2016 loans that are benchmarked to base rate.

Banks are now fixing their MCLR rates for different tenors as their internal benchmark rates and link the interest rate they quote to their borrowers with reference to MCLR. MCLRs of major banks in the country are given in the following table.

Current MCLR Rates 04 June 2021

Banks	3 years	2 years	1 year	6 months	3 months	1 month	Over-night
SBI MCLR	7.30%	7.20%	7.00%	6.95%	6.65%	6.65%	6.65%
HDFC MCLR	7.40%	7.30%	7.20%	7.05%	6.95%	6.90%	6.85%
ICICI MCLR	NA	NA	7.30%	7.25%	7.10%	7.05%	7.05%
Axis MCLR	7.55%	7.50%	7.40%	7.35%	7.30%	7.20%	7.20%
PNB MCLR	7.60%	NA	7.30%	7.00%	6.80%	6.70%	6.65%
Citibank MCLR	NA	NA	6.30%	6.15%	5.95%	5.90%	5.70%

Banks	3 years	2 years	1 year	6 months	3 months	1 month	Over-night
IndusInd MCLR	8.95%	8.90%	8.60%	8.50%	8.35%	8.30%	8.25%
RBL MCLR	NA	NA	8.65%	8.50%	8.20%	8.10%	8.10%
DBS MCLR	NA	NA	6.80%	6.60%	6.50%	6.35%	6.35%
Canara MCLR	NA	NA	7.35%	7.30%	6.95%	6.70%	6.70%
IDFC First Bank MCLR	9.20%	8.80%	8.40%	8.30%	8.10%	8.05%	8.05%
Bank of India MCLR	7.80%	NA	7.35%	7.30%	7.25%	7.20%	6.70%
Nainital Bank MCLR	8.10%	7.70%	7.40%	7.25%	7.15%	7.10%	7.10%
Jammu & Kashmir Bank MCLR	7.85%	7.80%	7.35%	7.20%	6.90%	6.70%	6.60%
Central Bank of India MCLR	NA	NA	7.10%	7.00%	6.85%	6.55%	6.55%
Bandhan Bank MCLR	10.86%	10.33%	8.94%	8.46%	8.27%	8.15%	8.08%
UBI MCLR	7.40%	7.35%	7.20%	7.05%	6.90%	6.70%	6.60%
UCO Bank MCLR	NA	NA	7.30%	7.20%	6.95%	6.85%	6.70%
Punjab and Sind Bank MCLR	NA	NA	7.65%	7.55%	7.45%	7.30%	7.15%
Bank of Baroda MCLR	NA	NA	7.40%	7.25%	7.15%	7.00%	6.55%
Federal Bank MCLR	NA	NA	7.90%	7.85%	7.80%	7.75%	7.65%
Standard Chartered MCLR	7.60%	7.25%	6.65%	6.50%	6.50%	6.40%	6.15%
IDBI Bank MCLR	8.60%	8.15%	7.80%	7.45%	7.30%	7.25%	7.05%
Indian Overseas Bank MCLR	7.45%	7.45%	7.45%	7.40%	7.40%	6.85%	6.85%

Source: bankbazar.com

While these are the benchmark rates of the respective banks, the actual rates applicable to each type of borrower will be based on the credit rating, purpose of loan, tenor of the loan, and the security cover for the loan. Hence loan interest rate will be worked out by the bank on individual cases. The loan interest rate will be either the minimum benchmark rate or by adding a spread over the MCLR. The spread can be up to 5-6% over MCLR benchmark.

To understand the rate of interest structure of bank loans we shall appreciate the bank lending practices in Indian banking. GOI had nationalised major banks in the country in 1969 and in 1980 with a view to dovetail the banking resources to the economic growth needs of the country. GOI and RBI have through the monetary and fiscal measures directed the bank loans to the economic growth areas. A concept of priority sector lending, export finance, and social lending to uplift the economically backward people were encouraged. Priority sector lending covers the agriculture and allied activities, housing, education, micro, small and medium enterprises segments. Poverty alleviation schemes for financing poor people to uplift them were encouraged. Govt. sponsored many schemes for this purpose and also provides subsidies. All these have made a very big difference in the approach of the banks towards bank loans to these segments. The interest rates are not totally based on the financial judgments. There is a social obligation attached to the pricing of loans to these segments. Banks in the country are obliged to lend 40% of their funds to priority sector.

The loans to these segments of priority sector are historically carried lower interest rates. Even now the banks are required to keep this in mind particularly for small loans of couple of lacs rupees to the small borrowers.

Hence a large portion of loans in priority sector segment is now priced at MCLR of banks or very close to MCLR rates. Home loans, education loans, loans to micro and small enterprises, export finance, crop loans to farmers, loans for allied activities in rural areas, loans under govt. sponsored schemes for poverty alleviation are loans for which generally banks offer the minimum lending rate i.e., MCLR.

RBI is not prescribing interest rate to any category of loans to priority sector and it is at the discretions of the banks. However, in case of govt. sponsored/supported loan schemes, banks are required to follow the specific directions, if any, on interest rates.

However, MCLR framework for bank lending rates was not to the satisfaction of RBI. RBI felt that the changes in the policy repo rate are not transmitted in MCLR rate changes by banks as was expected. In its press release dated 4 September 2019 RBI stated as under:

3. It has been observed that due to various reasons, the transmission of policy rate changes to the lending rate of banks under the current MCLR framework has not been satisfactory. The RBI therefore has today issued a circular making it mandatory for banks to link all new floating rate personal or retail loans and floating rate loans to MSMEs to an external benchmark effective October 1, 2019. The banks are free to choose one of the several benchmarks indicated in the circular. The banks are also free to choose their spread over the benchmark rate, subject to the condition that the credit risk premium may undergo change only when borrower's credit assessment undergoes a substantial change, as agreed upon in the loan contract.

RBI issued directions on the same date vide RBI/2019-20/53 DBR.DIR.BC.No.14/13.03.00/2019-20—September 04, 2019 amending the existing directions as under:

The existing paragraph No. 7 *of the aforesaid Master Direction stands replaced as under:*

(a) All new floating rate personal or retail loans (housing, auto, etc.) and floating rate loans to Micro and Small Enterprises extended by banks from October 01, 2019 shall be benchmarked to one of the following:

- Reserve Bank of India policy repo rate
- Government of India 3-Months Treasury Bill yield published by the Financial Benchmarks India Private Ltd. (FBIL)
- Government of India 6-Months Treasury Bill yield published by the FBIL
- Any other benchmark market interest rate published by the FBIL.

(b) Banks are free to offer such external benchmark linked loans to other types of borrowers as well.

(c) In order to ensure transparency, standardisation, and ease of understanding of loan products by borrowers, a bank must adopt a uniform external benchmark within a loan category; in other words, the adoption of multiple benchmarks by the same bank is not allowed within a loan category.

Most of the banks have now started using repo rate as the external benchmark and quote their rates for loans by adding the spread over this external benchmark. Thus, whenever there is change in repo rate, the lending rates of the banks corrects itself and pass on the benefit or burden to the borrowers immediately. The new interest rate based on repo benchmark rate is known as Repo Linked Lending Rate (RLLR) which will replace the MCLR of banks immediately for all the new floating rate loans.

Interest rates on other loans

Banks give all types of personal loans and business loans. Some types of loans are considered as the key types of loans having great demand and availed by large number of borrowers. Three such loans and the interest rates quoted by banks are as under:

Bank Lending Rates for Home Loans, Car Loans and Personal Loans in 2021

Banks/Lenders	Home loan Interest Rate	Car loan interest rate	Personal loan rate
State Bank of India	6.75%	7.70% onwards	9.60% onwards
Punjab National Bank	6.75%	7.30% onwards	8.95% onwards
Bank of Baroda	6.75%	7.25% onwards	10% onwards
Union Bank of India	6.80%	7.40% onwards	8.90% onwards
Canara Bank	6.90%	7.30% onwards	11.25% onwards
Indian Bank	7.55%	8.45% onwards	9.05% onwards
Punjab & Sind Bank	6.65%	7.00% onwards	
Central Bank of India	6.85%	7.50% onwards	8.45% onwards
Bank of India	6.85%	7.35% onwards	9.35% onwards
UCO Bank	6.90%	7.95% onwards	8.45% onwards
Indian Overseas Bank	7.05%	7.55% onwards	10.30% onwards
Bank of Maharashtra	7.05%	7.40% onwards	9.55% onwards

Banks/Lenders	Home loan Interest Rate	Car loan interest rate	Personal loan rate
HDFC Bank	6.75%	7.95% onwards	
ICICI Bank	6.75%	7.90% onwards	10.50% onwards
Yes Bank	8.95%		
Kotak Mahindra Bank	6.65%		10.50% onwards
Axis Bank	6.90%		
IDBI Bank	6.85%	7.50% onwards	9.50% onwards
Karnataka Bank	7.50%	8.05% onwards	
Federal Bank	7.65%	8.50% onwards	10.49% onwards
Standard Chartered Bank	7.99%		
J&K Bank	7.20%	7.95% onwards	
HSBC			9.75% onwards
Citi Bank			9.99% onwards

Source: paisabazar.com, Bankbazar.com and banks, August/September 2021

We can observe that home loans are generally at MCLR rates of the banks. Home loans are secured by mortgages and are considered as safe long-term loans for the banks.

We can also observe that the car loans are also offered at low rates as they are also secured loans. The rates are little over MCLR by about 1.50%.

Personal loan segment is a popular loan segment and even though it is unsecured loan banks are offering it at about 3% over MCLR.

Agricultural Loans

Agricultural loans are given for vide variety of purposes which includes crop loan, loan for farm mechanisation, loan for farm development, loan for allied activities, etc. We give below the present (Sept. 2021) SBI Agricultural Loan Interest Rates for few types of loans. This is to understand the interest rates and SBI is biggest bank of the country and its rates are the most competitive. Other bank's rates are generally higher.

Type of Agricultural Loan	Interest Rate*
SBI Crop Loan (Kisan Credit Card)	Simple interest at the rate of 7% per annum up to the repayment due date.
SBI Multipurpose Gold Loan	7.50% per annum
SBI Tractor Loan	10.25% onwards
SBI Dairy Loan	10.85% onwards
SBI Produce Marketing Loan	10.85% onwards

Other than agriculture, the important sector under priority sector is micro, small and medium enterprises (MSME) sector. MSME consists of micro units, small units and medium units in industrial or service sectors. The MSME sector comprises of many divergent activities and sizes of activities.

For MSME category the rate of interest is quoted individually by the banks for the large number of activities and types of borrowers, depending on nature of loan, tenor of loan, size of loan, credit rating and security covers. Hence the interest rates range from MCLR to 'MCLR + maximum spread'.

Other Important Interest Rates in the Indian Financial System

There are few other interest rates which are applicable to some of the important borrowing instruments prevalent in the Indian financial market they are:

Debentures: Debenture is document issued under the seal of the company. Debenture is an acknowledgment of the funds received by the company equal to the nominal value of the debenture. It includes the payment of interest at a fixed rate till the times the principal sum becomes repayable. Debentures can be secured against the securities of some assets of the company or can be Unsecured Debentures. Debentures can be convertible debentures which can be converted as equity at a subsequent date. Other category of dentures is non-convertible debenture (NCD) which is an instrument of borrowing by the corporates. Companies may issue debentures under the rules applicable. The tenor of debentures is generally 2 to 7 years and companies have discretion to fix the rate of interest payable.

As debentures are borrowings by the companies the rate of interest offered is generally nearer to banks' benchmark lending rates and also depends on the credit rating of the companies. Debenture issues by the companies will reduce their dependence on bank loans for their business. Debenture issue is considered as capital issue and can be listed and traded in the stock market.

RBI has approved the debentures issued by the companies for a tenor of less than one year to be a money market instrument which can be traded in money market also.

As the companies have the discretion to fix interest rates, companies will generally keep in mind the bank loan interest rate applicable to them in case they borrow from bank. Thus, they tend to fix debenture rate at a lower level than the bank loan rate. Hence the interest rate on debenture is closely connected to bank lending rates and move according to the movement in the bank lending rates.

The following table mentions some debenture issues by few companies in the past (from 2012 to 2019). Coupon rate is the interest rate. Debenture issue is a huge market in the country and companies raise huge amounts of capital from this market. The issues mentioned in the table below are just to give an idea about the interest rates offered by the companies. These are random cases only.

Name of the company	Tenor	Coupon rate	Year
Magma Fincorp	3 and 5 years	10.25%-10.5%	2019 April
Muthoot Homefin	2 and 5 years	9.5%-10%	2019 April
L&T Finance	3, 5 and 8 years	8.66%-9.05%	2019 April
Shriram City Union Finance	2, 3 and 5 years	9.55%-9.75%	2019 April
Shriram Transport Finance Company Ltd		9.70%	2018 Oct
JM Financial Credit Solutions Limited		10.25%	2018 Nov
SREI Equipment Finance Ltd		8.6%-9.75%	2017 Jan
Mahindra & Mahindra Financial Services		8.44%-9%	2016 May
Edelweiss Housing Finance		9.5%-10%	2016 July
Dewan housing finance corporation	7 year	9.05%-9.25%	2016 Aug
ECL Finance, an arm of Edelweiss Financial Services	3-5 year	11.85%	2014 Jan
Muthoot Finance	2-5 years	13%-13.25%	2012 Feb

Commercial Paper: Commercial Paper (CP) is a short-term unsecured promissory note with maturity period of 15 days to one year. Since it is unsecured, it is issued by the large and creditworthy companies to meet their short-term fund requirements.

Commercial paper was introduced in the year 1990 with the purpose to provide an additional window for short-term finance to companies and also to introduce a money market instrument in the financial market. CP can be issued in denominations of ₹ 5 lakh or multiples thereof. CP will be issued at a discount to face value as may be determined by the issuer.

Interest rate fixed by the companies is also connected to bank lending rates as CP is instruments of borrowings for short-term. The table below gives the range of interest rates offered by the companies for different maturities from the year 2010 to 2021.

The rates are though linked to bank lending rates, because of the unsecured nature of the instrument and short-term nature, we can observe that the rates are little higher than the debenture rates.

Commercial Paper Issued by Companies (At face value)

Amount in "crores"

Fortnight ended	Total Amount Outstanding	Reported During the Fortnight	Rate of Interest %
May 31, 2021	388707	61594	3.36-12.87
May 31, 2020	425817	52155	3.13-12.14
Dec 31, 2019	414906	83568	4.99-13.18
Mar 31, 2019	483084	101296	6.54-12.60
Mar 31, 2018	372577	99915	6.49-14.00
Mar 31, 2017	397965	109409	5.99-13.33
Mar 31, 2016	260244	67364	7.35-13.14
Mar 31, 2015	193268	69425	7.44-14.92
Mar 31, 2014	106614	25037	8.64-12.61
Mar 31, 2013	109255	19273	8.05-13.42
Mar 31, 2012	91188	17630	9.75-15.25
Jun 15, 2011	123400	20522	8.25-13.00
Jan 15, 2010	92363	11503	3.15-7.55

Source: RBI

Certificate of deposit: Certificates of deposit are short-term instruments issued by commercial banks and financial institutions to the individuals, corporations and companies. They are unsecured and negotiable.

Certificate of deposit interest rates

Fortnight ended	Total amount Outstanding 'In crores'	Issued during the fortnight 'In crores'	Minimum Rate of Interest %	Maximum Rate of Interest %
	1	2	3	4
May 21, 2021	90349	5836	3.43	4.01
May 22, 2020	160455	5705	3.50	7.83
Dec 20, 2019	160669	13837	4.97	5.84
Mar 29, 2019	272260	52412	7.09	8.45
Mar 2, 2018	194581	31905	7.16	7.80
Mar 31, 2017	155741	24597	6.21	6.70
Apr 1, 2016	244672	56703	7.79	8.53
Mar 20, 2015	280968	65095	8.38	9.10
Mar 21, 2014	375796	90848	8.94	10.35
Mar 22, 2013	389612	87753	8.80	10.12
Mar 23, 2012	419530	101450	9.30	11.90
Mar 25, 2011	424740	69713	9.00	10.60
Mar 26, 2010	341054	37356	4.52	7.12
Mar 27, 2009	192867		6.00	11.50
Mar 28, 2008	147792		9.00	10.75
Mar 30, 2007	93272	9428	10.23	11.90
Mar 31, 2006	43568	9028	6.50	8.94
Mar 18, 2005	12078	2594	4.21	6.34

Source: RBI

Certificate of deposits are introduced in the year 1989 as money market instrument in the financial market. A certificate of deposit can be issued at a discount on its face value. Furthermore, banks and financial institutions can issue certificates of deposits on a floating rate basis.

Minimum amount of a CD should be ₹ 1 lakh, and in multiples of ₹ 1 lakh thereafter (i.e., the minimum deposit that could be accepted from a single subscriber should not be less than ₹ 1 lakh). The maturity period of CDs issued by banks should not be less than 7 days and not more than one year, from the date of issue. The issuing bank/FI are free to determine the discount/coupon rate.

CD is issued as a transferable instrument unlike the term deposit receipt of the bank which is not transferable. Further banks cannot give loans against CDs and also CDs cannot be paid before maturity. CDs in physical form are freely transferable by endorsement and delivery. CDs in demat form can be transferred as per the procedure applicable to other demat securities. There is no lock-in period for the CDs.

As CD is same as bank term deposit with a change in transferability, the interest rates offered by the banks are close to their term deposit rates. The following table gives the interest rates of CDs from the year 2005 to 2021. We can observe that they have moved similar to bank term deposit rates over the years. In May 2021, the maximum rate was 4.01%.

Treasury Bills

This instrument is issued by Reserve Bank of India on behalf of the Central Government for government's short-term requirements of funds. Treasury bills are zero coupon securities and pay no interest. They are issued at a discount (at a reduced amount) and redeemed at the face value at maturity. The difference (discount) is the interest.

When the government wants to borrow from the financial market, it can do it by issuing two types of debt instruments—treasury bills (T-bills) and government bonds (G-secs). Treasury bills are issued when the government need money for a shorter period while bonds are issued when it need debt for longer period like five years and above. We have earlier studied the interest rates on govt. securities.

Treasury bills are the money market instruments. Banks can also subscribe to treasury bills issues as treasury bills are same as govt. securities for the purpose of SLR and also can be used in repo transactions.

Treasury bills are basically instruments for short-term (maturities less than one year) borrowing by the Central Government. Treasury bills were first issued in India in 1917.

Until 1988, the only kind of Treasury bill that was available was the 91-day bill, issued on tap; at a fixed rate of 4.5% (the rates on these bills remained unchanged at 4.5% since 1974). 182-day T-bills were introduced in 1987, and 364-day T-bill was introduced in April 1992. Now Treasury bills are issued in the three tenors of 91 days, 182 days and 364 days.

RBI manages the public debt office of the Central Government and also manages State Governments borrowings. The interest rates on treasury bills are as advised by RBI to GOI. Hence the interest rates are decided by RBI keeping in mind the benchmark rate and also the market situation like the liquidity position in the market.

The table given below gives the Treasury bill interest rates from the year 2011 to 2021. We can observe that the rates are close to repo rate of RBI.

Treasury bills—interest yield %

	(91-Day Treasury Bill Primary) Yield %	182-Day Treasury Bill (Primary) Yield %	364-Day Treasury Bill (Primary) Yield %
30-12-2011	8.48	-	8.35
28-12-2012	8.19	-	8.11
20-12-2013	8.65	8.84	-
19-12-2014	8.35	8.38	-
18-12-2015	-	7.23	7.25
23-12-2016	6.23	-	6.34
22-12-2017	6.19	6.33	6.40
21-12-2018	6.60	6.87	6.97
20-12-2019	5.03	5.22	5.30
28-10-2020	3.19	3.36	3.45
25-05-2021	3.40	3.60	3.72

Source: RBI

6

Demonetization in the Year 2016

Demonetisation of the currency notes in India in 2016 is not the first instance of demonetisation in the country.

The first demonetisation took place on 12 January 1946 during British rule when notes of ₹ 500, ₹ 1000, ₹ 10,000 were demonetised. The purpose was to curb and check the black money in the country.

In the year 1946, as mentioned in the Report of the Board of Directors of the Reserve Bank, total issue of these notes were ₹ 143.97 crore. RBI report stated that the High Denomination Bank Notes (Demonetisation) Ordinance applied to British India only but its provisions were extended, with suitable modifications to the Administered Areas on 22 January 1946 and many Indian States also issued parallel Ordinances. States which did not enact such legislation were required to exchange their holdings of demonetised notes before 7 March 1946. Out of a total of ₹ 143.97 crores of high denomination notes in circulation on 11 January 1946, notes of the value of ₹ 109.67 crores were exchanged before 26 January 1946, the total value of such notes exchanged up to 30 June 1946 being ₹ 128.02 crores.

It took long time to approve and exchange these notes as some of these notes were lying with many princely states then existing. Exchange was made by issuing ₹ 100 notes. It is reported that up to the end of 1947 total demonetised notes of the value of ₹ 134.9 crores were exchanged. Thus, notes worth only ₹ 9.07 crores were demonetised.

After the first demonetisation, the higher denomination banknotes of ₹ 1,000, ₹ 5,000 and ₹ 10,000 were reintroduced in the year 1954.

The second demonetisation took place on 16 January 1978 when all these high denomination notes were demonetised. The Preamble to the Demonetisation Act 1978 highlights "the need for demonetisation of high denominations, in the public interest. The usage of high-denomination bank notes was considered detrimental to Economy of India, due to illegal financial transactions facilitated by high-denomination bank notes".

The Finance Minister H.M. Patel in his budget speech on 28 Feb. 1978 remarked as under:

> The demonetisation of high denomination bank notes was a step primarily aimed at controlling illegal transactions. It is a part of a series of measures which government has taken and is determined to take against anti-social elements.

Six months after demonetisation, Finance Minister H.M. Patel presented the results on July 18, 1978 as under:

> The demonetisation of high-denomination notes had the limited objective of stopping the illicit transfer of money for financing transactions, which, apart from resulting in tax evasion, were harmful for a healthy growth of the economy. The measure resulted in the high-denomination banknotes of an approximate value of ₹ 16 crore (160 million) not having been tendered for exchange becoming valueless and therefore, would not form part of money supply. Apart from the psychological impact which such a measure has had on tax evaders, black-marketeers, etc., it has yielded valuable information to tax authorities in respect of persons who tendered high-denomination notes for exchange, which, it would appear, indicates tax evasion in a number of cases.

It was said that the total value of demonetised currency notes (₹ 1000 + 5000 + 10000) were around ₹ 73.1 crore in 1977-78. The chief economic advisor of the State Bank of India affirmed that 25% of the proscribed currency notes did not return to the banking system during the 1978 demonetisation episode.

Thereafter RBI introduced ₹ 500 note into circulation from October 1987 and ₹ 1,000 note made a comeback from November 2000.

Demonetisation on 8 November 2016

GOI demonetised the 500 and 1000 rupee notes on 8 November 2016 and the public were advised to deposit the demonetized notes with the banks. RBI simultaneously issued the new denomination notes of 500 rupees and 2000 rupee notes to the public.

While announcing demonetisation on 8 November 2016, Prime Minister Shri Narendra Modi had outlined three broad objectives to fight black money, control corruption and terror funding. GOI was very positive that the results of demonetization will be evident in about 50 days' time and the nation will be benefitted from this step, in terms of weeding out black money and terrorist activities and blocking of forged notes.

Surprisingly the public went with the GOI assurances and thought that demonetization will achieve the desired result and will help the country. Public generally accepted the demonetisation and cooperated with the GOI to the maximum extent possible. Even though few political parties have criticized the move, public opinion generally favoured govt.'s decision and its views. In view of this, the exercise though painful to the public and nation, continued without any noticeable resent from the public.

The Reserve Bank of India issued detailed guidelines and advised that the demonetised banknotes can be deposited with banks over a period of fifty days until 30 December 2016. The demonetised banknotes can also be exchanged for new note over the counter at all banks. The limit for such exchange was fixed at ₹ 4,000 per person from 8 to 13 November, was increased to ₹ 4,500 from 14 to 17 November, and reduced to ₹ 2,000 from 18 to 25 November. The exchange of banknotes was stopped completely on 25 November. International airports also facilitated exchange of banknotes for foreign tourists and out-bound travellers, amounting to a total value of ₹ 5,000 per person. Petrol pumps, government hospitals, railway and airline booking counters, state-government recognised dairies and ration stores, and crematoriums were allowed to accept the demonetised banknotes until 2 December 2016.

Cash withdrawals from bank accounts were restricted to ₹ 10,000 per day and ₹ 20,000 per week per account from 10 to 13 November. This limit was increased to ₹ 24,000 per week from 14 November 2016. Limits/restrictions on cash withdrawals from Current accounts/Cash credit accounts/ Overdraft accounts were withdrawn later. RBI increased the withdrawal limit from Savings Bank account to ₹ 50,000 on 20 February 2017 from the earlier ₹ 24,000 and then on 13 March 2017, removed restrictions on withdrawals from savings bank accounts.

In case of ATMs, limit on withdrawals was also imposed, ₹ 2,000 per day until 14th November, and ₹ 2,500 per day until 31st December. This limit was increased to ₹ 4,500 per day from 1st January and to ₹ 10,000 from 16 January 2017.

From 17 November 2016, as a special measure, families were allowed to withdraw ₹ 250,000 for wedding expenses. Farmers were permitted to withdraw ₹ 25,000 per week against crop loans.

Sudden withdrawal of currency notes of ₹ 500 and ₹ 1000 put the entire country in to a big task of exchanging the old notes or depositing them in the bank accounts. It created untold miseries to all citizens as in the absence of adequate cash they had to face lot of hardships. More than 100 deaths directly related to this exercise were reported. Further all economic activities like trade, industry, service sector and agriculture suffered due to non-availability of cash to carry on with the activities. Poor people and daily wage earners suffered the maximum due to loss of income.

The cash flow slowly came back to normal. However, during this exercise GOI also claimed that digitalisation of the economy is also one of the important purposes of this massive exercise.

GOI wanted that the reliance on cash be reduced in the system and in its place digital payments are used to transact.

Only after April 2017 the cash flow in the economy came back to near-normal status.

The Size of Demonetisation Exercise

As per RBI data, on November 4, 2016, before demonetisation (8-11-2016), India's money market had the overall circulation of banknotes worth ₹ 17.97 lakh crore. It is informed that the banned banknotes of 500 rupees and 1000 rupees constituted 86.4 per cent of the total money in circulation. Thus, the banned notes were worth ₹ 15.52 lakh crore. This was an unparalleled massive exercise as 86.4% of money was replaced with new notes.

In the year 2018, The Reserve Bank of India (RBI) has come out with details on this exercise in its annual report giving information on demonetisation implemented in 2016. It is said that of ₹ 15.41 lakh crore demonetised currency notes of ₹ 500 and ₹ 1,000 denominations, only ₹ 10,720 crore did not reach to the banks or the RBI.

This means 99.3% of demonetised notes were deposited back with banks and only 0.7 per cent of demonetised currency notes were junked in the exercise. Compared to this, the government had initially expected that approximately ₹ 3 lakh crore or approximately 20%, of the demonetised banknotes would not come back to the banking system, thus shedding the substantial weight of black money. Thus, it is evident that govt. expectation to weed out black money did not materialise.

Subsequent information given out by GOI and its depts., revealed that black money holders have used the bank accounts of poor and gullible to deposit permitted cash deposits. Some such cases are identified and tax dept. is collecting information of such transactions. GOI also claimed that the demonetisation has resulted in increase in number of first-time taxpayers and also increase in the level of returned income by existing taxpayers. According to government reports the no. of income taxpayers saw a record increase in the post-demonetization era. About 9.1 million new taxpayers were added which was an 80% rise over the typical yearly rise. Statistics on new taxpayers and increase in tax revenues were published. But this did not reveal any huge increase in tax collections that can be directly attributed to demonetisation.

Thus, it is now known that the purpose for which GOI has demonetised the ₹ 500 and ₹ 1000 notes did not fructify. It did not result in detection of black money and the exercise became futile. However, GOI has claimed that tax departments have received leads to many cases of black money. It also claimed that this exercise has resulted in increase of tax collections and also increase in taxpayer base.

Similarly, the other aims of demonetisation like reducing corruption and checking fake currencies used by terrorists are also could not be verified. RBI data on fake notes detected from the year 2017 onwards does not show any major variance from the past. Even some fake notes are being detected in the new ₹ 500 and ₹ 2000 denomination notes as per the table below.

Number of counterfeit banknotes detected in banks (April-March)

Denomination	2015-16	2016-17	2017-18
₹ 1	2	3	4
₹ 2 and ₹ 5	2	80	1
₹ 10	134	523	287
₹ 20	96	324	437
₹ 50	6,453	9,222	23,447
₹ 100	2,21,447	1,77,195	2,39,182
₹ 200	NA	NA	79
₹ 500 (old)	2,61,695	3,17,567	1,27,918
₹ 500 (new)	NA	199	9,892
₹ 1000	1,43,099	2,56,324	1,03,611
₹ 2000	NA	638	17,929
Total	6,32,926	7,62,027	5,22,783

Source: RBI.

GOI also claimed to push digital payments in the economy to reduce currency notes in circulation. Digital payments have definitely gown over the years.

In January 2020, RBI governor Shri Shaktikanta Das had claimed that digital payments account for around 97% of daily payment system transactions in terms of volume. He said that the government's drive towards cashless economy bore fruit as digital payments across India increased at a compound annual growth rate (CAGR) of 55.1% over the past five years, i.e., between the financial years (FY) 2015-16 and 2019-20. During this period, its value has grown from INR 920.38 lakh cr to INR 1,623.05 lakh cr, at an annual compounded rate of 15.2%.

Reserve Bank of India (RBI) data on digital payments:

Year	Nos	Value ₹
2015-16	593.61 crore	920.38 lakh crore
2016-17	969.12 crore	1120.99 lakh crore
2017-18	1459.01 crore	1369.86 lakh crore
2018-19	2343.40 crore	1638.52 lakh crore
2019-20	3434.56 crore	1623.05 lakh crore

Digital payments have increased over the years as per the data above which is a positive development. But we find that it had no impact on bank notes in circulation.

In fact, currency in circulation has increased over the years after demonetisation as shown in the table published by RBI shown below:

Table 6.1: Banknotes in Circulation

Denomination (₹)	Volume (million pieces)			Value (₹ billion)		
	Mar 2016	Mar 2017	Mar 2018	Mar 2016	Mar 2017	Mar 2018
1	2	3	4	5	6	7
2 & 5	11,626	11,557	11,425	45	45	44
	(12.9)	(11.5)	(11.2)	(0.3)	(0.3)	(0.2)
10	32,015	36,929	30,645	320	369	307
	(35.5)	(36.8)	(29.9)	(1.9)	(2.8)	(1.7)
20	4,924	10,158	10,016	98	203	200
	(5.4)	(10.2)	(9.8)	(0.6)	(1.5)	(1.1)
50	3,890	7,113	7,343	194	356	367
	(4.3)	(7.1)	(7.2)	(1.2)	(2.7)	(2.0)
100	15,778	25,280	22,215	1,578	2,528	2,222
	(17.5)	(25.2)	(21.7)	(9.6)	(19.3)	(12.3)

Denomination (₹)	Volume (million pieces)			Value (₹ billion)		
	Mar 2016	Mar 2017	Mar 2018	Mar 2016	Mar 2017	Mar 2018
200	-	-	1,853	-	-	371
	-	-	(1.8)	-	-	(2.1)
500	15,707	5,882	15,469	7,854	2,941	7,734
	(17.4)	(5.9)	(15.1)	(47.8)	(22.5)	(42.9)
1000	6,326	89	66	6,326	89	66
	(7.0)	(...)	(...)	(38.6)	(0.7)	(0.4)
2000	-	3,285	3,363	-	6,571	6,726
	-	(3.3)	(3.3)	-	(50.2)	(37.3)
Total	90,266	100,293	102,395	16,415	13,102	18,037

-: Not Applicable and ...: Negligible.

Note: Figures in parentheses represent the percentage share in total volume/value.

Source: RBI.

Currency in circulation, according to the RBI data, was ₹ 18.03 lakh crore in March 2018 and further increased to ₹ 24.2 lakh crore as at March 2020 and ₹ 28.2 lakh crore in March 2021, as compared to ₹ 16.4 lakh crore in 2016. Volume of currency notes have increased to 10.2 lakh pieces in 2018 and to 11.6 lakh pieces in 2020 and 12.43 lakh pieces in March 2021, from 9 lakh pieces in 2016.

The share of high denomination currency notes was 86.4 per cent at the time of demonetisation. In March 2021, the share of high denomination notes was 85.7% which is almost at same level.

Banknotes in circulation during the years 2019, 2020 and 2021 are given in the following table.

Table 6.2: Banknotes in Circulation (end-March)

Denomination (₹)	Volume (pieces in lakh)			Value (₹ crore)		
	2019	2020	2021	2019	2020	2021
1	2	3	4	5	6	7
2 and 5	1,13,025	1,12,203	1,11,728	4,372	4,331	4,307
	(10.4)	(9.7)	(9.0)	(0.2)	(0.2)	(0.2)
10	3,12,598	3,04,022	2,93,681	31,260	30,402	29,368

Denomination (₹)	Volume (pieces in lakh)			Value (₹ crore)		
	2019	2020	2021	2019	2020	2021
	(28.7)	(26.2)	(23.6)	(1.5)	(1.3)	(1.0)
20	87,127	82,994	90,579	17,425	16,599	18,116
	(8.0)	(7.2)	(7.3)	(0.8)	(0.7)	(0.6)
50	86,015	86,009	87,524	43,007	43,004	43,762
	(7.9)	(7.4)	(7.0)	(2.0)	(1.8)	(1.5)
100	2,00,738	1,99,021	1,90,555	2,00,738	1,99,021	1,90,555
	(18.5)	(17.2)	(15.3)	(9.5)	(8.2)	(6.7)
200	40,005	53,646	58,304	80,010	1,07,293	1,16,608
	(3.7)	(4.6)	(4.7)	(3.8)	(4.4)	(4.1)
500	2,15,176	2,94,475	3,86,790	10,75,881	14,72,373	19,33,951
	(19.8)	(25.4)	(31.1)	(51.0)	(60.8)	(68.4)
2,000	32,910	27,398	24,510	6,58,199	5,47,952	4,90,195
	(3.0)	(2.4)	(2.0)	(31.2)	(22.6)	(17.3)
Total	10,87,594	11,59,768	12,43,671	21,10,892	24,20,975	28,26,863

Notes: 1. Figures in parentheses represent the percentage share in total volume/ value. They may not add up to 100 due to rounding-off of numbers.

2. Figures may not add up to total due to rounding-off of numbers.

Source: RBI.

Thus, the demonetisation exercise of withdrawing the high value notes turned out to be a Damp squib.

Reactions from Public

After the demonetisation was announced by the government in 2016, there were lot of reactions from economists, political parties and even from the international community. A small section of businessmen and bankers supported the measures. However majority view was against the demonetisation. But public in general tacitly supported the govt. thinking that it will eliminate the menace of black money in the country. Probably they believed in government's view that a large chunk of high denomination notes will not be deposited with banks for fear of action against unaccounted money or black money.

However, it is pertinent to understand that in 2012, the Central Board of Direct Taxes recommended against demonetisation, saying in a report that "demonetisation may not be a solution for tackling black money or shadow economy, which is largely held in the form of benami properties, bullion and jewellery."

According to data from income tax probes, black money holders kept only 6% or less of their wealth as cash, suggesting that targeting this cash would not be a successful strategy.

According to Prof. R. Vaidyanathan's book *Black Money and Tax Havens* (published in October 2017), the amount of money Indians have stashed in tax havens could be around ₹ 65 lakh crore. Whereas the amount of domestic black money is estimated to be around ₹ 15 lakh crore, a good amount of that is in the form of assets such as real estate and financial investments.

Thus, it is pertinent to note that black money is generally parked in tax heavens, in real estate and in bullion and only a fraction is held in cash.

Now the question arises as to why the GOI decided to demonetise stating that it is aiming to hit at black money. In fact, there were many views and studies available on the role of black money in the economy and also on how hoarders park black money.

It appears that GOI gambled hoping that it can remove the menace of black money by forcing it out of circulation as hoarders may not dare to deposit it with banks.

Criticisms and Fact Check

Demonetisation has been one of the most criticized moves by PM Modi. Former Prime Minister Manmohan Singh and former RBI Governor Raghuram Rajan have condemned this move and its effects on the Indian economy. Many political parties in the country also opposed and criticized this move.

Demonetisation was initiated with a wide array of motives like stripping the Indian economy of its black money, push people to pay taxes for the unaccounted pile of cash, curb terrorism, promote the digital India movement and make India a cashless economy.

Demonetisation and Black Money

The most important point that pushed people to support demonetisation was its associating with bringing an end to the black money problem in India. However, almost 99% of the

money was deposited back with RBI. This means that either the hoarders found a way to legitimize their black money and deposit it in the bank or black money was not held in the form of cash. This was not a new revelation but known and discussed earlier also. It was always discussed that the bulk of black money is held in the form of real estate and gold and only a small percentage in cash. Even this small percentage of unaccounted cash found its way and was deposited in the banks. The Income Tax department is reported to have seized ₹ 474.37 crore in new and old currency from November 9, 2016 to January 4, 2017.

Demonetisation and Terror Funding

Second reason to support demonetisation was its role in curbing terrorism by increasing the obstacles in terror funding. Terrorist organisations were known to use fake Indian currency notes for funding their projects and the government believed that this could be contained with.

Fake notes are known to exist and rumoured sometimes even printed abroad and brought in to the country. News reports rumouring about printing of fake notes at Pakistan by terror groups and using it in India were common knowledge but there was no authentic news on this earlier and also now. It is informed by RBI that fake notes of newly designed 500 and 2000 rupee notes are already detected. But such detections are not alarming in terms of quantity of notes detected.

In view of limitations to get reliable information whether terror funding through fake notes existed and to what extent, cannot be known. Whether there is any positive change in such activities cannot be verified.

Demonetisation and Digital India

Pushing India towards cashless economy was another reason that demonetisation was publicized. People turned towards digital transactions for everything from buying groceries from a road side vendor, to paying utility bills during the time of demonetisation. However, as the flow of cash into the economy began to increase, the use of the apps and digital wallets saw a slide once again.

Reactions of Economists

Demonetisation is not commonly used as a tested economic step in the world so far, even though many countries have used it. It generally does not appeal to the economists who can be considered as professionals in this area.

It is pertinent to note that by and large economists did not approve demonetisation move by GOI.

- Nobel laureate Amartya Sen, severely criticised the demonetisation move calling it a "despotic action" among other things.
- Former Senior Vice-President and Chief Economist of the World Bank, Kaushik Basu, called it a 'major mistake' and said that the 'damage' is likely to be much greater than any possible benefits.
- Pronab Sen, former Chief Statistician and Planning Commission of India member, called it a "hollow move" since it did not really address any of the purported goals of tackling black money or fake currency.
- Prabhat Patnaik, a former professor of economics at the Jawaharlal Nehru University, Delhi called the move 'witless' and 'anti-people'. He criticised the simple way in which black money was assumed as "a hoard of cash", saying that it would have little effect in eliminating "black activities" while "causing much hardship to common people."
- Nobel laureate Paul Krugman said that it is difficult to see gains from demonetisation, while there may be significant costs to it.

Source: wikipedia.

Former prime minister and former finance minister of our country criticised demonetisation as under:

> On 24 November 2016, former Prime Minister Shri Manmohan Singh said "this scheme will hurt small industries, the farming sector. The GDP can decline by about 3 per cent due to this move". He termed the

demonetisation as organised loot, legalised plunder of the common people.

Former Finance Minister Shri P. Chidambaram launched an attack on the Modi Government saying that the country paid a huge price for demonetisation by way of job loss, closure of industries and the GDP growth.

"Indian economy lost 1.5 per cent of GDP in terms of growth. That alone was a loss of ₹ 2.25 lakh crore a year. Over 100 lives were lost. 15 crore daily wage earners lost their livelihood for several weeks. Thousands of SME units were shut down. Lakhs of jobs were destroyed," Chidambaram said in a series of tweets.

GDP growth rate is given in the table below:

Real GDP growth rate (base year 2011-12)

Financial Year	Quarter	Quarterly	Yearly
2015-16	Q1 (April–June)	7%	8%
	Q2 (July–September)	7.4%	
	Q3 (October–December)	7.2%	
	Q4 (January–March)	9.1%	
2016-17	Q1 (April–June)	7.9%	7.1%
	Q2 (July–September)	7.5%	
	Q3 (October–December)	7%	
	Q4 (January–March)	6.1%	
2017-18	Q1 (April–June)	5.7%	6.5%
	Q2 (July–September)	6.3%	
	Q3 (October–December)	7.2%	
	Q4 (January–March)	7.6%	
2018-19	Q1 (April–June)	7.7%	
	Q2 (July–September)	8.2%	
	Q3 (October–December)		
	Q4 (January–March)		

*GDP estimate for 2018-19—6.8%

From the table above we can note that GDP came down from 8% in the year 2015-16 to 7.1% in the year 2016-17, a drop of 0.9%. GDP depends on overall growth in all sectors of the country. GDP was also lower in the year 2017-18 at 6.5%. For the year 2018-19 it is estimated to be 6.8%.

Ministry of Finance Department of Economic Affairs Economic Division—MONTHLY ECONOMIC REPORT January 2019 said that—

> The growth of real GDP for 2018-19 is estimated to be 7.0 percent (2nd Advance Estimate). The revised growth rates of GDP, released by Central Statistics Office for the years 2015-16, 2016-17 and 2017-18 are 8.0 percent, 8.2 percent and 7.2 percent respectively.

It is difficult explain the reason for GDP coming down over the years. Demonetisation of notes can be a contributory factor in this downfall along with many other economic developments over these years.

Direct Cost of Demonetisation

It is said that around ₹ 8000 crore for printing new notes during the period July 2016-June 2017. RBI expenses for printing new notes were as under:

- 2015-16–₹ 3421 crore
- 2016-17–₹ 7965 crore
- 2017-18–₹ 4912 crore

Cost of printing notes is a regular feature with RBI expenses as it prints notes for replacement of soiled notes and also for additional currency requirement during the year. Increase in such cost in the year 2016-17 as compared to previous year is ₹ 4544 crore.

Demonetisations in other Countries of the World

Demonetisation was attempted by many countries in the world during past 50-60 years for various purposes. We observe that many countries attempted it to curb black money. Some countries have used it as a measure to fight against soaring inflation. There were other purposes also as we can observe from the table below.

Year	Country	Details
1969	USA	In 1969, the United States of America under President Richard Nixon declared all bills above $100 null and void in United States of America to curb the existence of black money in the nation and restore the country's sheen. The move was highly successful and is claimed to have been the starting of development of the American banking system. The $100 bill is the most widely circulated denomination till date.
1971	United Kingdom	In 1971, the United Kingdom adopted decimal currency against pounds, shillings, and pence. In 1968 and 1969 decimal coins which had precise equivalent values in the old currency were introduced.
1982	Ghana	To reduce tax evasion and clear excess liquidity, the country demonetized its 50 cedi currency. The exercise was highly unsuccessful as the public started turning towards foreign currency and physical assets. Moreover, the general public lost confidence in the banking system and a fresh black market for currency cropped up.
1984	Nigeria	During the military government of Muhammadu Buhari in 1984, Nigeria introduced new currency and banned the old notes. However, the debt-ridden and inflation hit country did not take the change well and the economy collapsed.
1987	Myanmar	The military invalidated nearly 80 percent of the value of money in circulation with the motive to curb the rising black economy. It resulted in a student demonstration followed by a government crackdown the very next year.
1991	Soviet Union	Under the leadership of Mikhail Gorbachev, 50 and 100 ruble notes were removed from circulation in an attempt to combat the parallel economy. The removed notes formed about one third of the total money in circulation. There were economic dislocations and several Soviet republics such as Kazakhstan and Ukraine were severely affected. Economic activity headed towards a major downturn and people began to lose faith in the government. The demonetization exercise was unsuccessful as Gorbachev faced a coup merely months later in August. Some historians also suggest that these series of events fuelled the eventual break-up of the USSR.

1993	Zaire	Under the dictatorship of Mobutu Sese Seko, successive currency reforms were rolled out. Obsolescent currency was withdrawn from the system in 1993. Increasing economic disruptions resulted in ouster of Mobutu in 1997.
1996	Australia	In 1996, in order to curb black money and improve the security features, the Australian government replaced its paper-based notes with polymer bank notes of the same denomination. The first polymer-based note was introduced in Australia in 1992. The move didn't have any impact any side-effects on the economy but made Australia a business-friendly country.
2002	European Union	Introduction of a unified currency 'Euro' on Jan. 1, 2002 called for demonetization of the existing currencies of 12 countries under the European Union. About eight billion notes and 38 billion coins were distributed through 218,000 banks, post offices and 2.8 million sales outlets. Simultaneously a large proportion of the nine billion national notes and 107 billion national coins were collected. Prior preparations starting from mid-1998 and informing the citizens well in advance resulted in this successful currency changeover.
2010	North Korea	In order to halt black market and improve the economy, Kim Jong Il government introduced currency changes. Kim Jong Il introduced reform that knocked off two zeros from the face value of the old currency. The move backfired as the price of necessity goods increased and people strongly resisted the move. This was followed by the murder of the finance minister.
2015	Zimbabwe	In order to stabilize its economy racked by hyperinflation, the government decided to replace the Zimbabwe dollar with the American dollar in 2015. The process took three months to make US dollar as the country's legal tender. The move, turned out to be unsuccessful as most wealth holders saw the value of their accumulated savings receding. Along with resentment among people, there were adverse effects on the economy as exports took a major hit due to loss of competitiveness.

2016	Pakistan	In December 2016, in order to improve security and durability of the bank notes, State Bank of Pakistan (SBP) issued new designs' bank notes. The move was applicable to 10, 50, 100 and 1,000 rupee notes' older design. The country issued a tender 18 months back and gave citizens enough time to exchange their old notes for the newly design notes. Earlier, Pakistan had demonetised 5 and 500 Pakistani rupee notes. On Dec. 19, Pakistan's senate passed a resolution to phase out its ₹ 5,000 notes in an attempt to curtail black money. In value terms, ₹ 5,000 bills account for 30% of the currency in circulation in the country. Pakistan's government plans to implement this demonetisation over the next three to five years, in contrast to India's approach. Much like India, Pakistan is on a mission to fight tax evasion and the stashing of illegal wealth.
2016	Venezuela	On Dec. 11, In order to curb the rising inflation rate that reached 425% and tackle the growing threat of the transnational mafias breeding in the country, the Nicolas-Maduro led government announced demonetization of its 100 Bolivar notes (which form 77% of the nation's cash in circulation). The citizens were given a 72 hour window before withdrawal of currency. Following violent protests including destruction of shops, road blockages and break down of ATMs, the government was forced to extend the deadline for use of old currency.

Sources: *Neha Borkar Updated: March 23, 2017 and *Team Groww - https://groww.in/- 17 July 2019.

It is observed that demonetisation is generally not effective to control black money. It also did not help to fight inflation. It was success in few cases and achieved some specific purposes.

During the time when India went through this exercise international community has been watching it closely. Countries in the world were interested to know whether this exercise will succeed in controlling black money.

But the Indian experiment proved ineffective. It is pertinent to note that the economists all over the world generally do not favour demonetisation as a measure to achieve control on black money.

7

Urban Co-operative Banks

Brief History of Coop Banks

Urban coop banks are a category of banks in our country which is in lime light now particularly after the Punjab and Maharashtra coop bank came into trouble in September 2019 and the matter is just resolved in January 2022.

Urban coop banks in the country have a very long history and these banks have been existing since more than 100 years.

Cooperative movement probably started in the country from the year 1890 onwards and mainly it was aimed at the rural population to assist the farmers to get credit at reasonable cost and not to borrow from money lenders at exorbitant interest rates.

As per the history of cooperative movement in India, 'Nidhis' or Mutual-Loan Associations based on the Co-operative Principle were organised in the Madras Presidency. By 1901, there were 200 nidhis with more than 36000 members and subscribed capital of more than 2 crores of rupees.

In Punjab, a society on co-operative lines was started as early as 1891 at Panjawar in Hoshiarpur district. The state of Mysore introduced Agricultural Banks in 1894. In U.P. also the village banks were established. All these efforts were purely voluntary, and non-official.

Govt. later in the year 1904 enacted The Co-operative Societies Act, 1904 as the first legislation about the cooperative societies. Under this Act:

(1) Any ten persons living in the same village or town or belonging to the same class or tribe could form a co-operative credit society for the encouragement of thrift and self-help among the members.

(2) Societies were classified as Rural and Urban. A society in which 80% of the total membership was agricultural was classed as rural, and the one in which 80% of the membership was non-agricultural, was classed as urban.

However, after the passing of the Act, the coop movement did not make much progress as expected of it. By 1911, there were about 8177 credit societies all over the country with a share capital of ₹ 50.5 lakhs and a membership of a little over 4 lakhs.

In view of this, govt. enacted The Cooperative Society's Act 1912 and made some improvements in the Act.

Under this Act

(1) Any society, credit or otherwise, could be registered which had as its objective, the promotion of the economic interest of its members.

(2) A federal society like the central bank or union could be registered.

(3) Every society registered earlier under the act of 1904 was deemed to be registered under the act of 1912.

With the enactment of this Act, the coop movement picked up. A number of new societies sprang up for purposes like the sale of agricultural produce, cattle insurance, the purchase of seeds, manures and implements, and the promotion of irrigation projects. District unions of primary societies and central banks began to be established.

The period from 1913 to 1928 saw substantial progress in the field of cooperation. The number of societies increased to 96091, membership to 37.80 lakhs and working capital to rupees 76.70 crores.

Then under the Reforms Act of 1919, the subject: 'co-operation' was transferred to the control and direction of the new Provincial govts. Provincial govts. (later states) enacted their own provincial laws (state laws) regulating cooperative movements.

The first urban coop bank was The Anyonya Sahayakari Mandali opened in Baroda (Vadodara) in 1889. This credit society was later named as Anyonya Sahayakari Mandali Cooperative Bank. This bank is said to be the first coop bank in Asia. Unfortunately, this bank was closed down in the year 2008.

Basically, urban coop banks were started as coop credit societies under the coop societies acts of the respective state governments. Coop societies are governed by the State Acts. There are different types of coop societies formed for many purposes. Credit societies are one type of coop societies permitted to be started under the society's Acts of the states. Credit societies are basically doing banking activities. But they cannot call themselves as banks under the banking regulations Act. However, they can call themselves as coop bank, only after obtaining the licence from RBI as RBI is the authority which controls banking activities in the country.

We must understand that the cooperative sector is legally recognised much earlier before the formation of RBI, and its role in the economy is encouraged by the laws of the country since long. Forming Credit cooperatives are permitted under coop societies acts. In view of this existing recognised status of credit cooperatives, RBI allowed them to be registered as coop banks with it on the basis of certain stipulations mainly on its capital base.

The Banking Regulation Act, 1949 gave RBI the authority over banks in India. But as credit coop societies are formed under coop society's acts which are older to the Banking Regulation Act, 1949, these credit cooperatives were not under RBI's control. In order to give RBI control over coop banks, govt. amended the banking regulation act in the year 1965 and from the year 1966 coop banks came under the supervision of RBI for all banking related matters. The Banking Laws (Application to Co-operative Societies) Act, 1965 (23 of 1965) amended the Banking Regulation Act, 1949.

Section 56(ccv) of banking regulation act defines the status of urban coop banks as under:

Section 56(ccv) in Banking Regulation Act, 1949

(ccv) "primary co-operative bank" means a co-operative society, other than a primary agricultural credit society,

(1) the primary object or principal business of which is the transaction of banking business;

(2) the paid-up share capital and reserves of which are not less than one lakh of rupees; and

(3) the bye-laws of which do not permit admission of any other co-operative society as a member: Provided that this sub-clause shall not apply to the admission of a co-operative bank as a member by reason of such co-operative bank subscribing to the share capital of such co-operative society out of funds provided by the State Government for the purpose.

We may observe from the definition in the section that the term 'urban coop bank' is not used. Instead, the term 'primary coop bank' is used. A credit coop society other than primary agricultural credit society is covered by this section.

This is because GOI had earlier decided to use the primary agricultural credit societies (PACS) for delivery of agriculture credit under its rural development programmes. All these PACS and also the other rural coop banks are promoted by the govts. Besides PACS, central and state governments have created and promoted many types of rural coop banks. These rural coop banks are dedicated banks for rural development. Present status of Rural coop banks is discussed in a separate chapter.

All other primary coop credit societies which became coop banks are promoted by groups of individuals and are started in urban centres. Hence the coop banks promoted by groups of individuals in urban places are called the urban coop banks (to differentiate them from the rural coop banks mentioned above). These banks are in private sector.

RBI report on growth of Urban Coop Banks stated under:

1. Data prior to 1948 about the urban cooperative banking sector is, unfortunately, not available. As at the end of financial year 1948-49, the number of UCBs stood at 815 and rose to become 1106 by the end of financial year 1966-67. During this period, the deposits held by UCB sector rose from ₹ 17 crores to ₹ 153 crores, registering a growth of 800% [Urban Cooperative banks were brought under the purview of B.R. Act, effective from 1 March 1966].

2. Between 1966-93, the resources mobilised by way of deposits by the UCBs have registered a phenomenal growth. From a meagre ₹ 153 crores as at the end of June 1967, they rose to ₹ 13531 crores by the end of March 1993. The credit base surged from ₹ 167 crores to ₹ 10132 crores during this period. Year wise key financial indicators of UCBs are given in Annexure IV. The annualised average growth of deposits and advances was found to be quite impressive. The number of urban cooperative banks had grown from 1106 to 1399 during the corresponding period.

3. The year 1993 was a watershed in the annals of urban cooperative banking movement. After Narasimham Committee (Report I) addressed the ills of banking system in 1991, and suggested a road map for liberalising the banking sector, a similar need was also felt to look de novo at the regulatory issues relating to UCBs. Accordingly, RBI appointed the Marathe Committee in 1991 to address these issues. Recommendations of this Committee were quite far reaching, particularly, in the realm of new bank licensing, branch licensing and area of operation, etc. Essentially, Marathe Committee, suggested to dispense with the "one district-one bank" licensing policy and recommended organisation of banks based on the need for an institution and potential for a bank to mobilise deposits and purveying of credit. It also felt that existence of commercial banking network should not prevent the cooperative initiative. RBI accepted these recommendations and had come out with its new policy approach in May 1993. Between May 1993, when the revised policy was put in place and 31 March 1999, RBI has issued as many as 537 licenses for setting up new banks. The liberalised branch licensing policy's stress was more on

bank's inherent financial strength rather than assessing the need for a branch and its viability in a given centre. As a result, the branch network of UCBs has increased from 3691 as at the end of March 1993, to 6619 by 31 March 1999. Urban cooperative banks were also allowed to extend their area of operation to the entire district without specific approval from RBI and banks, with deposits of ₹ 50 crores and above, were permitted to cross the borders of the States of their registration. Banks complying with certain norms can now also open extension counters without RBI permission. There were 1499 UCBs in the year 1999.

4. Besides, easing regulatory restrictions, a number of policy pronouncements were made in the operational sphere too. UCBs can now invest 10% of their surplus funds outside cooperative fold. Ceiling on quantum of advances to nominal members has been increased substantially and scheduled UCBs have been allowed to do merchant banking/forex operations. Effective from November 1996, urban cooperative banks have been given freedom to finance direct agricultural operations. The interest rates on deposits of urban banks have been deregulated from 21 October 1997. They can also install ATMs without prior approval of RBI.

As per above report of RBI, at the end of financial year 1948-49, the number of UCBs stood at 815 and rose to become 1106 by the end of financial year 1966-67. The number of urban cooperative banks had grown from 1106 to 1399 during the period 1966-93. From the year 1993 RBI started issuing licences to open new UCBs as recommended by Marathe Committee Report.

As on 31 March 1999 there were 1499 UCBs, an addition by new 100 UCBs.

Total deposits of all UCBs as on March 1999 is given in the table below. There were 1499 UCBs out of which 29 were scheduled UCBs. The table also gives the deposit size wise break up of UCBs.

Table 7.1: As on 31 March 1999

Banks with deposits base	No. of Reporting Banks	Deposits (₹ in crores)	% to total deposits
Scheduled UCBs	29	17464.46	34.55
Others above ₹ 100 crore	60	10030.48	19.84
Above ₹ 50 crore and upto ₹ 100 crore	123	8538.27	16.89
Above ₹ 25 crore and upto ₹ 50 crore	186	6412.68	12.69
Above ₹ 10 crore and upto ₹ 25 crore	322	5138.50	10.17
₹ 10 crore and below	779	2960.02	5.86
Total	1499	50544.41	100.00

In May 1993, RBI liberalised licensing norms for UCBs. Due to this, 823 new bank licences were issued up to June 2001. The number of UCBs went up from 1499 in March 1999 to 1,926 in March 2004. But it was observed that the performance of these new UCBs started deteriorating.

K. Madhava Rao Committee in 1999

This committee was formed mainly to study the status of UCBs with reference to large no. of UCBs have been started after 1991 and that many of them have become weak financially causing concern to all interested parties.

The RBI committee chaired by K. Madhava Rao in 1999 had raised concerns over rise in number of urban cooperative banks and their weak financial performance. The number of urban cooperative banks had risen as licensing was liberalised following the 1991 reforms. The Rao Committee also pointed to a lack of professionalism and corporate governance which was leading to these cooperative banks being in weak health. The committee was of the view that entry barriers for cooperative banks were low and had to be upgraded.

The committee also said that state governments and the RBI maintaining dual control over cooperative banks is "one of the most vexatious problems of urban cooperative banking movement".

The committee views and recommendations were as under:

UCBs are not same as other coop societies as they accept deposits from the public. In view of this interests of the depositors shall be protected.

The committee was of the view that entry barriers for cooperative banks were low and had to be upgraded. Efficient management of the bank could also be ensured by specifying criteria like the composition of the board of directors, the suitability of the promoters and the adequacy of the proposed management.

The annual financial statements of UCBs shall be similar to the financial statements of commercial banks and that they are prepared with the same discipline as regards provisioning and valuation norms. They shall be audited by independent auditors similar to commercial banks. UCBs shall be inspected by the regulatory authority. They must be required to furnish to the regulatory authority the same information as is required from commercial banks.

The tools by which the financial soundness of commercial banks is measured must also be made applicable to UCBs. These would include (i) capital adequacy norms, (ii) permissible limits of non-performing assets, (iii) exposure limits, etc.

Subject to the normal regulatory safeguards, an UCB be allowed to operate in all lines of business available to a commercial bank and be given such freedom in its operating practices as is necessary.

Committee observed that though UCBs are brought under the Banking Regulation Act, 1949, some of the provisions which enable RBI to take immediate action in case of commercial banks are not made applicable to UCBs. Sections 35B, 36 (in so far as it relates to changes in management) and Parts II-A, II-C and the relevant clauses of Part III are inapplicable to urban cooperative banks. This restricts RBI authority to rehabilitate weak UCBs, in comparison to commercial banks.

The most significant factor is the dual control over the urban cooperative banking sector. The Committee recommended that the dual control is replaced by unitary control. This unitary control must recognise that the cooperative character of UCBs may be controlled by the Registrar of Cooperative Societies, its banking functions must be under the sole control of the RBI.

The above committee recommendations brought out the issues facing the UCBs. While credit societies were created as self-help groups for taking care of banking needs of the group, over a period they have evolved as commercial banks in terms of their functioning and reach. Even though they are catering to the banking needs of lower income groups to some extent, over the period this distinction has blurred as UCBs are accepting deposits from public who are not their members. In case of borrowers, they are issuing shares to them and making them as nominal members with no voting rights. Thus, the management of the society remained in the hands of promoters. As depositors of UCBs are non-members they have no say or control on the working of the UCB.

It was felt that UCBs are posing a threat to depositor's interest. In case of commercial banks, the depositor's interests are generally protected by the supervisory authority of RBI who has been given legal authority to look in to the affairs of the bank. But the authority of RBI on UCBs is limited to banking activities. This does not give authority to RBI to control the management.

In the banking history, failures of UCBs are a regular feature. There were cases of mismanagements by the promoters. Large no. of UCBs are non-scheduled and also small banks. There are About 58 UCBs which are multistate coop banks with branches in more than one state. Other UCBs are operating within one state only. Only 54 UCBs are under the category of scheduled banks. But at the same time the business of the UCBs is continuously increasing. Some of the top UCBs are now comparable to commercial banks in terms of their business levels.

Historically UCBs and commercial banks are operating in the same area and offering similar banking services. There is no segregation of their role. But their constitutions are different. Commercial banks are limited companies registered under company's act and UCBs are cooperative societies registered under state coop societies acts. Cooperative movement is an accepted mode for development and is identified by the GOI as desirable and important. Coop movement is encouraged in all possible economic activities of the country. Primary credit coop societies are permitted to undertake banking business.

Prior to the latest changes made in the year 2021 by GOI, RBI had specific powers over UCBs only in the following areas:

1. Laying down prudential norms on capital adequacy, accounting standards, classification of assets, provisioning, etc.;
2. Fixing single/group exposure norms and sectoral exposures;
3. Conducting on-site and off-site supervision;
4. Calling for statutory/other returns;
5. Off-site monitoring of the financial position of banks;
6. Initiating supervisory actions against individual UCB to improve the financial position;
7. Giving directions and operational instructions; and
8. Imposition of penalty.

However regular feature of UCB failures proved that RBI is not in a position to ensure safety of UCBs and protect the interests of depositors of these banks.

In the year 2001, a major UCB; Madhavpura Mercantile coop bank from Ahmedabad came into trouble as it was found that it had very large exposure to share brokers. It is a big UCB and its failure badly affected the depositors of the bank and also other coop banks in state of Gujarat. This UCB could not be revived and after long time a final decision was taken to close the bank. RBI cancelled the bank's licence in June 2012. Liquidation process was started in 2013 and is still going on.

The RBI found that nearly a third of the newly licensed UCBs became financially unsound within a short period. In its 2004-05 policy statement, RBI said that it would consider issuance of fresh licences only after a comprehensive policy on UCBs, including an appropriate legal and regulatory framework was put in place.

Thereafter many working groups and committees were set up to study the urban cooperative banks and give recommendations for improving their workings. These are:

- In 2006-07, a working group was established to examine augmenting capital of urban cooperative banks, chaired by N.S. Vishwanthan.
- In 2007-08, another group, chaired by R. Gandhi, was established to improve information technology systems in urban cooperative banks.
- In 2009, another such group, chaired by V.S. Das, deliberated on establishing an umbrella organisation for the urban cooperative banking sector.
- In 2011, a committee was formed to study licensing of new urban cooperative banks, chaired by Y.H. Malegam. This committee noted that only 57 per cent of urban cooperative banks were financially sound and one should be careful in granting new licences. It raised the entry-point norms for new players and said that all new urban cooperative banks should meet conditions related to Board governance.
- In 2015, the RBI formed yet another committee, led by Shri R. Gandhi, to study urban cooperative banks.

Presently RBI is framing its policies on UCBs based on the recommendations of R. Gandhi Committee to address the issues facing UCBs. This committee report is discussed later in this chapter.

The urban coop banks are a distinct category. They are in private sector and are located in urban centres. They function like commercial banks. They are also permitted to become scheduled banks by complying certain requirements prescribed by RBI, for this purpose. Initially there were some restrictions on them to undertake certain types of banking activities. They were not allowed to lend to agriculture. They were not allowed to enter into foreign exchange business. They were not allowed to open branches in other states. But over years all these restrictions were removed. Now these banks are very similar in their functioning to commercial banks in the country.

There are many scheduled urban coop banks now. There are also many big urban coop banks now with branches in many states. The banks with branches in many states are termed as multi-state urban coop bank. Few urban coop banks are now bigger in size in terms of business, than some of the private sector commercial banks.

As stated earlier urban coop banks are basically societies registered under the societies' acts of the respective states. Their registration, management, liquidation is controlled by the state govts. Hence the authority of RBI on them is only in respect of banking activities. The scheduled urban coop banks are bound by RBI rules for scheduled banks with regard to minimum capital, reporting to RBI on many matters, and inspection by RBI.

But RBI has no authority to exercise control on the management. In case an urban coop bank is in trouble, RBI has no full authority for resolution. Authority lies with the state govt. Thus, urban coop banks are under dual control of RBI and the state govt.

UCBs are the weak links in the Indian banking structure. They are governed by the society's acts of state govts. RBI control on these banks is considered limited. In view of this, there has been views to convert these urban coop banks as commercial banks as limited companies. RBI in the past, considered voluntary conversion of urban coop bank into commercial bank. One urban coop bank namely the development coop bank was converted itself as commercial bank and named itself as DCB bank.

RBI generally issues separate guidelines for urban coop banks on banking related matters. Generally, they are allowed some relaxations or they are given extra time to comply with the guidelines. Urban coop banks have developed themselves like commercial banks and they are competing with them for business. UCBs are also subjected to the credit policy of RBI in relation to prudential norms and capital adequacy norms. In view of this, practically there are no differences now between them and commercial banks.

As discussed above, urban coop banks are functioning like commercial banks but RBI control on them is considered weaker in comparison to that of commercial banks. This is reflected in the health and continuation of urban coop banks. Since 1960s there were very few commercial bank failures as compared to failures of urban coop banks. In case of commercial banks RBI is empowered to merge the weak banks with other banks and save the closure of commercial banks to protect depositors. RBI has even the authority to compulsorily merge weak banks. Due to this reason, there has been no closure of commercial banks for quite some years now.

But failures of urban coop bank have been a regular feature almost every year. RBI has no independent authority to merge or close the failed urban coop bank. This authority is with the state govt. In view of this, even when the decision is taken for closure of bank the process is very tedious and time taken for this process is very long. It does not help the depositors of the bank as they have to wait indefinitely even for getting a part of their deposits as final payment.

As per reports of DICGC in its annual accounts for the year ending March 2019, DICGC has paid claims to failed banks since its inception in 1962 to March 2019 as under:

	Type of banks	No. of failed banks	Total claims paid "₹ in millions"
1	Commercial banks	27	2959
2	Co-op banks	351	48223
	Total	378	51182

Failure of commercial banks was in the initial years and there have been no failures for past few decades. But failure of coop bank has been a regular feature almost every year. Generally, the failed urban coop banks are small and the news does not get attention at national level. Only when a fairly big urban coop bank fails or gets into trouble then the news gets national attention. The examples are the failure of Madhavpura Mercantile coop bank in the year 2001 and the present case of Punjab and Maharashtra coop bank getting into trouble. Otherwise, the failures of urban coop banks have not got the attentions of govt. and RBI. The failure of these two urban coop banks is discussed later in this chapter.

As stated earlier, all UCBs are not scheduled banks as it is optional for them. There are 53 scheduled UCBs as on May 31, 2021. These are generally the bigger UCBs and 33 of them are multi-state UCBs.

List of Scheduled Urban Co-operative Banks
(Updated as on May 31, 2021)

Sr. No.	Bank Name	Multi-state status
1	Ahmedabad Mercantile Co-Op Bank Ltd., Ahmedabad	Multi state
2	Kalupur Commercial Coop Bank Ltd., Ahmedabad	Multi state
3	Mehsana Urban Co-Op Bank Ltd., Ahmedabad	Multi state
4	Nutan Nagarik Sahakari Bank Ltd., Ahmedabad	Multi state
5	Rajkot Nagrik Sahakari Bank Ltd., Ahmedabad	Multi state
6	SBPP Co-operative Bank Ltd., Killa Pardi, Dist Valsad (Gujarat)	
7	Surat Peoples Coop Bank Ltd., Surat, Gujarat	Multi state
8	Amanath Co-operative Bank Ltd., Bangalore	
9	Andhra Pradesh Mahesh Co-Op Urban Bank Ltd., Hyderabad	
10	Indian Mercantile Co-operative Bank Ltd., Lucknow	
11	Abhyudaya Co-operative Bank Ltd., Mumbai	Multi state
12	Apna Sahakari Bank Ltd., Mumbai	Multi state
13	Bassein Catholic Co-operative Bank Ltd., Mumbai	
14	Bharat Co-operative Bank (Mumbai) Ltd., Mumbai	Multi state
15	Bharati Sahakari Bank Ltd., Mumbai	Multi state
16	Bombay Mercantile Co-operative Bank Limited, Mumbai	Multi state
17	Citizen Credit Co-operative Bank Ltd., Mumbai	Multi state
18	Cosmos Co-operative Bank Ltd., Pune	Multi state
19	Dombivli Nagari Sahakari Bank Ltd., Dombivli (East), Maharashtra	Multi state
20	G.P. Parsik Janata Sahakari Bank Ltd., Thane	Multi state
21	Greater Bombay Co-operative Bank Limited, Mumbai	
22	GS Mahanagar Co-operative Bank Ltd., Mumbai	
23	Jalgaon Janata Sahakari Bank Ltd., Jalgaon, Maharashtra	
24	Jalgaon People's Co-operative Bank Ltd., Jalgaon, Maharashtra	Multi state
25	Janakalyan Sahakari Bank Ltd., Mumbai	
26	Janalaxmi Co-operative Bank Ltd., Nashik, Maharashtra	

Sr. No.	Bank Name	Multi-state status
27	Janata Sahakari Bank Ltd., Pune	Multi state
28	Kallappanna Awade Ichalkaranji Janata Sahakari Bank Ltd., Ichalkaranji, Maharashtra	Multi state
29	Kalyan Janata Sahakari Bank Ltd., Kalyan, Maharashtra	Multi state
30	Kapol Co-operative Bank Ltd., Mumbai	Multi state
31	Karad Urban Co-operative Bank Ltd., Karad, Maharashtra	
32	Nagar Urban Co-operative Bank Ltd., Ahmednagar, Maharashtra	Multi state
33	Nasik Merchant's Co-operative Bank Ltd., Nasik, Maharashtra	Multi state
34	New India Co-operative Bank Ltd., Mumbai	
35	NKGSB Co-operative Bank Ltd., Mumbai	Multi state
36	Pravara Sahakari Bank Ltd., Tahasil Rahata, Dist. Ahmednagar, Maharashtra	
37	Punjab & Maharashtra Co-operative Bank Ltd., Mumbai	Multi state
38	Rajarambapu Sahakari Bank Ltd., Dist. Sangli, Maharashtra	
39	Rupee Co-operative Bank Ltd., Pune, Maharashtra	
40	Sangli Urban Co-operative Bank Ltd., Sangli, Maharashtra	
41	Saraswat Co-operative Bank Ltd., Mumbai	Multi state
42	Shamrao Vithal Co-operative Bank Ltd., Mumbai	Multi state
43	Solapur Janata Sahakari Bank Ltd., Solapur, Maharashtra	Multi state
44	Thane Bharat Sahakari Bank Ltd., Thane (W), Maharashtra	
45	TJSB Sahakari Bank Mumbai Thane, Maharashtra	Multi state
46	Vasai Vikas Sahakari Bank Ltd., Vasai (W), Maharashtra	
47	Zoroastrian Co-operative Bank Ltd., Mumbai	Multi state
48	Nagpur Nagrik Sahakari Bank Ltd., Nagpur, Maharashtra	Multi state
49	Shikshak Sahakari Bank Ltd., Nagpur, Maharashtra	
50	The Akola Janata Commercial Co-operative Bank Ltd., Akola, Maharashtra	Multi state
51	The Akola Urban Co-operative Bank Ltd., Akola, Maharashtra	Multi state
52	The Khamgaon Urban Co-operative Bank Ltd., Khamgaon, Maharashtra	Multi state
53	Goa Urban Co-operative Bank Limited, Goa	

Though UCBs are functioning at par with commercial banks, it was observed that UCBs as a group is facing problems. Failure cases are more and frequent. Large percentage of UCBs is considered weak financially. Weaknesses are attributed generally to weak and unprofessional management, dual control of RBI and state govt., incidence of wrong or influenced credit decisions, etc. These are said to be the specific problems contributing to failures of UCBs.

At the same time, it is also observed that UCBs are increasing their business satisfactorily and particularly the bigger UCBs are able to grow fast and compete with commercial banks. Further as an accepted policy of the govt., cooperative movement in the country is a success story in many areas and it has a crucial role in the economy to assist lower income groups.

Failures in UCBs is not new but the two failures of major UCBs; Madhavpura mercantile coop bank in 2001 and Punjab and Maharashtra coop bank getting into trouble in 2019 have raised the seriousness of the issue.

In fact, after the Madhavpura mercantile coop bank episode, the real issues facing the UCBs and its management have been brought out to the front. We can observe that RBI has set up many committees to go into these issues and suggest remedies after the failure of Madhavpura mercantile bank. But these attempts have been proved inefficient and insufficient as seen in PMC bank episode in 2019. Though RBI tried to bring in many changes to improve the management of UCBs and also the supervision on them, it could not implement any effective system to control and safeguard the health of UCBs. PMC bank episode in 2019 is a glaring proof of the failure of control system.

Thus, the issues facing the RBI and govt. were twofold. One issue is the basic weakness existing in the functioning of UCBs due to its constitution under society's acts. The other issue is defining the role of UCBs in the emerging banking structure in the country. It is now important to decide the positioning of UCBs within the present banking structure. Whether they should remain in cooperative sector or they shall be transformed as companies. This is for the reason that there is no difference between UCB and commercial bank in their operations. Hence it is logical to have both of them under same controlling authority. Further the model of coop society is for promoting self-help groups to develop themselves through their combined efforts. But in case of UCBs their main base of resources (deposits) is not from the members but from the public who are not their members. Even the borrowers are nominal members without voting rights. This structure of UCB is illogical as the depositor's interest is not protected nor they have any role in the management.

Report of the High-Powered Committee on Urban Co-operative Banks (UCBs) 2015 (R. Gandhi Committee 2015 recommendations)

This committee has made few recommendations and also some suggestions to improve the working of the UCBs and bring them to new standards so that they can play an effective role in the banking sector and to bring stability in their workings. The main issue facing the UCBs are their weak financials, lack of professional management, ineffective and slow resolution system to deal with failures. Committee recommendations address these issues. The recommendations are also based on the present status of UCBs and how they can be fitted into the banking system of the country. It gives a blue print for the transition of UCBs into the mainstream banking.

The Committee made the following recommendations:

1. *Business size and conversion of MS-UCBs into joint stock banks*: The Committee feels that a business size of ₹ 20,000 crore or more may be the threshold limit beyond which a UCB may be expected to convert to a commercial bank.

2. *Conversion of other UCBs into Small Finance Banks*: As per the Committee smaller UCBs voluntarily willing to convert to SFBs can do so irrespective of the threshold limit provided they fulfil all the eligibility criteria and selection process prescribed by RBI and further provided that the small finance banks licensing window is open.

3. *Issue of fresh licences*: The Committee unanimously recommends that licenses may be issued to financially sound and well-managed co-operative credit societies having a minimum track record of five years which satisfy the regulatory prescriptions set by RBI as licensing conditions.

4. *Board of Management in addition to Board of Directors*: The Committee recommends that the concept of BoM put forward by the Malegam Committee has to be one of the mandatory licensing conditions for issuing licenses to new UCBs and in the expansion of existing UCBs.

5. *Entry Point Norms*: The Committee also feels that licenses may be issued to well-managed co-operative credit societies which satisfy the following capital requirements:

- To operate as a Multi-State UCB—₹ 100 crore
- To operate beyond two districts and as a state level UCB—₹ 50 crore
- To operate as district level UCB (upto 2 districts)—₹ 25 crore
- In case of conversion of co-operative credit societies in unbanked areas and in the North-East, suitable relaxations may be made by RBI.

6. *Depositors as voting members*: It was concluded that depositors ought to have a say on the boards of UCBs. For this, a majority of the board's seats be reserved for depositors by making suitable provisions in the bye-laws.

Suggestions made by the committee:

1. At present, no powers are available with RBI for constituting boards of UCBs, removal of directors, supersession of BoD, auditing of UCBs and winding up and liquidation of UCBs. However, such powers for commercial banks are vested with RBI. There are certain sections in the BR Act, 1949 such as provisions of Section 10A (professional BoD), 10B (removal of a whole-time chairman), 30 (Audit), 44 (winding-up of banks), 44A (amalgamation of banking companies) and 45 (suspension of business) which were not replicated while amending Section 56 of the BR Act, 1949. These amendments can be incorporated in Section 56 of the Act ibid for effective regulation and supervision of UCBs.

2. Resolution Mechanism: As time is of essence in any resolution framework, there is a need to review the existing supervisory action, revisiting existing guidelines on mergers, revision in instructions on restructuring negative net-worth UCBs including revisiting instruments for augmenting capital for UCBs.

   There should be a regulatory set up to provide legal backing for RBI to play a central role in the winding up of the banking business of UCBs without the intervention of the authorities under the co-operative societies' laws. The possibility of winding up the banking business of UCBs by RBI directly by appointing DICGC as the liquidator for liquidating the banking business of a UCB may also be explored.
3. Umbrella Organisation: The Committee recommends that given the importance of the issue RBI may expedite the decision on the structure of the urban co-operative banking system and appropriate Umbrella Organization/s.

(Extracted from report published by RBI)

The main recommendations are with regard to transition of UCBs to commercial banks or to small finance banks, providing for the safeguards to take care of depositors of UCBs and quicker resolution mechanism in case of failures. It also recommended for entry level restrictions for UCBs to ensure the financial strength of UCBs.

The committee made recommendations to set up Board of Management in UCBs to ensure professional management in the bank.

RBI has accepted many recommendations and from 2018 onwards RBI and made desired changes in the workings of UCBs. The following two points which were hindering the transition of UCBs to commercial banks have been resolved by making necessary changes.

1. Transition of UCB into a commercial bank is not feasible as the present guideline of RBI for commercial

bank is ₹ 500 crore capital to start a new bank. This will be very high for most of the present day UCBs. Further at present there is limited scope for UCBs to raise capital. The bigger UCBs may have built up sizeable net worth due to reserves created over the years. But for medium and small sized UCBs it will act as handicap in their transition to commercial banks.

2. UCBs are allowed conversion as Small Finance Banks, but under the existing guidelines UCBs are functioning similar to commercial banks without any restrictions. Small fiancé banks are not universal banks like commercial banks. There are many restrictions on them which are at present not applicable to UCBs. UCBs are not willing to let go the advantages they have at present. One example is priority sector lending prescription of 75% applicable to SFBs. UCBs have presently 40% prescription applicable to them. This will be a major change in the working of UCBs.

The subsequent changes brought in by GOI and RBI to establish UCBs under the banking system and to re-define their role in the banking system are discussed little later.

Business Share of UCBs

UCBs were started in 1889 the progress was not much till 1966. There were 1100 UCBs in 1966. From the year 1966 UCBs came under the purview of the Banking Regulation Act. After this there was good progress in UCB sector. From 1,100 UCBs in 1966, their number went up to 1,941 in March 2003. Thereafter the numbers started coming down gradually to 1534 in 2021. This was mainly due to the fact that 351 UCBs were closed from 1962 to 2018. Many UCBs were also merged with other banks.

Business of UCBs has grown consistently over the years. The following tables show the performance of UCBs from the year 2001 to 2021.

Performance of UCBs—Deposits and Advances

(₹ in crores)

As on March 31	Total No. of UCBs	Deposits	Advances
2001	1618	80840	54389
2002	1854	93069	62060
2003	1941	101546	64880
2004	1926	110256	67930
2005	1872	105021	66874
2006	1853	114060	71641
2007	1813	121391	79733
2008	1770	1399	904
2009	1721	1570	962
2010	1674	1831	1124
2011	1645	2119	1365
2012	1618	2386	1578
2013	1606	2768	1810
2014	1589	3155	1996
2015	1579	3551	2243
2016	1574	3922	2449
2017	1562	4435	2612
2018	1551	4565	2805
2019	1544	4843	3030
2020	1539	5012	3054
2021	1534	5269	3127

Data source: RBI.

We may observe that between the years 2001 to 2021 (in 20 years) the deposits have increased from ₹ 808 bn to ₹ 5269 bn (6.52 times). Advances have gone up from ₹ 544 bn to ₹ 3127 bn (5.74 times).

Balance Sheet of Urban Co-operative Banks (At end-March)

In the year 2021, there were 1534 UCBs in the country and out of which 53 are scheduled urban coop banks and 1481 are non-scheduled urban coop banks.

Table 7.2: Balance Sheet of Urban Co-operative Banks
(At end-March)

(Amount in ₹ crore)

Items	Scheduled UCBs		Non-Scheduled UCBs		All UCBs		Rate of Growth (%)	All UCBs
	2020	2021	2020	2021	2020	2021	2019-20	2020-21
1	2	3	4	5	6	7	8	9
Liabilities								
1) Capital	4,415	4,467	9,696	9,765	14,111	14,233	3.9	0.9
	(1.5)	(1.5)	(2.9)	(2.7)	(2.3)	(2.2)		
2) Reserves and Surplus	14,896	15,836	18,423	21,354	33,319	37,190	-10.6	11.6
	(5.1)	(5.3)	(5.5)	(6.0)	(5.3)	(5.7)		
3) Deposits	2,29,706	2,39,576	2,71,124	2,87,406	5,00,830	5,26,982	3.4	5.2
	(78.9)	(79.5)	(81.4)	(80.7)	(80.3)	(80.1)		
4) Borrowings	5,003	3,748	334	314	5,337	4,062	-1.0	-23.9
	(1.7)	(1.2)	(0.1)	(0.1)	(0.9)	(0.6)		
5) Other Liabilities and Provisions	36,950	37,913	33,518	37,471	70,467	75,385	20.4	7.0
	(12.7)	(12.6)	(10.1)	(10.5)	(11.3)	(11.5)		
Assets								
1) Cash in Hand	1,797	1,676	4,037	4,212	5,835	5,888	8.3	0.9
	(0.6)	(0.6)	(1.2)	(1.2)	(0.9)	(0.9)		
2) Balances with RBI	9,804	11,121	2,792	3,418	12,595	14,539	-8.4	15.4

Items	Scheduled UCBs		Non-Scheduled UCBs		All UCBs		Rate of Growth (%)	All UCBs
	2020	2021	2020	2021	2020	2021	2019-20	2020-21
	(3.4)	(3.7)	(0.8)	(1.0)	(2.0)	(2.2)		
3) Balances with Banks	18,526	21,906	47,719	47,694	66,245	69,600	8.6	5.1
	(6.4)	(7.3)	(14.3)	(13.4)	(10.6)	(10.6)		
4) Money at Call and Short Notice	6,260	5,087	2,135	1,792	8,395	6,879	39.8	-18.1
	(2.2)	(1.7)	(0.6)	(0.5)	(1.3)	(1.0)		
5) Investments	75,175	80,278	86,328	99,872	1,61,504	1,80,150	3.0	11.5
	(25.8)	(26.6)	(25.9)	(28.0)	(26.0)	(27.4)		
6) Loans and Advances	1,41,151	1,43,201	1,64,138	1,69,564	3,05,289	3,12,765	0.7	2.4
	(48.5)	(47.5)	(49.3)	(47.6)	(48.9)	(47.5)		
7) Other Assets	38,257	38,271	25,945	29,760	64,201	68,031	20.8	6.0
	(13.2)	(12.7)	(7.8)	(8.4)	(10.3)	(10.3)		
Total Liabilities/Assets	2,90,970	3,01,540	3,33,094	3,56,311	6,24,064	6,57,851	4.2	5.4
	(100.0)	(100.0)	(100.0)	(100.0)	(100.0)	(100.0)		

Notes: 1. Data for March 2021 are provisional.

2. Figures in parentheses are proportion to total liabilities/assets (in per cent).

3. Components may not add up to the whole due to rounding off.

Source: Off-Site surveillance returns, RBI.

53 scheduled UCBs are the bigger UCBs and many of them are multi-state UCBs. The table below shows business share of scheduled and non-scheduled UCBs.

31-3-2021	Scheduled UCBs (53)		Non-scheduled UCBs (1481)		Total UCBs 1534
	₹ crore	% to total UCBs	₹ crore	% to total UCBs	₹ crore
Total assets	3,01,540	45.84	3,56,311	54.16	6,57,851
deposits	2,39,576	45.46	2,87,406	54.54	5,26,982
advances	1,43,201	45.78	1,69,564	54.22	3,12,765

We may observe that 53 scheduled UCBs hold nearly half (45.84%) of assets of total UCBs. They account for 45.46% of deposits and 45.78% of advances of total UCBs.

Business Share of UCBs in Total Banking Business in the Country

Scheduled commercial banks in the country are the biggest group of banks and they consist of public sector banks, private sector banks, small business banks, payment banks, local area banks, foreign banks and regional rural banks. This group is having over 90% share of banking business in the country. Remaining banks are the UCBs and Rural Coop Banks. The following chart shows the business share of banks in March 2020.

31-3-2020 (₹ in crores)	Assets	Deposits	Advances
Total Banking sector	1,98,98,496	1,52,01,156	1,13,37,453
Scheduled Commercial Banks (SCBs)	1,80,14,425	1,39,75,045	1,03,01,897
Share of SCBs %	90.53	91.93	90.87
Urban coop banks	6,24,064	5,00,830	3,05,289
Share of UCB %	3.14	3.30	2.69
Rural coop banks	12,60,007	7,25,281	7,30,267
Share of RCBs %	6.33	4.77	6.44

We may observe that SCBs account for 90.53% share in total banking assets of the country and UCB share is small just 3.14%. RCB share is 6.33% in total banking assets.

We can observe that in March 2020, UCBs accounted for 3.30% share in deposits and 2.69% share in bank credit.

Though it is a small share, in terms of their reach UCBs play an important role in mobilising deposits from lower income groups and also extends loans mainly to small borrowers.

The Relevance of Urban Coop Banks

Coop banks are working on cooperative principles. This means that the bank is promoted to take care of the financial needs of a group on self-help basis. This group formation may be for any legitimate purpose. It can be on the basis of community, activities, region, etc. Urban coop banks can accept deposits from public but they can give loan assistance to only members of the bank. In this they are different form the commercial banks.

But in practice the member ship of these coop banks is open and even a person who is not a member can become a member and be eligible for loan assistance. Thus, practically urban coop bank can give loan to anyone by making him a nominal member of the bank. Under this arrangement the depositors of the bank and also the borrowers of the bank have no say in the management of the bank. Management is vested with the original members or group who are the promoters of the coop credit society.

As regards the scope of operations they are at par with commercial banks at present. They are allowed to finance agriculture, priority sector, trade, exports, all kinds of personal loans, etc. The deposit schemes are also similar to commercial banks. Generally, UCBs offer higher interest rates on deposits than the commercial banks. Thus, they are in position to attract deposits from the public.

UCBs are also similar to commercial banks as the banking regulations of RBI on matters like maintaining CRR and SLR, credit policy, observing prudential norms for credit (income recognition, asset classification and provisioning), capital adequacy requirements, etc. Most of the larger UCBs are also working with computerised system on core banking platforms and are in a position to provide delivery channels and banking products similar to commercial banks.

Though UCBs are in coop sector the present working of them has made the status of a coop society has become redundant for them. It is not providing them any advantage rather it is hindering their growth. As many coop banks have grown big and became scheduled banks and multi-state coop banks, the original concept of helping some group or segment on self-help basis is no longer pertinent for them. If UCB is looking for growth then it would like to expand its horizon and become a bank at national level. Scheduled bank status and multi-state bank status are the steps in this direction. As UCB aims to get deposits from larger public it will have to project its image as a well-managed and fairly big size bank to instil confidence in the public dealing with it.

Actually, the bigger UCBs are now finding that the tag of a coop bank is not helping them and rather it is acting as a weak identity. This we can observe from the behaviour of larger UCBs and the way they are projecting themselves in the market. The tag of coop bank is a legal necessity and they cannot change it. But they are creating trade names for the bank where the word co-op is not used. The biggest UCB, saraswat coop bank is using the trade name as saraswat bank. Then there is SVC bank (shamrao vithal coop bank), NKGSB bank (NKGSB coop bank), PMC Bank (Punjab and Maharashtra coop bank), etc. Almost all bigger UCBs are using the trade names in their advertisements and communications. This trend clearly shows that the bigger UCBs will be eager to leave behind the UCB tag and become commercial banks.

The top ten urban coop banks and their workings as under:

Saraswat coop bank is biggest UCB in the country with deposits of ₹ 38083 crores and advances of ₹ 25338 crores as at 31-3-2020. Punjab and Maharashtra coop bank which ranked 5th in 2019 has run into trouble this year and RBI has placed it under directions restricting withdrawals by the depositors of the bank. In March 2020, the audited statements of this bank showed negative networth of ₹ 2840 crores.

We may also observe that the net owned funds of all these banks are over ₹ 500 crores, the minimum capital now

As at 31-3-2020

	31/03/2020 (₹ in crores)	Deposits	Advances	Own Funds	Net NPA %	Capital Adequacy %	Branches
1	Saraswat co-op bank Ltd	38083	25338	3522	1.56	14.75	284
2	SVC co-op bank Ltd	16500	11607	1698	1.81	12.96	198
3	Cosmos co-op bank Ltd	15195	11503	1974	7.15	12.30	140
4	Bharat co-op bank Ltd	11529	7853	1252	4.69	13.81	102
5	Punjab and Maharashtra co-op bank Ltd	10727	4472	-(2840)			137
6	Abhyudaya co-op bank Ltd	10838	6654	1380		12.60	111
7	TJSB sahakari bank Ltd	11373	5641	1191	0.46	15.38	136
8	Janata sahakari bank Ltd	8904	5253	998	9.95	12.32	71
9	NKGSB co-op bank Ltd	7876	4904	781	5.09	13.18	109
10	Kalupur commercial co-op bank	7837	4918	1446	0	17.60	56

Source: Annual reports of respective banks.

prescribed for starting a commercial bank. Net npa position of five banks is high now. Kalupur commercial coop bank has zero net npa status.

Urban coop banks as discussed earlier is a weak link in the banking sector due to its unique positioning. Though the cooperative movement is laudable and has its benefits, UCBs are losing the relevance of coop principles in their growth and progress. Their future is definitely in commercial banking which is more suitable in the present conditions.

This aspect of the urban banks has engaged the attention of both GOI and RBI. There were many committees set up in the past to consider the future of UCBs and transition of them to commercial banking.

We can compare the business figures of these top UCBs with private sector banks. The table below shows the workings of top 10 UCBs and bottom ten private sector commercial banks.

Deposits, Advances and Assets of top ten UCBs and bottom ten Private Sector Banks (As on March 31, 2019)

(Amount in ₹ crore)

Top 10 UCBs	Deposits	Advances	Total Assets	Bottom 10 Private Sector Banks	Deposits	Advances	Total Assets
Saraswat Co-op Bank	36014	25797	50026	RBL Bank	58394	54308	80358
Cosmos Co-op Bank	15353	11599	19650	Karnataka Bank	68452	54828	79045
Shamrao Vithal Co-op Bank	16263	11500	19378	Karur Vysya Bank	59867	48580	69340
Bharat Co-operative Bank	11882	8575	14143	City Union Bank	38447	32673	45258
TJSB Sahakari Bank	10700	5660	13486	Tamilnad Mercantile Bank	35136	26487	40532
Abhyudaya Co-op Bank	11022	5798	12808	DCB Bank	28435	23568	35547
Punjab & Maharashtra Co-op Bank	11617	8383	11660	Lakshmi Vilas Bank	29279	20103	33046
Janata Sahakari Bank	8713	5238	10172	Catholic Syrian Bank	15123	10615	16911
Kalupur commercial co-op bank	6939	4676	9479	Dhanlaxmi Bank	10603	6289	11798

Top 10 UCBs	Deposits	Advances	Total Assets	Bottom 10 Private Sector Banks	Deposits	Advances	Total Assets
NKGSB Co-op Bank	7601	5251	8831	Nainital Bank	7286	3515	8101

Note: Top and bottom banks are based on their total asset size.
*The data is extracted from annual reports of the banks

The above table provides an interesting study. In this top 10 urban coop banks and bottom 10 private sector commercial banks (there are only 21 private sector commercial banks) are compared in terms of total assets of the banks. We can observe that saraswat coop bank is bigger than 7 private sector commercial banks. The second and third ranked UCBs (cosmos bank & svc bank) are bigger in assets size than 3 private sector commercial banks.

Failures of UCBs

As many of smaller UCBs are financially weak or mismanaged, failures are a persistent problem with UCBs. Since UCBs are under banking regulation act and are under the supervisory control RBI, failure of number of UCBs on regular basis is a matter of concern. This is mainly attributed to dual control on UCBs and poor professionalism in smaller UCBs.

RBI has the authority to conduct inspections of these banks and call for returns from them. But it appears that RBI supervision on them is ineffective. This is leading to non-detection of incipient weaknesses and timely corrective actions could not be enforced on them. The main sufferers are the depositors of these banks as they have no recourse. The deposit insurance scheme is awfully inadequate at ₹ one lac per depositor (now increased to ₹ 5 lacs).

At present when an UCB is in crisis, RBI firstly puts some restrictions on the bank. These are called the directions of RBI under section 35a of Banking Regulation Act, 1949. Mainly it is restricting withdrawals by depositors by prescribing maximum withdrawal limit, and restriction on bank to sanction fresh loans. Such action is aimed at to avoid run on the bank and to gain time to study the possibilities of turning the bank into health and avoid closure. But it is tedious process and in the

meantime the depositors are put to inconveniences as they could not use their money. It creates economic hardship for them. They also do not know about the safety of their money. There is also distinct possibility of their losing money.

Resolution becomes difficult if the problem is due to mismanagement or frauds. Resolution will also depend on the size of the bad loans and misappropriations as percentage to the total working of the bank. If it is high then saving the bank may not be feasible.

RBI will consider whether the bank can be saved by any means and also examines whether the UCB can be merged with any other bank. At this stage since the UCB is a society registered under societies act, state govt. is required to be involved in the process of resolution. If there is no scope to revive the UCB or its merger with another bank, RBI may have to finally cancel the banking licence issued to the UCB. Thereafter the UCB shall have to be liquidated as per the provisions of the society's act of the state.

The depositors in such case shall get the deposit insurance cover upto ₹ 5 lacs per depositor and the depositors may get refund of their deposits depending on the liquidation process and depending on the amount the liquidator is able to realise by disposing the assets.

It is generally experienced that the resolution is long drawn process, as by law, only the state govt. can take necessary actions in the matter and RBI cannot act on its own. This delays the process sometimes over 10-15 years or even more.

MOUs between RBI and State Govts.

Recognising the importance of urban co-operative banks in providing banking services to the middle and lower income group of people, the Reserve Bank drafted a Vision Document for UCBs in March 2005, to address the problem of dual control which is inhibiting RBI's ability to handle the resolution of the weak UCBs. The vision document envisages close cooperation between RBI and state govts. by way of signing a memorandum of understanding (MOU) between state govts. and RBI and between RBI and GOI (for multi-state UCBs).

At present, as per provisions of the State Cooperative Societies Act and also the BR Act 1949, the Reserve Bank is not empowered to take action against the management of an urban cooperative bank, whereas in respect of commercial banks it has the authority. MOU provides a mechanism for resolution and the State Governments may agree to take immediate action on the requisitions of RBI for supersession of the Board of Directors, appointment of liquidators, for removal of CEO/ Chairman of a bank, enhancing quality of HR and IT resources in the UCBs, as required by RBI.

After the state govt. signs the MOU, Task Force for Cooperative Urban Banks (TAFCUBs) is set up in states. It is formed with the RBI director in the state as the chairman and the registrar of coop societies (RCS) of the state as the vice chairman and also it will have representatives of other interested agencies as members. TAFCUBs will make its recommendations regarding the UCBs in general and also on individual UCB, to the state govt. for approval of the proposed actions. This mechanism thus will ensure quick responses to the issues faced by the UCBs. This will also speed up the resolution mechanism for weak UCBs.

It is informed that so far 23 State Governments and Central Government (in case of multi-State UCBs) have signed the Memorandums of Understanding (MOUs) with the Reserve Bank covering 98.6 per cent of the total number of the UCBs representing 99.2 per cent of deposits of the sector. The State level Task Force for Cooperative Urban Banks (TAFCUBs) have been set up in these states to identify the potentially viable and non-viable UCBs in the State and to chart out the revival path and non-disruptive exit route for the UCBs.

The process of merger and amalgamation:

RBI generally encourages mergers of weak UCBs with the strong and bigger banks. This is considered to protect the depositors of the UCB in duress.

The application for merger giving the proposed scheme has to be submitted by the acquirer bank to the Registrar of Cooperative Societies (RCS)/Central Registrar of Co-

operative Societies (CRCS) and a copy of the proposal is simultaneously forwarded to the Reserve Bank along with certain specified information. The Reserve Bank examines the proposals and places the same before an expert group for screening and recommendations. On evaluation, if the proposal is found to be suitable, the Reserve Bank issues no objection certificate (NOC) to the RCS/CRCS and the banks concerned. RCS/CRCS, being the authority vested with the responsibility of administering the Co-operative Societies Act, then issues the order of amalgamation of the weak UCB with the acquirer bank.

The chart given below gives the information about mergers of UCBs state wise from 2004 to 2020. In the last 15 years 136 UCBs were merged with other banks.

	States	Nos.
1	Punjab	1
2	Telangana	2
3	Uttarakhand	2
4	Uttar Pradesh	2
5	Chhattisgarh	2
6	Rajasthan	3
7	Karnataka	4
8	Andhra Pradesh	12
9	Gujarat	35
10	Maharashtra	73
	Total	136

Source: RBI.

Classification of UCBs on Deposit Base

At present UCBs are classified into two categories: Tier-I and Tier-II categories as under

Tier-I UCBs are defined as:

(a) deposit base below ₹ 100 crore operating in a single district, or deposit base below ₹ 100 crore operating in more than one district, provided that the branches of the bank are in contiguous districts, and deposits and advances of branches in one district separately constitute at least 95 per cent of the total deposits and advances, respectively;

(b) deposit base below ₹ 100 crore, with branches originally in a single district which subsequently became multi-district in their operations due to a re-organisation of the district.

Tier-II UCBs—All other UCBs are defined as Tier-II UCBs

The position of business of Tier-I and Tier-II UCBs at the end of year 31st March 2021 is given in the table below.

Table 7.3: Tier-wise Distribution of Urban Co-operative Banks (At end-March 2021)

(Amount in ₹ crore)

Tier Type	Number of Banks		Deposits		Advances		Total Assets	
	Number	% to Total	Amount	% to Total	Amount	% to Total	Amount	% to Total
1	2	3	4	5	6	7	8	9
Tier-I	846	55.1	33,854	6.4	19,188	6.1	44,120	6.7
Tier-II	688	44.9	4,93,128	93.6	2,93,577	93.9	6,13,731	93.3
All UCBs	1,534	100.0	5,26,982	100.0	3,12,765	100.0	6,57,851	100.0

Note: Data are provisional.

Source: Off-site surveillance returns, RBI.

We can observe that Tier-II UCBs which are 688 in numbers account for 93.6% deposits, 93.9% in advances and the assets are 93.3% of total UCB sector.

Capital Adequacy of UCBs

Table 7.4: Component-wise Capital Adequacy of UCBs (At end-March)

(Amount in ₹ crore)

	Scheduled UCBs		Non-Scheduled UCBs		All UCBs	
	2020	2021	2020	2021	2020	2021
1. Capital Funds	13,407	13,794	25,408	27,610	38,815	41,404
i) Tier-I Capital	7,521	8,000	22,009	24,011	29,530	32,011
ii) Tier-II Capital	5,886	5,794	3,399	3,600	9,285	9,393

2. Risk-Weighted Assets	1,42,573	1,45,767	1,75,015	1,68,622	3,17,588	3,14,388
3. CRAR (1 as % of 2)	9.4	9.5	14.5	16.4	12.2	13.2
Of which:						
Tier-I	5.3	5.5	12.6	14.2	9.3	10.2
Tier-II	4.1	4.0	2.0	2.1	2.9	3.0

Source: Off-site returns, RBI.

Capital adequacy ratio of all UCBs as at March 2021 was 13.2% which is good and as per the present requirements. But the bigger scheduled UCBs have lower ratio at 9.5% as compared to the present requirement of 11.5% CRAR.

NPA Position of UCBs

The following table gives NPA position of UCBs:

Table 7.5: Non-Performing Assets of UCBs (At end-March)

Sr. No.	Items	Scheduled UCBs		Non-Scheduled UCBs		All UCBs	
		2019-20	2020-21	2019-20	2020-21	2019-20	2020-21
1	2	3	4	5	6	7	8
1	Gross NPAs (₹ crore)	13,779	14,785	18,443	21,674	32,222	36,459
2	Gross NPA Ratio (%)	9.8	10.3	11.3	12.8	10.6	11.7
3	Net NPAs (₹ crore)	5,051	5,264	8,167	7,981	13,217	13,245
4	Net NPA Ratio (%)	3.8	3.9	5.3	5.1	4.6	4.6
5	Provisioning (₹ crore)	8,728	9,521	10,276	13,693	19,004	23,214
6	Provisioning Coverage Ratio (%)	63.4	64.4	55.7	63.2	59.0	63.7

Note: Data for 2020-21 are provisional.
Source: Off-site surveillance returns, RBI.

In March 2021, gross NPA of all UCBs was 11.7% with net NPA of 4.6% which are quite high. In case of scheduled UCBs it was; gross NPA at 10.3% and net NPA at 3.9% which is slightly better but still considered as high.

UCBs under the Directions of RBI

We have earlier discussed that RBI places UCBs which are identified as weak and when there is threat of run on these UCBs, such UCBs are placed on moratorium with some directions to be followed in their operations. RBI from time to time undertakes this exercise and such directions will continue till such time a final decision is made on the future of the UCBs concerned. The final decisions may be either merger with some other bank or closure of the UCB. In such cases the banking licence issued earlier to the UCB will be cancelled by RBI. With the cancellation of licence UCB cannot continue functions as bank.

There were many UCBs which were merged or closed during past many years. In case of closures the process takes long time as the liquidator takes over to liquidate the assets and distribute the recovered amount to the depositors. There may be many UCBs under closure and the process is still continuing. It is difficult to get information on those banks.

However, there are many UCBs which are still under the directions from RBI pending for decision on their final fate. The following table gives a list of such banks. However, this list may not be the complete list. We have made our best attempt to collect information on such UCBs and they are mentioned in the table.

Generally, RBI places UCBs under directions for a period varying from three months to six months. During this period the banks shall have to work with the restrictions with a purpose to revive the bank and bring it back to health. At the end of the period RBI conducts review to decide the future course of action. In case the financials are improving then RBI may extend the period to help the bank to get the weaknesses removed and return back to health. When the bank becomes healthy RBI will withdraw its directions issued earlier on those banks and allows them to resume normal functions (see Table 7.7).

Depending on the individual status of the bank RBI allows time to the bank if there is an attempt to merge the bank with stronger bank. If RBI finds that there is no chance of revival or merger, and the bank remains weak, RBI then cancels the banking licence issued to the bank and the bank will then be liquidated (see Table 7.8).

The list of 25 banks presently under the directions is given in the Table 7.6 below:

These UCBs were placed under directions by RBI in the last few years and the directions imposing certain restrictions are still continuing on them. They are listed below:

Table 7.6

	Name of the UCB	Present position
1	Rupee Co-operative Bank, Pune	The RBI imposed directions on Rupee Cooperative Bank on February 22, 2013. Reserve Bank of India, as per the directive DOR. MON/D-10/12.22.218/2021-22 dated May 28, 2021, directs that the aforesaid Directions shall continue to apply to the bank till August 31, 2021 subject to review. RBI has further extended the directions to continue on the bank till February 28, 2022 subject to review.
2	The Vaish Co-operative Commercial Bank Ltd., New Delhi	Reserve Bank of India, issued directions to the bank by the Directive dated August 28, 2015. The directions shall continue to apply to the bank for a further period of three months from February 09, 2021 to May 08, 2021 subject to review.
3	The Maratha Sahakari Bank Ltd., Mumbai, Maharashtra	The Maratha Sahakari Bank Ltd. was placed under directions from close of business on August 31, 2016 vide directive dated August 31, 2016. Directions shall continue to apply to the bank till February 28, 2022 as per the directive DOR. MON/D-49/12.22.140/2021-22 dated November 29, 2021.
4	Kapol Co-operative Bank, Mumbai	The Mumbai-based Kapol Cooperative Bank was placed under directions on March 31, 2017. Directions shall continue to apply to the bank till April 30, 2022 as per the directive DOR. MON.D-43/12.22.111/2021-22 dated October 27, 2021.
5	The City Co-operative Bank, Mumbai	The City Cooperative Bank, the Mumbai-based bank was placed under directions on April 17, 2018. Directions shall continue to apply to the bank till January 16, 2022 as per the directive DOR. MON.D-42/12.22.039/2021-22 dated October 14, 2021, subject to review.
6	Padmashri Dr. Vitthalrao Vikhe Patil Co-operative Bank Ltd., Nashik, Maharashtra	Reserve Bank of India, had issued directions to the bank, from the close of business on May 19, 2018. These directions shall continue to apply to the bank for a further period of three months from December 18, 2021 to March 17, 2022, subject to review.

7	The Needs of Life Co-operative Bank, Mumbai	The Mumbai-based bank was placed under directions from October 29, 2018. The direction on the Needs of Life Co-op Bank Ltd., Mumbai shall continue to apply to the bank for a further period of six months from November 01, 2020 to April 30, 2021 and as per the recent order, this direction has been extended further until October 31, 2021.
8	The Adoor Co-operative Urban Bank Ltd., Adoor, Kerala	The Reserve Bank of India issued Directions dated November 02, 2018, from close of business on November 9, 2018. On 9-12-2021 RBI continued it for a further period of three months, from December 10, 2021 to March 09, 2022, subject to review.
9	Sikar Urban Co-operative Bank Ltd., Sikar, Rajasthan	Bank was placed under Directions from close of business on November 09, 2018. The order is now continued for a further period of three months from December 10, 2021 to March 09, 2022, vide Directive dated December 09, 2021, subject to review.
10	Bidar Mahila Urban Co-operative Bank Ltd., Bidar, Karnataka	Reserve Bank of India issued Directive dated February 21, 2019, on Bidar Mahila Urban Co-operative Bank Ltd. It shall continue to apply to the bank for a further period of six months from September 01, 2021 to February 28, 2022, subject to review.
11	The Mudhol Co-operative Bank Limited, Mudhol, Dist. Bagalkot, Karnataka	The Reserve Bank of India issued Directions vide Directive dated April 2, 2019. Directions are continuing Vide Directive DOR.CO.AID.No.D-02/12.23.094/2020-21 dated April 05, 2021, for a further period of six months from July 08, 2021 to January 07, 2022, subject to review. The directions shall continue to apply to the bank for a further period of six months from July 08, 2021 to January 07, 2022, subject to review.
12	Millath Co-operative Bank Ltd., Davangere, Karnataka	Reserve Bank of India issued Directive dated April 26, 2019, to Millath Co-operative Bank Ltd. The directions shall continue to apply to the bank for a further period of three months from February 08, 2022 to May 07, 2022, subject to review.
13	Shri Anand Co-operative Bank Ltd., Chinchawad, Pune, Maharashtra	Bank was placed under directions from close of business on June 25, 2019, vide Directive No. DCBS.CO.BSD-I/D-16/12.22.474/2018-19 dated June 21, 2019. Directions shall continue to apply to the bank till February 24, 2022 as per the directive DOR.MON.D-48/12.22.474/2021-22 dated November 24, 2021, subject to review.

14	Punjab and Maharashtra Cooperative Bank (PMC), Mumbai	The Reserve Bank of India (RBI) imposed restrictions on the Punjab and Maharashtra Cooperative Bank (PMC) on September 24, 2019. This bank which was among the top 10 urban cooperative banks, was placed under an RBI administrator on September 2019 for six months due to massive under-reporting of dud loans. On 25-01-2022 GOI approved the amalgation of this bank with Unity Small Finance Bank. (Details of this UCB is discussed in chapter 2 of this book.)
15	Guru Raghavendra Sahakara (co-operative) Bank Niyamitha Bengaluru-based	RBI placed withdrawal limit of ₹ 35,000 per account on bank's customers in January 2020. The central bank allowed the depositors to withdraw only ₹ 35,000 per month for six months. The ceiling was later raised to ₹ 1 lakh. The Reserve Bank of India has extended the Directions for a further period of six months from July 11, 2021 to January 10, 2022, subject to review.
16	People's Co-operative Bank Ltd., Kanpur, Uttar Pradesh	On June 11, 2020 the RBI issued directions to the People's Co-operative Bank Ltd., Kanpur for a period of six months from December 11, 2020 to June 10, 2021, subject to review. RBI has further been extended for a period of three (03) months from December 11, 2021 to March 10, 2022 vide directive order DOR.MON.D-52/12.28.059/2021-22 dated December 08, 2021.
17	Mantha Urban Cooperative Bank Ltd., Mantha District: Jalna, Maharashtra	Reserve Bank of India (RBI) has issued certain Directions to Mantha Urban Cooperative Bank Ltd., Mantha District: Jalna, Maharashtra, as from the close of business on November 17, 2020. The Reserve Bank of India has now further extended the Directions for a period of two months from December 17, 2021 to February 16, 2022.
18	Deccan Urban Co-operative Bank, Karnataka	Bank has been put under restriction by Reserve Bank of India for a period of six months from the close of business on February 19, 2021 and are subject to review. These directions shall continue to apply to the bank for a further period of six months from August 20, 2021 to February 19, 2022, subject to review.
19	Garha Co-operative Bank Ltd., Guna	The Reserve Bank of India (RBI) vide Directive dated February 23, 2021 has issued certain Directions to Garha Co-operative Bank Ltd., Guna, whereby, as from the close of business on February 24, 2021. The directions shall continue to apply to the bank for a further period of three months from November 25, 2021 to February 24, 2022, subject to review.

20	Independence Co-operative Bank Limited, Nashik	Reserve Bank of India (RBI) vide Directive Ref. No. DoS. CO.UCBs-West/D-2/12.07.005/2020-21 dated February 09, 2021, has issued certain Directions to Independence Cooperative Bank Limited, Nashik, from the close of business on February 10, 2021. These directions shall continue to apply to the bank for a further period of two months from January 11, 2022 to March 10, 2022, subject to review.
21	Sarjeraodada Naik Shirala Sahakari Bank Ltd., Shirala, Dist. Sangli, Maharashtra	Reserve Bank of India (RBI) vide Directive Ref. No. DoS. CO.UCBs-West/D-1/12.07.157/2020-21 dated February 03, 2021 has issued certain directions to Sarjeraodada Naik Shirala Sahakari Bank Ltd., Shirala, as from the close of business on February 03, 2021. These directions shall continue to apply to the bank till March 03, 2022 as per the directive DOR. MON/D-57/12.07.157/2021-22 dated December 30, 2021, subject to review.
22	The Laxmi Cooperative Bank Limited, Solapur	Reserve Bank of India (RBI) vide Directive DoS.Co.UCBs-West/S1910/12.07.005/2021-22 dated November 12, 2021, has issued certain Directions to The Laxmi Cooperative Bank Limited, Solapur, from the close of business on November 12, 2021. The bank will continue to undertake banking business with restrictions. These directions shall remain in force for a period of six months from the close of business on November 12, 2021 and are subject to review.
23	Babaji Date Mahila Sahakari Bank Ltd., Yavatmal	Reserve Bank of India vide Directive Ref. No. NGP.DOS. SSM-2 No.S-817/15.04.168/2021-22 dated November 08, 2021, has issued certain Directions to Babaji Date Mahila Sahakari Bank Ltd., Yavatmal. These directions shall remain in force for a period of six months from the close of business on November 8, 2021 and are subject to review.
24	The Seva Vikas Cooperative Bank Limited, Pune	Reserve Bank of India vide Directive Ref. No. DoS. CO.NSUCBs-West/D-1/12.22.252/2021-22 dated October 12, 2021, has issued certain Directions to The Seva Vikas Co-operative Bank Limited, Pune. These directions shall remain in force for a period of six months from the close of business on October 12, 2021 and are subject to review.

25	Indian Mercantile Cooperative Bank Ltd., Lucknow	Reserve Bank of India (RBI) vide Directive Ref. No. DoS. CO.OCCD/185569/12.28.007/2021-22 dated January 28, 2022, has issued certain Directions to Indian Mercantile Cooperative Bank Ltd., Lucknow. These directions shall remain in force for a period of six months from the close of business on January 28, 2022 and are subject to review.

Following UCBs were put under directions by RBI during last few years, and subsequently as their working positions improved, RBI removed the restrictions imposed on them and they are allowed to function normally.

Table 7.7

1	Amanath Cooperative Bank Ltd., Bengaluru	Reserve Bank of India issued directive dated April 1, 2013. RBI withdraws with effect from January 3, 2020, All Inclusive Directions issued to Amanath Co-operative Bank Limited, Bengaluru.
2	U.P. Civil Secretariat Primary Co-operative Bank Ltd., Lucknow	The bank has been under directions since September 25, 2018 vide directive dated September 19, 2018. On 10-12-2020, Reserve Bank of India (RBI) has lifted restrictions on the bank.
3	Sri Bharathi Co-operative Urban Bank Ltd., Hyderabad	The Reserve Bank of India issued directions on January 02, 2019. RBI withdraws with effect from March 19, 2020. All inclusive directions issued to Sri Bharathi Co-operative Urban Bank Ltd., Hyderabad.
4	Youth Development Cooperative Bank, Kolhapur	Youth Development Cooperative Bank. The Kolhapur-based bank was placed under directions on January 4, 2019. Reserve Bank of India, withdraws with effect from April 05, 2021, All-Inclusive Directions issued to Youth Development Co-operative Bank Limited.

5	Hindu Co-operative Bank Limited, Pathankot, Punjab	Reserve Bank of India had, issued Directions to Hindu Cooperative Bank Limited, from the close of business on March 25, 2019. Reserve Bank of India, on being satisfied, withdraws with effect from October 14, 2021, the said directions issued to Hindu Cooperative Bank Limited.
6	Kerala Mercantile Cooperative Bank Ltd., Kozhikode, Kerala	The Reserve Bank of India, vide directive dated May 29, 2019 has placed the Kerala Mercantile Cooperative Bank Ltd. under Directions. RBI withdraws with effect from August 28, 2020, the said Directions so issued to Kerala Mercantile Cooperative Bank Ltd., Kozhikode.
7	Kolikata Mahila Cooperative Bank Limited, Kolkata, West Bengal	Reserve Bank of India (RBI) has issued certain Directions to Kolikata Mahila Cooperative Bank Limited, from the close of business on July 9, 2019. Reserve Bank, on being satisfied withdraws from April 10, 2021, the said directions so issued to Kolikata Mahila Cooperative Bank Limited, Kolkata, West Bengal.

Some UCBs which were put under directions earlier but subsequently their banking: licences were withdrawn in the years 2020 and 2021 asking the banks to close down and go into liquidation process. They are as under:

Table 7.8

1	Mapusa Urban Co-operative Bank of Goa Ltd., Goa	The Reserve Bank of India issued directions under Section 35A to The Mapusa Urban Co-Operative Bank of Goa Ltd., Goa vide Directive dated July 24, 2015. On 16-4-2020 licence was cancelled by RBI.
2	CKP Cooperative Bank, Mumbai	The 103-year old cooperative bank was put under directions on May 2, 2012. Reserve Bank of India (RBI) has canceled the license of CKP Cooperative bank on 2nd May 2020.

3	Karad Janata Sahakari Bank, Karad, Maharashtra	The bank was placed under directions on November 7, 2017. The Reserve Bank of India (RBI) has, vide order dated December 7, 2020 cancelled the licence of the bank to carry on banking business, with effect from the close of business on December 7, 2020.
4	Shivajirao Bhosale Sahakari Bank, Pune	RBI placed the Pune-based bank under directions in May 2019. The Reserve Bank of India (RBI) has cancelled the licence and said the bank ceases to carry on banking business, with effect from the close of business on May 31, 2021.
5	Bhagyodaya Friends Urban Co-operative Bank Ltd., Warud, Dist. Amravati, Maharashtra	Reserve Bank of India, had issued directions from the close of business on January 17, 2019. The RBI has, vide its order dated April 20, 2021, cancelled the licence of Bhagyodaya Friends Urban Co-operative Bank. Consequently, the bank ceased to carry on banking activities, with effect from 22nd April 2021.
6	Dr. Shivajirao Patil Nilangekar Urban Co-operative Limited Nilanga, Dist. Latur, Maharashtra	Reserve Bank of India, had issued directions from the close of business on February 16, 2019. The Reserve Bank of India (RBI) has, vide order dated July 08, 2021, cancelled the license of the bank. Consequently, the bank ceases to carry on banking business, with effect from the close of business on July 14, 2021.
7	Shivam Sahakari Bank, Ichalkaranji, Kolhapur	Shivam Sahakari Bank was placed under directions on May 19, 2018, vide order dated January 28, 2021 RBI cancelled the licence of the bank. Consequently, the bank ceases to carry on banking business, with effect from the close of business on January 29, 2021.
8	United Co-operative Bank Limited, Bagnan, West Bengal	Reserve Bank of India had issued Directions from the close of business on July 18, 2018. In May 2021, The Reserve Bank of India cancelled the licence of the bank.

9	Vasantdada Nagari Sahakari Bank Ltd., Osmanabad, Maharashtra	Reserve Bank of India, had issued directions from the close of business on November 13, 2017. The Reserve Bank of India (RBI) has, vide order dated January 08, 2021 cancelled the licence of the bank to carry on banking business, with effect from the close of business on January 11, 2021.
10	Karnala Nagari Sahakari Bank Ltd., Panvel, Raigad, Maharashtra	The Reserve Bank of India vide directive DoS.CO.UCBs-West/D-1/12.07.157/2019-20 dated June 15, 2020 had placed Karnala Nagari Sahakari Bank Ltd., under Directions from the close of business on June 15, 2020. Reserve Bank of India has, vide order dated August 09, 2021 cancelled the licence of Karnala Nagari Sahakari Bank Ltd., Panvel (District - Raigad), Maharashtra. Consequently, the bank ceases to carry on banking business, with effect from the close of business on August 13, 2021.
11	The Madgaum Urban Cooperative Bank based in South Goa	RBI first imposed sanctions on TMUCB in 2014-15. This UCB tried to merge with the Thane Janata Sahakari Bank (TJSB) but it did not work out. Reserve Bank of India has, vide order dated July 27, 2021 cancelled the licence of The Madgaum Urban Cooperative Bank Limited, Margao, Goa. Consequently, the bank ceases to carry on banking business, with effect from the close of business on July 29, 2021.

Control on UCBs Working

It is observed that the weakness in the working of UCBs is mainly due to mismanagements particularly in the area of sanction of loans. UCBs are getting into trouble mainly due to inept handling of loan sanctioning. Many committees have pointed out this aspect and have recommended that professionalism shall be induced into the management. Coop banks are managed by board of directors elected amongst the members/promoters who may not have the necessary competence. The process of UCBs chief executive's appointment is also felt to be weak. Thus, the credit decisions of UCBs are a weak area in their operation. Many a times the credit decisions are taken due to extraneous considerations.

It was felt that there shall be a professionally competent committee in the UCB to look into the operational areas of the bank. Idea of creating board of management (BoM) comprising of experienced members was mooted for the UCBs which shall work under the overall supervision of board of directors of the bank. This idea was first mooted in the report of Y.H. Malegam committee (2011) and R. Gandhi committee (2015) supported it and made recommendation for making it mandatory for UCBs. Similarly, the appointment of chief executive officer of the UCB shall be based on some criteria suitable for the job.

It was learnt that UCBs were not happy about the concept of BoM in the bank. It was probably considered as dilution of the power of board of directors.

RBI has decided to introduce BoM in UCBs and issued Guidelines on Board of Management for Primary (Urban) Co-operative Banks on December 31, 2019. RBI's guidelines state as under:

1. *Objective*

Under the present legal framework, the Board of Directors of a UCB perform both the executive and supervisory roles and has the responsibility to oversee the functioning of UCB as a co-operative society as well as its functions as a bank. Since UCBs are accepting public deposits, it is imperative that a separate mechanism be put in place to protect the interests of depositors. Accordingly, it is proposed to implement a Board of Management consisting of members with special knowledge and practical experience in banking to facilitate professional management and focussed attention to banking related activities of UCBs.

2. *Constitution of Board of Management (BoM)*

2.1 There shall be a Board of Management (BoM) in every UCB with deposit size of ₹ 100 crore and above in addition to the Board of Directors. BoM shall be constituted by the Board of Directors (BoD) of such UCBs within a period of one year from the date of the circular. In addition to the functions as furnished in Para 4 below, the BoD may delegate such powers as deemed necessary for the proper functioning of the bank.

2.2 Other UCBs including Salary Earners' Banks may also constitute BoM voluntarily. For the UCBs with deposit size of ₹ 100 crore and above, constitution of BoM shall be a mandatory condition for opening of new branches/expansion of area of operation.

3. *Functions of Board of Management*

The BoM shall exercise oversight over the banking related functions of the UCBs, assist the BoD on formulation of the policy and any other related matters specifically delegated to it by the Board for proper functioning of the bank. The functions of the BoM shall include the following:

(i) Rendering expert advice on all proposals being put up to the Board or any Committee of the Board for sanction of loans.

(ii) Recommending action for recovery of NPAs, One Time Settlement or Compromise Settlement and assisting the Board in monitoring the same.

(iii) Overseeing the management of funds and borrowings in the bank.

(iv) Recommending proposals for investment of bank's funds as per the board approved policy.

(v) Oversight on internal controls and systems and risk management in the bank.

(vi) Exercising oversight on implementation of computerisation, technology adoption and other incidental issues in the bank.

(vii) Overseeing internal audit and inspection functions including compliance.

(viii) Oversight on complaint redressal system.

(ix) Assisting the Board in formulation of policies related to banking functions, illustratively loan policy, investment policy, recovery policy, ALM and Risk management, etc. to ensure that policies are in tune with RBI guidelines.

(x) Any other responsibility as may be delegated to it by the BoD.

NB: In the event where the BoD differs with the recommendations of BoM, it shall do so by recording, in writing, the reasons thereof.

As per RBI guidelines the size of BoM shall be minimum five and maximum twelve. The CEO would be a non-voting member. RBI has also fixed the qualification criteria for the members of BoM as practical experience in accountancy, banking, economics, finance, law, industry, rural economy and few other related fields. Members of board of the UCB can also be placed in BoM if they are qualified but such members shall not be more than 50% of BoM strength.

RBI has issued guidelines that UCBs having deposits of ₹ 100 crore and above shall obtain prior approval of RBI for appointment of CEO. RBI shall have power over BoM and CEO as provided in the guideline as under:

4. *RBI's powers over BoM and CEO*

RBI shall have powers to remove any member of BoM and/or the CEO if the person is found to be not meeting the criteria prescribed by RBI or acting in a manner detrimental to the interests of the bank or its depositors or both. The BoD shall seek concurrence from RBI before removing any member of the BoM/accepting the resignation tendered by any member of the BoM. RBI shall also have powers to supersede the BoM if the functioning of BoM is found unsatisfactory. After removal of the member of BoM or CEO or supersession of BoM, BoD shall appoint a new member or CEO or constitute a new BoM as the case may be within a period of three months. As an interim arrangement, BoD may carry out the functions of BoM.

RBI guideline requires UCBs to make suitable amendments to their bye-laws, with the approval of the General Body and

Registrar of Co-operative Societies to provide for constitution of BoM, in addition to the BoD.

It may be noted that due to the constitution of UCBs as cooperative society governed by the state societies acts, and in the absence of specific provisions in the banking regulation act 1949, the control of RBI on UCBs are not at par with commercial banks. To overcome the lacunae, RBI has evolved firstly a system of signing MOUs with state govts. which enables immediate response from state govt. on resolution matters in respect of UCBs. Now with the present guidelines on the formation of BoM and with the authority over BoM and CEO of the UCBs, RBI will be better equipped to supervise UCBs on same line as of commercial banks.

Single Party Limit and Priority Sector Lending by UCBs

Prior to 13 March 2020, UCBs were permitted to have exposures up to 15% and 40% of their capital funds to a single borrower and a group of borrowers, respectively. It was observed that Punjab and Maharashtra coop bank which is in difficulty now is mainly due to the fact that this bank has taken a very big exposure to one HDIL group. As the urban coop banks are positioned as banks to function for the benefits of lower income group in the society, their sanctioning big loans is not in sync with their role in the economy. Further UCBs being small banks, any large exposure to single borrower or group will weaken the bank in case of default by this single borrower. In view of this RBI has now decided to reduce the existing exposure limit fixed for UCBs mentioned above.

Similarly, the urban coop banks are to be discouraged from sanctioning big loans, and in their own interest they shall have to be directed to give smaller loans to larger number of borrowers in order to spread the credit risk. Hence RBI has now proposed to increase priority sector lending targets for UCBs.

Priority sector lending targets for UCBs prior to 13 March 2020 were 40% same as commercial banks. Whereas in case of newly created Small Finance Banks in commercial sector it has been fixed at 75%. This was one of the reasons for UCBs not keen to convert themselves as Small Finance Banks. In order to encourage UCBs to become small finance banks, RBI has increased the priority sector lending targets to 75%, same as small finance banks. RBI is also proposing to start on-tap scheme for issue of Small Finance Bank licences.

On 13 March 2020, RBI (vide RBI/2019-20/171 DOR (PCB). BPD.Cir.No.10/13.05.000/2019-20 March 13, 2020) issued fresh guidelines to UCBs on single party and group exposure limits, priority sector targets and target for small loans as under:

1. *Prudential Exposure Limits*

1.1 In terms of our circular UBD.DS. Cir. No.44/13.05.00/2004-05 dated April 15, 2005, Primary (Urban) Co-operative Banks (UCBs) were permitted to have exposures up to 15 per cent and 40 per cent of their capital funds to a single borrower and a group of borrowers, respectively. On a review, it has been decided that, henceforth, the prudential exposure limits for UCBs for a single borrower/party and a group of connected borrowers/parties shall be 15 per cent and 25 per cent, respectively, of their tier I capital.

1.2 UCBs shall have at least 50 per cent of their aggregate loans and advances comprising loans of not more than ₹ 25 lakh or 0.2% of their tier I capital, whichever is higher, subject to a maximum of ₹ 1 crore, per borrower/party. Tier I capital for this purpose shall be reckoned in the manner provided in paragraph 1.1 above. Notwithstanding the above, UCBs shall adhere to the revised exposure limits stipulated at para 1.1 above. UCBs which do not, at present, comply with the prescribed threshold shall be in conformity with the above requirements by March 31, 2024.

2. *Revised Priority Sector Lending Target*

2.1 In terms of the circular DCBR.BPD (PCB).Cir. No.07/09.09.002/2017-18 dated May 10, 2018, the overall priority sector lending (PSL) target for UCBs stood at 40% of the adjusted net bank credit (ANBC) or credit equivalent amount of off-balance sheet exposure (CEOBSE), whichever is higher. On a review, it has been decided that the overall PSL target for UCBs shall stand increased to 75 per cent of ANBC or CEOBSE, whichever is higher.

2.1.1 UCBs shall comply with the above target by March 31, 2024 as per the following milestones:

PSL targets to be achieved by			
March 31, 2021	March 31, 2022	March 31, 2023	March 31, 2024
45% of ANBC or CEOBSE, whichever is higher	50% of ANBC or CEOBSE, whichever is higher	60% of ANBC or CEOBSE, whichever is higher	75% of ANBC or CEOBSE, whichever is higher

2.1.2 The extant sub-targets under the priority sector shall remain unchanged.

We can observe that with these changes in the credit policies applicable to UCBs RBI has now paved the way for UCBs to transform to small finance bank status and become a commercial bank, if they chose so.

More Powers to RBI to Supervise UCBs

In June 2020, the Union Cabinet had approved an ordinance to bring cooperative banks under the supervision of the Reserve Bank of India (RBI). It also extended the provisions applicable on commercial banks to cooperative banks. GOI took this action as after the impact of COVID-19 in the year 2020 it was observed that many UCBs are faced with the problem of increased NPAs and also that the CAR of these banks came down.

On 16 September 2020, GOI moved the Banking Regulation (Amendment) Bill, 2020 in the Lok Sabha and it was approved and made into an Act replacing the ordinance passed earlier in June 2020.

Moving the Banking Regulation (Amendment) Bill, 2020 in the Lok Sabha, the finance minister said the government was compelled to come out with an ordinance during the lockdown period as the condition of the cooperative banks was 'grave'.

The finance minister stated that the Gross non-performing assets (NPAs) of cooperative banks increased from 7.27 per cent in March 2019, to over 10 per cent by March 2020, and as many as 277 urban cooperative banks have reported losses in 2018-19 fiscal.

Finance Minister Nirmala Sitharaman further said that over 100 urban cooperative banks were unable to meet the minimum regulatory capital requirement and 47 had negative networth at the end March 2019.

Finance Minister said amendments to the banking regulation law seeking to extend the supervision of RBI to cooperative banks are aimed at improving their governance and protecting depositors' money.

Effect of Banking Regulation Amendment Act 2020

The provisions of amended act bring coop banks like UCBs, State Coop Banks and District Central Coop Banks under RBI control similar to commercial banks. While the provisions are made immediately applicable to UCBs, for State Coop Banks and District Central Coop Banks the GOI shall separately issue notifications later.

With this amendment, the long pending issue of inadequate authority of RBI to deal with UCBs facing financial weakness or closure is settled. As discussed earlier, the problem is due to the dual control of state governments and RBI on UCBs. This amendment act empowers RBI now to take immediate and appropriate action independently on similar lines as its authority on commercial banks. These powers include:

1. RBI may prescribe conditions on and qualifications for employment of Chairman of co-operative banks. RBI may remove a chairman not meeting 'fit and proper' criteria and appoint a suitable person. It may issue directions to reconstitute the Board of Directors in order to ensure sufficient number of qualified members.
2. To enable making of a scheme of reconstruction or amalgamation of a banking company for protecting the interest of the public, depositors and the banking system and for securing its proper management, even without making an order of moratorium, so as to avoid disruption of the financial system.

3. Supersession of Board of directors of a multi-State co-operative bank—The Reserve Bank may, for reasons to be recorded in writing, by order, supersede the Board of directors of such multi-State co-operative bank for a period not exceeding five years.
4. RBI is empowered to give approval to Co-operative banks for raising equity or unsecured debt capital from the public.

We can observe that with this Amendment Act passed by GOI it is now clear that GOI has addressed the issue of weak RBI governance on UCBs due to the existing cooperative laws passed by the state govts. We may also note that due to inherent supervisory weakness in controlling coop banks, RBI has opened a window for UCBs to get converted into small finance banks by becoming a limited company under companys act.

The present amendment act has done away with all the weak points existing in the supervision of UCBs by bringing them at par with commercial banks. Thus, the RBI supervision and authority will be same for both commercial banks and UCBs. Further the Amendment act also takes care of capital requirement of UCBs by permitting them to raise capital from the public.

This development is a welcome measure for the coop banks as now coop banks will be at par with commercial banks, without losing their constitution and identity as a cooperative society, and continue to perform their assigned role in the economy.

The coop banking has travelled a long way eversince they are brought under the perview of Banking Regulation Act in 1960s. But the coop banks were under the dual control of RBI and state govts. and RBI authority over these banks were limited to banking business only. As the failure rate in coop banks continued to be high it was argued that the solution is in empowering RBI to handle coop banks on similar lines as commercial banks. It was pointed out that RBI is quite successful in its handling commercial banks and managed to merge weak commercial banks with bigger banks and save the weak bank from closing. In case of weak coop bank, RBI alone cannot decide on any scheme to protect the bank from closing. State govts. are in fact having control on management and also on the issue of forming any scheme for revival or merger.

Many committees that were set up to study the cases of UCBs recommended unitary control of RBI on them. GOI in the past made many changes and gave more powers to RBI to deal with weak UCBs. But the failure of two big UCBs; Madhavpura mercantile coop bank in 2001 and crisis of PMC bank in 2019 showed that the changes made were inadequate and could not save UCBs from closing down.

The Banking Regulation Amendment Act 2020 approved by GOI appears to be the final solution as it places coop banks now under the control of RBI on the same footing as that of commercial banks.

We can now hope that the major debacles like Madhavpura mercantile coop bank in 2001 and Punjab and Maharashtra coop bank in 2019 will not recur in future and that even if such like cases of failures recur, the matter will be resolved quickly. We can also hope to see stability in coop sector banks similar to commercial banks, under the uniform supervisory control of RBI.

However, there will be pressure on RBI to supervise and control UCBs which are large in numbers as compared to commercial banks. It will definitely stretch the capability of RBI to handle UCBs on the same line that of commercial banks. There can be additional man power requirements to conduct on-site inspections of all banks atleast once in a year. RBI may have to evolve a system of supervision of all UCBs on the similar lines of its supervision of commercial banks.

Madhavpura Mercantile Coop Bank in 2001

Madhavpura Mercantile Cooperative Bank was registered as a cooperative society in Gujarat on 27 September 1968. It began business in Ahmedabad's Madhavpura spice-market area. In the year 1994, it received its banking licence and it became a multistate cooperative bank in April 1996. In 1999, it became a scheduled bank.

Madhavpura Mercantile Cooperative Bank was the largest urban cooperative bank in Gujarat in 2001 with deposit base of ₹ 1,200 crore as at in March 2001. Besides public deposit it had deposits from other coop banks. Nearly 50% of its deposit was from other banks.

Its operations are confined to Gujarat and Maharashtra States. It had a network of 28 branches—23 in Ahmedabad, one each in Baroda, Surat and Rajkot and two in Maharashtra i.e. Mumbai, Vashi-Navi Mumbai.

In 1999-2000, it started lending out large sums of money to stock brokers. It took large exposure to stock broker Ketan Parekh who was the leading bull operator in the stock exchange then. The bank had issued pay orders worth ₹ 1,200 crore to Ketan Parekh, which he discounted at Bank of India. The bank had also lent money to Mukesh Babu and Sirish Maniar of the brokerage firm Maniar Group.

Advances to these stock brokers were in gross violation of Reserve Bank of India (RBI) rules and regulations which only allowed banks to lend maximum of ₹ 15 crore to stock brokers.

In the early 2001, Ketan Parekh was active during the Bull Run in the stock exchanges. It was said that he and many others made huge money. This was followed by a Bear phase in Bombay stock exchange and the sensex dropped in March 2001. It was said that Ketan Parekh and many others lost heavily during this crash. On 8 March 2001, the news broke out that Madhavpura bank had issued huge amount of guarantees to Ketan Parekh and that Ketan Parekh had lost heavily in the stock crash. This news resulted in a rush to withdraw money by the depositors of Madhavpura bank.

Seeing the condition of the bank facing a run on it, RBI stepped in and restricted the bank's operations on 13 March 2001. This crisis put another 210 urban cooperative banks that kept money with Madhavpura Mercantile in trouble and some of them had to be liquidated. Some of the deposits of other coop banks were in the form of call money. The Deposit Insurance and Credit Guarantee Corp. (DICGC) that offers insurance cover to individual deposits up to ₹ 1 lakh had to pump in hundreds of crores to rescue stranded depositors.

With a view to protecting the interests of the depositors, RBI issued directions to the bank on March 13, 2001 under Section 35A of the Banking Regulation Act, 1949 restricting certain operations. Central Registrar of Co-operative Societies (CRCS) passed order to supersede the Board of Directors of the co-operative bank under Section 48 of the Multi State Co-operative Societies Act, 1984 and appointed an Administrator on March 14, 2001 to oversee the affairs of the co-operative bank.

RBI conducted the statutory inspection of Madhavpura mercantile co-operative bank with reference to financial position of the bank as on March 31, 2001 and the inspection revealed the precarious financial position of the bank as under:

The co-operative bank's net worth was assessed at (-) ₹ 1147.13 crore and the bank was not having adequate assets to meet its liabilities as required under Section 22(3)(a) of the Act.

(i) The co-operative bank had not complied with the requirements of minimum capital and reserves in terms of the provisions of Section 11(1) of the Act.

(ii) The entire capital and reserves of the co-operative bank had eroded and the deposit erosion was to the extent of 90.9%.

(iii) The gross NPAs formed 88.2% of the gross advances.

(iv) The co-operative bank had a net loss of ₹ 1192.81 crore.

Government of India/CRCS formulated a Scheme of Reconstruction for the co-operative bank from 23-8-2001 for a period of ten years. This scheme was to safeguard the interests of the depositors and a large number of UCBs who had placed deposits with the co-operative bank.

The scheme envisaged infusion of funds to run the bank, retention of existing deposits, converting call money borrowings from banks/institutions into term deposits, DICGC giving deposit insurance claims (₹ one lac per depositor) to all eligible depositors, and restrictions on new loans, etc.

Joint committee of parliament on Stock Market Scam and matters relating thereto (Thirteenth Lok Sabha) was constituted and it presented a report to both houses of parliament on 19-12-2002. This report also looked into the affairs of Madhavpura mercantile coop bank and some of the observations are as under. The report also contained the financial position of the bank which is given hereunder:

Source: Report Joint Committee on Stock Market Scam and Matters Relating Thereto (Thirteenth Lok Sabha) (Volume I & II) presented to Lok Sabha on 19 December 2002 laid on the Table of Rajya Sabha on 19 December 2002 Lok Sabha Secretariat New Delhi December 2002.

The financial position (trial balance) of the Bank as on 31.3.2001 is given at Appendix-I.

Salient Features of Scrutiny

The snap scrutiny by RBI of books of the Bank at Ahmedabad and Mumbai has revealed following irregularities in the working of the Bank:

(i) Of the advances outstanding at ₹ 1594.17 crore (as on 16.3.2001), a sum of ₹ 1082.22 crore constituting 68% of the advances were in the nature of unsecured advances, granted mainly to 21 borrowal accounts belonging to or related to stockbrokers. At least 10 such accounts indicated linkages with Shri Ketan Parekh a leading stock broker with an exposure of ₹ 843.57 crore i.e. 77.9% of total advances to share brokers.

(ii) The Bank had been resorting to large borrowing through Call Money Market for the purpose of lending to these big borrowal accounts. The exposure of the Bank to call money market as on 16/3/2001 aggregated ₹ 197 crore. (Appendix-I). It is observed that the Bank's borrowing was excessive in the call money market since last week of December 2000.

(iii) The Bank has blatantly violated RBI directive with respect to credit exposure for single borrower (20% of capital funds) or group of borrowers (50% of capital funds) by sanctioning credit limits much in excess of its credit exposure ceiling.

(iv) It had granted total credit facility of ₹ 21.00 crore to the group (M/s. Madhur Food Products Ltd.) belonging to

APPENDIX-I

Trial Balance of Madhavpura Mercantile Co-Operative Bank Ltd.
AS ON 31 MARCH 2001

@(₹ in crore)

Sr. No.	Liabilities	Amount	Sr. No.	Assets	Amount
1	Paid up Capital	13.87	1	Cash & balance with RBI/SBI	59.49
2(a)	Statutory Reserves	13.97	2	Balance with other banks	10.46
(b)	Other Reserves	17.94	3	Investments	64.65
3	Provisions (BDDR)	132.16	4	Loans and Advances	1717.37
4	Deposits	1262.38	5	Premises	10.46
5	Borrowings	# 193.11	6	Furniture and Fixture	9.87
6	Bills Payable	4.38	7	Interest Receivable	75.10
7	Interest Payable	7.72	8	Bills for collection as per contra	4.38
8	Overdue Interest Reserve	69.72	9	Other Assets	3.14
9	Branch Adjustments	0.04			
10	Other Liabilities	219.29			
11	Profit and Loss A/c	20.34			
	Total	1954.92		Total	1954.92

@ Source Annexure IX of Report of the Committee on revival of MMCB.

Includes borrowings of ₹ 192 crore from 15 participants in the call money market. As on March 16, 2001 the outstanding was ₹ 197 crore. The difference of ₹ 5 crore is due to adjustment of call money lending of Federal Bank Ltd., against the security of the deposits maintained by MMCB with it.

its chairman in violation of RBI directive on Credit Exposure norms which was much more than the prescribed limit of 20% of its Capital Funds of ₹ 27.52 crore.

(v) The Bank's deposits as on 16.3.2001 aggregated ₹ 1212.56 crore; of which institutional deposits, mostly from large number of cooperative Banks, aggregated to ₹ 590.13 crore forming 46.4% of the Bank's total deposits.

Further Developments

During the period of ten years starting from 23.8.2001, the reconstruction scheme did not make much progress mainly due to insufficiency in infusion of funds and non-recovery of loans mainly from Ketan Parekh and others. The reconstruction scheme expired on August 23, 2011.

RBI conducted statutory inspection of the co-operative bank with reference to its financial position as on March 31, 2011. Inspection report revealed that the co-operative bank's assessed net worth was (-) ₹ 1316.50 crore, CRAR was (-) 1941.1%, gross NPAs were ₹ 1126.55 crore i.e. almost 99.99% of its gross advances, accumulated losses were ₹ 1357.41 crore and deposit erosion was 100%. Due to precarious financial position, RBI placed the bank under Directions from the close of business of August 23, 2011 for a period of six months and extended up to August 23, 2012, subject to review.

The co-operative bank in its reply dated April 18, 2012 to the show cause notice issued by RBI, accepted the precarious financial position of the co-operative bank and attributed it to the fraud amounting to ₹ 1200.00 crore committed on the co-operative bank by the share broking community including Ketan Parekh and his associates in collusion with the then members of the Board of Directors. As per the bank, an amount of ₹ 803.00 crore constituting 72% of the total advances were unsecured due to unenforceable securities and defective documentation and hence not recoverable.

Finally, RBI decided to cancel the banking licence issued to the bank and allow the bank to go for liquidation. GOI also agreed on this and Reserve Bank of India (RBI) passed an order cancelling the banking licence issued to the co-operative bank with effect from the close of business on June 04, 2012.

A retired IAS officer has been appointed as the liquidator and another three members were nominated as members of liquidation committee. It is said that in 2012 the bank owed a total of ₹ 1,596 crore as under:

- 665 crore to 281 banks
- 436 crore to Deposit Insurance & Credit Guarantee Corporation
- 166 crore as interest
- 144 crore to Bank of India
- 98 crore to public account holders
- 87 crore to Reserve Bank of India

In 2013, the bank had to recover ₹ 1,467 crore from a total number of 851 defaulters including 18 members of the broker Ketan Parekh's group which owed ₹ 1,117 crore and another ₹ 350 crore owed by other 833 defaulters.

Gujarat urban coop banks federation (GUCBF) in the year 2018 in a statement said that that 45000 depositors of Madhavapura mercantile coop bank with deposits up to ₹ 2 lakh will get their deposits back as welcome gesture. Depositors were already earlier paid by DICGC as the deposit insurance claim of ₹ one lac per depositor.

Criminal actions were initiated against the stockbrokers involved and also the erstwhile management of the coop bank.

Sources: RBI press release, Wikipedia, and DNA news.

Punjab and Maharashtra Cooperative Bank

This bank is now taken over by Unity Small Finance Bank on 25-01-2022.

This case is discussed in detail under Chapter-2.

Sources: For brief history of coop banks:

- Co-operative Movement in India—Economics Discussion—www.economicsdiscussion.net-india-co-operative-movement-in-india.
- RBI.

8
Rural Coop Banks

History of both rural coop banks and urban coop banks are common and is already mentioned in the chapter on urban coop banks. The segregation of rural coop banks and urban coop banks happened after the year 1950 as mentioned therein.

In the year 1951, RBI appointed a committee known as the All-India Rural Credit Survey Committee headed by Shri A.D. Gorwala (Chairman). The objective of this committee was to study the problems of rural credit and explore possibilities of expanding agricultural credit through cooperative credit system.

The committee submitted its report in December 1954 and it highlighted the vital importance of rural credit by cooperatives and suggested to earmark and strengthen the cooperative credit societies that were then existing and to support them for delivery of rural credit. This was recommended after studying the existing sources of credit available to farmers which was mainly the money lenders and traders in the rural area. Commercial banks were not having any network in rural areas to finance farmers. Thus, it was recommended that cooperative system be used to reach the farmers and the govt. and banks can perform supporting role by providing finance to coop banks engaged in disbursing agricultural loans.

The important recommendations of the committee were as under:

> The Report suggested cooperative sector to play a vital role to reach grass roots i.e., farmers for agricultural credit. The major recommendations of the RCS Committee were as following:

- There shall be large-sized primary agricultural credit societies, primary land mortgage banks, grain banks and primary marketing societies at the primary level.
- At the district level, there should be preferably a District Central Cooperative Bank (DCCB) or a branch of state cooperative bank, a primary-level mortgage bank and a district marketing society.
- There should be a state cooperative bank, a central land mortgage bank and a state cooperative marketing society at the apex in each state.
- Visualizing cooperatives as an exclusive agency for providing credit to agriculture, the committee urged a well-defined role for the commercial banks in delivering credit in specialized areas, such as marketing, processing, storage and warehousing.
- RBI to create two funds to support agriculture.
- For the success of cooperative credit movement, the Survey Committee suggested an integrated scheme of rural credit based on the following fundamental principles:
  (a) state partnership in cooperative credit institutions;
  (b) full coordination between credit and other agricultural activities, particularly, marketing and processing; and
  (c) administration through adequately trained and efficient personnel, responsive to the needs of the rural population.
- The Committee recommended that the state govts. shall provide minimum 51% as capital to these banks and credit societies to strengthen them financially and also to provide guidance. Legal provisions to be made for this state partnership with rural credit institutions.

Government of India accepted these recommendations and implemented them. The following steps were taken by GOI.

In the year 1955, State Bank of India was formed by an Act of Parliament which took over from The Imperial Bank of India.

Eight banks that were existing in the erstwhile princely states were made as the subsidiaries of SBI in 1959. SBI was given a mandate to open maximum branches (about 400 branches) in the country covering all districts and centres. SBI opened more than 400 branches in the next few years.

The RBI Act was amended in 1955 to provide for the establishments of two funds, namely:

- The National Agricultural Fund (NAF) for long-term operations; and
- The National Agricultural Credit (Stabilization) Fund.

These funds were created to support the apex cooperative banks in the states.

In February 1956, the NAF was created to provide loans to the states to enable them to subscribe to the share capital of cooperative credit institutions. This Fund is also allowed to be used to give long-term support to Central Land Mortgage Banks (later known as SCARDBs).

GOI started the concept of five-year plans to direct and monitor the progress of the country and the First five-year plan period was the 1951-56. The first five-year plan is the period when GOI set up cooperatives as the purveyor of rural development backed by the state governments.

As per information available the existing agricultural credit societies and banks in the year 1950-51 and thereafter were as under:

	Co-operatives	1950-51	1955-56	1960-61	1965-66	1990-91	March 2005	March 2010	March 2019
1	PACS	115462	159939	212129	191904	82905	108779	94647	95995
2	DCCBs	505	478	390	346	356	367	370	363
3	State coop banks	15	24	21	22	24	31	31	33
4	PCARDBs	286	302	463	673	711	727	697	602
5	SCARDBs	5	9	18	19	19	20	20	13

Source: Collected from various sources and RBI

In the first five-year plan 1951-56, the structure of agriculture credit cooperatives was streamlined as per the recommendations.

Existing primary agriculture credit societies at village levels, Central coop banks, state coop banks, were identified and given their new roles under the new system. Their role is to provide short-term loans to agriculture.

For extending long-term loans to agriculture and allied activities, the existing land mortgage banks were identified and new banks were promoted. GOI decided on two-tier set up for long-term lending banks. These banks were later renamed as PCARDBs at ground level and apex bank at state level created is known as SCARDBs. At some states, there are unitary system of SCARDB with branches at district levels. In some state a mixed set up of PCARDBs and also branches of SCARDBs exist.

This exercise also resulted in closure of redundant cooperatives, merger of central coop banks within the districts and merger of state coop banks in many states. New district coop banks were also started in many districts and state coop banks in many states. In view of these changes, the numbers of cooperatives in each category of banks are seen changing with the years.

These banks are called the Rural coop banks.

State govts. started partnership with these institutions by providing capital and also other financial supports. State govts. started providing guarantees selectively for the loans/bonds/debentures raised by the state coop banks and SCARDBs. State govts. are also involved in the management of these banks.

RBI was extending refinances and also loans to state coop banks in the beginning. Then RBI set up the Agricultural Refinance Corporation (ARC) in 1963 to work as a refinancing agency to provide medium-term and long-term agricultural credit. In 1975, ARC was renamed as Agriculture Refinance and Development Corporation (ARDC). In 1982, National bank for agriculture and rural development (NABARD) was formed, and it took over the functions of ARDC and also took over the functions of Agricultural Credit Department (ACD) and Rural Planning and Credit Cell (RPCC) of RBI.

After nationalisation of 14 banks in the year 1969, GOI directed these banks to support agriculture activities in the country. This has changed the scenario of rural credit disbursal. Nationalised banks have grown very fast and have opened large number of branches in rural areas in a decade's time. Bank credit to agriculture by these banks showed phenomenal growth-out-performing the rural coop banks.

In 1975, GOI also started Regional Rural Banks as commercial banks (sponsored by mostly nationalised banks) and dedicated them for rural development.

At present agricultural loans are provided by all the banks in the country under their obligation to give priority sector advances as per the credit policy of RBI. Now the commercial banks are having major share in agricultural lending.

Table 8.1: Share in Credit Flow to Agriculture

(Per cent)

	Share in Credit Flow to Agriculture		
	Co-operative Banks	RRBs	Commercial Banks
1	2	3	4
2014-15	16.4	12.1	71.5
2015-16	16.7	13.0	70.2
2016-17	13.4	11.6	75.0
2017-18	12.9	12.1	74.9
2018-19	12.1	11.9	76.0
2019-20(P)	11.3	11.9	76.8

Note: (P) Data are provisional

Source: Data submitted by Banks on ENSURE portal of NABARD.

In the year 2019-20, commercial bank's share in agricultural lending is 76.8% as against RCB share of 11.3% and RRBs share of 11.9%.

However, the role of rural coop banks is continued. Rural coop banks are different from other banks in many respects. They are totally dedicated for rural development and is mainly appreciated for its cooperative movement which involves the farmers to form groups and work for self-development. The short-term loans, mainly the crop loans, are disbursed by the PACS which are located in villages and the farmers are the members of this society.

PACS are not banks but credit societies. Their main function is to provide short-term loans to its members. For this purpose, they have borrowing arrangement with the DCCBS. PACS are also allowed to collect deposits from their members. Besides these functions, they also make the arrangement of supplying of the agricultural inputs like seeds, fertilizers, insecticides, kerosene, etc. PACS also help its members by guiding and providing help to market/sell their agricultural products in the market at the proper prices.

DCCBs and State coop banks function like regular banks and accepts deposits from public and also from cooperatives. They have good deposit base as source for their lending and also refinance facility is available from NABARD. Many State govts. have made rules that the cooperative societies shall maintain their accounts with these banks. This was done with a view to keep funds of the cooperative sector within the sector. There may be certain exceptions to this rule also.

DCCBs are non-scheduled banks. They enjoy the privilege to open branches within their districts and they need not obtain permission from RBI for this. The State Coop Banks have the option to become scheduled banks and 23 of state coop banks is in scheduled bank category now. However, State coop banks will require to obtain branch licence from RBI for opening any branch.

PCARDBs and SCARDBs are non-scheduled banks. They extend long-term loans to agriculture. These banks are not allowed to accept deposits from public. From the year 1997, SCARDBs are allowed to mobilise term deposits from public for periods not less than 12 months subject to the condition that aggregate deposits accepted and outstanding at any point of time are not to exceed their net owned funds. However, there is not much progress made by these banks in procuring deposits. Resources for these banks are mainly from their borrowings.

As at March 1999 the resource base of rural coop banks were as under:

Resource base of Cooperative Banks

(₹ crore)

Agency	Share Capital		Reserves		Deposits		Borrowings	
	Amount	%	Amount	%	Amount	%	Amount	%
StCBs	585	2	2,917	7	25,786	66	9,849	25
DCCBs	2,484	4	4,801	7	45,609	69	12,796	20
PACS	3329*	15	-	-	5,255	24	13,299	61
SCARDBs	582	4	1,440	11	240	2	11,093	83
PCARDBs	610	7	559	7	152	2	6,849	84
TOTAL	7,590	5	9,717	7	77,042	52	53,886	36

*Includes Reserves

Sources: NABARD, NAFSCOB and NCARDBF.

We can observe that the deposits of StCBs and DCCBs accounted for 66% and 69% of their total resources. PACS share of deposits was 24% of its total resources. PACS could not improve their deposits due to many reasons. We can also observe that PCARDBs and SCARDBs mainly depend on their borrowings for their resources.

Guidelines for Implementing Prudential Norms

RBI issued guidelines to rural coop banks to comply with prudential norms from 1996-97. In order to bring about transparency in financial operations, prudential norms covering income recognition, asset classification and provisioning were made applicable to StCBs and DCCBs from the year 1996-97. In respect of SCARDBs and PCARDBs, the prudential norms were made applicable from the year 1997-98. To mitigate the hardships faced by these banks in making full provisioning, RBI permitted phasing of provisioning spread over a four-year period (upto 1999-2000) in the case of the short-term lenders and three years (upto 1999-2000) in the case of the long-term lenders.

Thus, under rural coop banks following are the types of banks as of March 2020:

Rural Co-op banks	Banks	Nos.
Short-term lenders	PACS*	97006
	District central coop banks - DCCBs	363
	State coop banks - StCBs	33
Long-term lenders	Primary Co-operative Agriculture and Rural Development Banks - PCARDBs	602
	State Co-operative Agriculture and Rural Development Banks - SCARDBs	13

In March 2021, there are 34 state coop banks and 23 of them are under scheduled category as under:

List of state coop banks

	State Co-operative Banks	State/Union Territory	Scheduled Status
1.	The Andaman and Nicobar State Co-operative Bank Ltd., Port Blair - 744101	Andaman and Nicobar Isls-UT	
2.	The Andhra Pradesh State Co-operative Bank Ltd., Vijayawada - 520002	Andhra Pradesh	Scheduled
3.	The Arunachal Pradesh State Co-operative Apex Bank Ltd., District - Papum Pare Naharlagun - 791110	Arunachal Pradesh	
4.	The Assam Co-operative Apex Bank Ltd., Guwahati - 781001	Assam	
5.	The Bihar State Co-operative Bank Ltd., Patna - 800 004	Bihar	Scheduled
6.	The Chandigarh State Co-operative Bank Ltd., Chandigarh - 160022.	Chandigarh-UT	
7.	The Chhattisgarh Rajya Sahakari Bank Maryadit Raipur - 492001	Chhattisgarh	Scheduled
8.	The Delhi State Co-operative Bank Ltd., New Delhi - 110002	Delhi	Scheduled
9.	The Goa State Co-operative Bank Ltd., Panaji - 403001	Goa	Scheduled
10.	Gujarat State Co-operative Bank Ltd., Ahmedabad - 380013	Gujarat	Scheduled
11.	The Haryana State Co-operative Apex Bank Ltd., Chandigarh - 160017	Haryana	Scheduled
12.	The Himachal Pradesh State Co-operative Bank Ltd., Shimla - 171001	Himachal Pradesh	Scheduled
13.	The Jammu and Kashmir State Co-operative Bank Ltd., Srinagar - 190008	Jammu & Kashmir	
14.	Jharkhand State Co-operative Bank Ltd., Ranchi - 834005	Jharkhand	

State Co-operative Banks		State/Union Territory	Scheduled Status
15.	The Karnataka State Co-operative Apex Bank Ltd., Bangalore - 560018	Karnataka	Scheduled
16.	The Kerala State Co-operative Bank Ltd., Thiruvananthapuram - 695033	Kerala	Scheduled
17.	The Madhya Pradesh Rajya Sahakari Bank Maryadit, Bhopal - 462003	Madhya Pradesh	Scheduled
18.	The Maharashtra State Co-operative Bank Ltd., Mumbai - 400001	Maharashtra	Scheduled
19.	The Manipur State Co-operative Bank Ltd., Imphal - 795001	Manipur	
20.	The Meghalaya Co-operative Apex Bank Ltd., Shillong - 793001	Meghalaya	Scheduled
21.	The Mizoram Co-operative Apex Bank Ltd., Aizawl-796001	Mizoram	
22.	The Nagaland State Co-operative Bank Ltd., Dimapur - 797112	Nagaland	
23.	The Odisha State Co-operative Bank Ltd., Bhubaneswar - 751001	Odisha	Scheduled
24.	The Puducherry State Co-operative Bank Ltd., Puducherry - 605004	Puducherry-UT	Scheduled
25.	The Punjab State Co-operative Bank Ltd., Chandigarh - 160022	Punjab	Scheduled
26.	The Rajasthan State Co-operative Bank Ltd., Jaipur - 302015	Rajasthan	Scheduled
27.	The Sikkim State Co-operative Bank Ltd., Gangtok - 737101	Sikkim	
28.	The Tamil Nadu State Apex Co-operative Bank Ltd., Chennai - 600001	Tamil Nadu	Scheduled
29.	The Telangana State Cooperative Apex Bank Ltd., Hyderabad - 500001	Telangana	Scheduled
30.	Tripura State Co-operative Bank Ltd., Agartala Dist.- West Tripura - 799001	Tripura	Scheduled
31.	The Uttar Pradesh Co-operative Bank Ltd., Lucknow - 226001	Uttar Pradesh	Scheduled
32.	The Uttarakhand State Co-operative Bank Ltd., Haldwani, Nainital - 263139	Uttarakhand	Scheduled
33.	The West Bengal State Co-operative Bank Ltd., Kolkata - 700069	West Bengal	Scheduled
34.	The Daman and Diu State Co-operative Bank Ltd.* Nani Daman - 396210	Daman and Diu-UT	

*New state coop bank

In March 2021, there are 13 SCARDBs as under:

List of SCARDBs

	SCARDB	State/UT	Structure*
1	Gujarat State Cooperative Agriculture & Rural Dev. Bank Ltd, Ahmedabad	Gujarat	unitary
2	Haryana State Cooperative Agriculture & Rural Dev. Bank Ltd, Panchkula	Haryana	federal
3	Himachal Pradesh State Cooperative Agri. & Rural Dev. Bank Ltd, Shimla	Himachal Pradesh	mixed
4	Jammu & Kashmir State Cooperative Agri. & Rural Dev. Bank Ltd, Srinagar	Jammu & Kashmir	unitary
5	Karnataka State Cooperative Agriculture & Rural Dev. Bank Ltd, Bangalore	Karnataka	federal
6	Kerala State Cooperative Agriculture & Rural Dev. Bank Ltd, Thiruvananthapuram	Kerala	federal
7	Pondicherry Cooperative Central Land Dev. Bank Ltd., Puducherry	Puducherry-UT	unitary
8	Punjab State Cooperative Agricultural Development Bank Ltd, Chandigarh	Punjab	federal
9	Rajasthan Rajya Sahakari Bhoomi Vikas Bank Ltd, Jaipur	Rajasthan	federal
10	Tamil Nadu Cooperative State Agriculture & Rural Dev. Bank Ltd, Chennai	Tamil Nadu	federal
11	Tripura Cooperative Agriculture & Rural Dev. Bank Ltd, Agartala	Tripura	unitary
12	Uttar Pradesh Sahakari Gram Vikas Bank Ltd, Lucknow	Uttar Pradesh	unitary
13	West Bengal State Coop. Agriculture & Rural Dev. Bank Ltd, Kolkata	West Bengal	mixed

SCARDBs in five states (Gujarat, Jammu & Kashmir, Puducherry, Tripura, and Uttar Pradesh) have a unitary structure i.e., they operate through their branches with no separate PCARDBs. SCARDBs in six states (Haryana, Karnataka, Kerala, Punjab, Rajasthan, and Tamil Nadu) have a federal structure where they operate through PCARDBs. Two states (Himachal Pradesh and West Bengal) have a mixed structure with SCARDBs operating through PCARDBs as well as through their branches.

Health of Rural Coop Banks

However, the health and functioning of the rural coop banks did not improve over the years despite govt. support. It was observed that they are not growing as expected. This was mainly because of the weak recovery position of their loans. Their working rather went down as many state govts. from time-to-time announced loan waiver schemes for farmers. This vitiated the recovery atmosphere of loans. Even farmers who could have repaid the loans delayed repayment hoping for waiver of loans.

Even after banking sector reforms were introduced in the country, rural coop banks were treated differently as they are supported by the govts. As stated earlier the prudential norms were prescribed for rural coop banks in the year 1997. In the year 2004 and 2005 NABARD and then RBI issued guidelines to rural coop banks to implement KYC norms.

Probably GOI overlooked the problems facing the rural coop banks for quite some time as the commercial banks and newly created Regional Rural Banks acquired major share in financing the farm sector over the years. There was no pressure on GOI as adequate agricultural credit was made available, mainly by commercial banks.

The financial position of rural coop banks continued to deteriorate due to high overdue loans, accumulated losses and inadequate capital. It was also observed that the banks who are allowed to collect deposits from the public are also unable to attract deposits. They are mainly dependent on support from their apex banks, state govts., central govt. and refinance from NABARD for lending to farm sector.

The position of rural coop banks as at end March 2005 was as under:

RBI observations on the financials were as under:

The share of the co-operative banks in agricultural credit declined from 62.0 per cent in 1992-93 to 34.0 per cent in 2002-03.

The financial health of co-operative banks has also deteriorated. As on March 31, 2005, four out of 31 StCBs, 71

Table 8.2: A Profile of Rural Co-operative Credit Institutions*
(As at end-March 2005)

(Amount in ₹ crore)

		Item	Short-Term			Long-Term		Total
			StCBs	DCCBs	PACS	SCARDBs	PCARDBs	
		1	2	3	4	5	6	7
A.		No. of Co-operative Banks	31	367	1,08,779	20	727	1,09,924
B.		Balance Sheet Indicators						
	i)	Owned Fund (Capital+Reserves)	9,495	20,495	9,197	5,022	3,494	47,703
	ii)	Deposits	44,316	82,098	18,976	566	365	1,46,321
	iii)	Borrowings	14,608	22,568	40,250	17,180	12,873	1,07,479
	iv)	Loans and Advances Issued	44,452	66,266	39,212	3,292	2,569	1,55,791
	v)	Loans and Advances Outstanding	37,346	73,091	48,785	17,422	12,763	1,89,407
	vi)	Total Liabilities/Assets	71,806	1,33,331	75,407 **	24,271	20,355	3,25,170
C.		Financial Performance						
	i)	Institutions in Profit						
		a) Number	26	296	47,015	11	262	47,610
		b) Amount of Profit	328	1,379	728	81	665	3,181

Item			Short-Term			Long-Term		Total
			StCBs	DCCBs	PACS	SCARDBs	PCARDBs	
1			2	3	4	5	6	7
	ii)	Institutions in Loss						
		a) Number	4	71	61,323	9	465	61,872
		b) Amount of Loss	37	405	1,989	244	274	2,949
	iii)	Overall Profit/Loss (-)	291	974	-1,261	-163	391	232
	iv)	Accumulated Loss	274	4,723	N.A.	1,098	2,313	N.A.
D.		Non-performing Assets						
	i)	Amount	6,072	14,520	16,052 @	5,437	4,056	46,138
	ii)	As Percentage of Loans Outstanding	16.3	19.9	33.6 #	31.3	31.9	24.4
	iii)	Recovery of Loans to Demand (%)	83.5	71.2	66.4	43.7	50.6	

N.A.: Not Available.

* : Based on reporting institutions.

@ : Total overdues.

** : Working capital.

: Percentage of overdues to demand.

Source: NABARD and NAFSCOB.

out of 367 DCCBs, 61,323 out of 1,08,779 PACS, nine out of 20 SCARDBs and 465 out of 727 PCARDBs incurred losses.

Accumulated losses as on March 31, 2005, in the short-term co-operative credit structure have been estimated at about ₹ 10,000 crore, and those in the long-term co-operative credit structure at about ₹ 4,000 crore.

We can also observe that NPA position was also very high. SCARDBs and PCARDBs had more than 30% NPAs. PACS had 33.6% NPAs. StCBs had 16.3% and DCCBs had 19.9% NPAs.

Task Force on Revival of Rural Cooperative Credit Institutions in August 2004 (Chairman: Prof. A. Vaidyanathan)

Concerned with the need for strengthening the co-operative credit structure in the country, the Government of India constituted a Task Force on Revival of Rural Cooperative Credit Institutions in August 2004 (Chairman: Prof. A. Vaidyanathan) to formulate a practical and implementable action plan to rejuvenate the rural credit co-operatives.

The Task Force submitted its report to the Government of India in February 2005 and recommended a financial package together with reforms to be brought about in the credit cooperatives with a view to making the credit cooperatives truly democratic, autonomous, vibrant, member driven, professionally managed and financially strong.

The task force recommended the reforms in the workings of rural coop banks as at present state govts. have contributed sizeable share capital in these cooperatives and dominated the management of these banks. This has, in fact, destroyed the democratic and autonomous functioning of these banks. This was evident from the fact that state govts. have superseded many boards of the RCBs and election of new boards were delayed. Effectively state govts. were managing these banks.

The govt. has accepted the recommendations and decided to revamp the workings and set up of these banks in their rightful position to support farm sector. Though the share in agriculture financing business has come down due to involvements of commercial banks and RRBs, it is observed and felt that the

PACS are serving the farmers at village level. They have very important role and their reach is still better than the commercial banks.

RBI in its publication headed as Developments in Co-operative Banking—Dated: Nov. 14, 2006 gave indications of the proposed changes in the working of these banks. The major points discussed in RBI report were as under:

- Co-operative banks have been displaying several weaknesses which have been inhibiting their ability to effectively compete with commercial banks in the emerging financial market. These weaknesses include low resource base, dependence on higher financing agencies, poor business diversification and recoveries, huge accumulated losses, lack of professionalism and skilled staff, weak MIS, poor internal check and control systems.
- In February 2005, StCBs and DCCBs were advised to formulate a customer acceptance policy and customer identification procedures to be followed while opening an account. It was decided in August 2005 to further simplify the KYC procedure for opening accounts for those persons who intend to keep balances not exceeding ₹ 50,000 in all their accounts taken together and the total credits in all the accounts taken together is not expected to exceed ₹ 1 lakh in a year.
- Out of 1,08,779 PACS as on March 31, 2005, 66,756 (61.4 per cent) were viable, 32,614 (30.0 per cent) potentially viable, 4,741 (4.4 per cent) dormant, 2,033 (1.9 per cent) defunct and 2,635 (2.4 per cent) others.
- As at end-March 2005, the long-term cooperative credit structure consisted of 20 State Co-operative Agriculture and Rural Development Banks (SCARDBs) and 727 Primary Co-operative Agriculture and Rural Development Banks (PCARDBs). Of the 20 SCARDBs, having 864 branches, eight were with unitary structure with branches, while twelve were federal/mixed in nature.

Recommendations of the Task Force on Revival Package for Short-term Co-operative Credit Structure

- The Revival Package for short-term co-operative credit structure envisages provision of financial assistance aggregating ₹ 13,596 crore to the short-term co-operative credit institutions to be shared by the Government of India, the State Governments and units of co-operative credit structure, subject to certain legal and institutional reforms to be initiated by the State Governments.
- The assistance will be available for: (i) wiping out accumulated losses; (ii) covering invoked but unpaid guarantees given by the State Governments; (iii) increasing the capital to achieve a minimum level of seven per cent CRAR; and (iv) technical assistance (including cost of special audit, human resources development and computerisation).
- The sharing pattern shall be based on origin of losses. While the broad share of the Government of India, the State Governments and CCS units works out approximately to 68:28:04, the share, however, would depend on the pattern of loan portfolio and accumulated losses in each CCS unit, the extent of guarantees issued by the State Governments and the amount of other receivables from the State Governments. This, however, would be finalised based on special audit to be conducted.

Recommendations of the Task Force on Revival of Long-term Rural Co-operative Credit Institutions

Financial assistance estimated at ₹ 4,839 crore, be provided to cover accumulated losses, cost of special audit and other technical assistance.

- The Government of India to bear all losses arising out of long-term loans for agriculture and related activities and entire cost of special audit, technical assistance, including HRD efforts and implementation costs;

- The State Governments to bear all dues payable by them to the long-term co-operative credit institutions and 50 per cent of losses arising from non-agricultural loans; and
- The LTCCI to bear 50 per cent of losses arising from non-agricultural loans.

Recommendations of the Task Force—Amendments to the State Co-operative Societies Act and Banking Regulation Act, 1949

Proposed Amendments to the State Co-operative Societies Act

- Ensuring full voting membership rights for all users of financial services, including depositors in co-operatives other than co-operative banks.
- Removing State intervention in all financial and internal administrative matters in co-operatives.
- Providing a cap of 25 per cent on government equity in cooperatives and limiting participation in the boards of cooperative banks to only one nominee. Any State Government or a co-operative wishing to reduce the state equity further would be free to do so and the co-operative will not be prevented from doing so.
- Permitting co-operatives under the parallel Acts (wherever enacted) to be members of upper tiers under the existing co-operative societies Acts and vice versa.
- Limiting powers of the State Governments to supersede Boards.
- Ensuring timely elections before the expiry of the term of the existing Boards.
- Facilitating regulatory powers for the Reserve Bank in the case of co-operative banks.
- Prudential norms, including CRAR for all financial cooperatives, including PACS.

As per the Revival Package approved by the Government of India, NABARD has been appointed as the implementing agency for the scheme.

The revival package considered the accumulated losses of these banks up to 31-3-2004 and suggested to wipe out the same. It also recommends state govt. investment in capital to the extent of maximum 25%. GOI is not to contribute any capital and its support shall be in the forms of grants or loan.

The important issue is the reviving the cooperative principle/ structure of these banks and not to allow them to be state controlled. It was observed that in many cases the state govt. share in the capital was high to the extent of 50% and above. This made the banks to be controlled by state governments who nominated three or four nominees in the management committees. Under cooperative rules each member is having one vote only and it is not based on shareholding as in the case of limited company. This was considered as going against the cooperative principle and the committee recommended to revert to the cooperative principle. In view of this state govts. are now allowed maximum 25% share in capital and appoint only one nominee. The excess shareholding, if any, shall be converted as loan or grant.

The recommendations also include the provision for membership and voting rights for all users of financial services, including depositors in co-operatives other than co-operative banks. This is an important and path-breaking step in the direction of the management control of cooperatives i.e., PACS. The depositors and borrowers of the PACS will get membership and voting rights. This can make a huge difference and protect the interests of all stakeholders in the credit society.

The task force has also recommended for bringing the rural coop banks (RCBs) to the standards of commercial banks with automation in working (computerisation), implementing KYC norms, implementing prudential norms for asset classification and improving the capital adequacy ratios over a period of five years to accepted level starting with a minimum level of 7% CAR.

The task force has also recommended for amending the existing laws like the Societies Acts of the states and The Banking Regulation Act so that RCBs come under the supervisory control of RBI, like other banks in the country. This means that the existing authority of state govts. under The Societies Acts will be passed on to RBI. These changes will enable RBI to have the authority to merge or consider closure of these banks.

Implementations of These Recommendations

GOI has accepted the recommendations and appointed NABARD as the agency to oversee the implementations. By the year 2012 NABARD has signed MOUs with maximum state govts. and GOI for bringing in the necessary changes in the working of these banks. The state govts. are required to amend the state laws to bring in the required legal provisions. It is a slow process.

Further, it was decided to have special audits of PACS to arrive at the correct position of accumulated losses and the required provisions for bad loans. It was also decided to start the funding with PACS first, so that their financial positions are streamlined. Under the existing three-tier arrangement of short-term credit institutions, once PACS are funded they will repay their dues to the DCCBs who in turn will repay their dues to state coop banks. There are also involvements of the state govts. in this, as they have given loans or provided guarantees to the banks. Hence state govts. shall also clear their obligations to these banks which will improve the position of recovery in loans guaranteed by state govts.

It can be observed that the financial package worked out by the task force is not very large and it is about ₹ 13596 crores for short-term credit institutions and about ₹ 4839 crores for long-term credit institutions. GOI is expected to contribute 68% and state govts. are expected to contribute 28%. But the major task is reorganising the workings of rural coop banks which shall take time.

Another issue under consideration is to rejig the three-tier short-term lending banks. It is now proposed that DCCBs can be merged with state coop banks so that two-tier structures of PACS and state coop banks is created. This change will also require the agreements of state govts. Besides there are recommendations regarding broad basing the deposit getting and borrowing arrangements for RCBs to improve their loanable funds without over dependence on apex banks and govts. as at present.

Legal Hurdles

GOI has amended the Multi State Coop Societies Act and the Banking Regulation Act in the year 2020, giving full authority to RBI to deal with urban and rural coop banks. Many state govts. have also amended the State Acts to give authority to RBI for resolution matters of these banks.

The Banking Regulation (Amendment) Act, 2020 has amended the provisions enabling RBI to supervise all coop banks in all respect. While the Amendment Act came into effect immediately for urban coop banks, for rural coop banks, it was mentioned that the effective dates will be separately notified in future.

Now GOI by notification dated December 23, 2020 notified that the effective date of the Banking Regulation (Amendment) Act, 2020 is from April 1, 2021 for DCCBs and state coop banks. With this the hurdle for amalgamation of DCCBs with state coop banks has been removed.

RBI has already framed and issued guidelines for merger of DCCBs with state coop banks.

As per the guidelines, RBI will consider proposals for amalgamation "when the state government of the state makes a proposal to amalgamate one or more DCCB/s in the state with the StCB after conducting a detailed study of the legal framework".

The scheme of amalgamation has to be approved by the requisite majority of shareholders.

"The proposal for amalgamation of DCCBs with the StCB will be examined by Reserve Bank in consultation with NABARD and the sanction/approval will be a two-stage process," the guidelines said.

In the first stage, an 'in-principle' approval will be accorded subject to fulfilment of certain conditions, following which the processes for amalgamation may be initiated by all concerned.

After completion of the first stage, NABARD and RBI may be approached for final approval along with compliance report, as per the guidelines.

Amalgamation of DCCBs with state coop banks is now on voluntary basis. Due to this we can know the progress in this exercise at some future date.

Present Status of Rural Coop Banks

Compilation of data on their working results of RCBs is often delayed. The data given in the table below is of March 2020. 23 out of 33 state coop banks are in scheduled category and DCCBs are in non-scheduled category. PACS are not banks but credit coop societies. But they are linked to DCCBs and act as conduit through which agricultural credit is disbursed to farmers. State coop banks and DCCBs provide short-term loans to farm sector. Long-term lending to farm sector is done by SCARDBs and PCARDBs.

Table 8.3: A Profile of Rural Co-operatives (At end-March 2020)

(Amount in ₹ crore)

Item	Short-term			Long-term	
	StCBs	DCCBs	PACS	SCARDBs (P)	PCARDBs (P)
1	2	3	4	5	6
A. Number of Cooperatives	33*	351**	95,509	13	602
B. Balance Sheet Indicators					
i. Owned Funds (Capital + Reserves)	21,900	43,246	43,741	4,859	3,673
ii. Deposits	2,10,342	3,45,682	1,65,476	2,409	1,372
iii. Borrowings	85,723	97,448	1,38,571	13,710	16,643
iv. Loans and Advances	1,99,943	2,79,272	2,14,533	20,700	15,819
v. Total Liabilities/Assets	3,40,267	5,35,977	3,25,322	27,104	31,337
C. Financial Performance					
i. Institutions in Profits					
a. No.	32	291	47,027	10	227
b. Amount of Profit	1,740	1,887	6,531	287	86
ii. Institutions in Loss					
a. No.	1	60	37,369	3	375
b. Amount of Loss	16	1,041	8,325	35	657
iii. Overall Profits (+)/Loss (-)	1,724	846	-1,794	252	-571

Item	Short-term			Long-term	
	StCBs	DCCBs	PACS	SCARDBs (P)	PCARDBs (P)
D. Non-performing Assets					
i. Amount	13,477	35,298	70,160	6,836	6,815
ii. As percentage of Loans Outstanding	6.7	12.6	31.0	33.0	43.1
E. Recovery of Loans to Demand Ratio***(Per cent)	94.4	70.2	69.3	43.1	44.1

Notes: 1. StCBs: State Co-operative Banks; DCCBs: District Central Co-operative Banks; PACS: Primary Agricultural Credit Societies; SCARDBs: State Co-operative Agriculture and Rural Development Banks; PCARDBs: Primary Co-operative Agriculture and Rural Development Banks.

2. (P): Data are provisional.
3. *: Data of Daman & Diu StCB (which is yet to be bifurcated completely from Goa StCB) is reported as a part of Goa StCB.
4. **: Excluding Tamil Nadu Industrial Co-operative Bank Limited (TAICO).
5. ***: Denotes the share of outstanding NPAs that have been recovered and on June 30, 2019.

Source: NAFSCOB and NABARD.

Financial performance of these banks shows that the position has not improved yet. Revival package is still in the process. One state coop banks, 60 DCCBs and 37,369 PACS were in loss in the year March 2020. Three SCARDBs and 375 PCARDBs were also in loss.

However, the accumulated losses of these banks were wiped out by infusion of funds from the govt. as per the revival plan. Own funds were ₹ 47703 crores in the year 2005 and now in the year 2020 the same is at ₹ 117,419 crore, which is substantially higher.

NPA position is still very high. StCBs had 6.7% DCCBs had 12.6%, PACS had 31% NPA. PCARDBs had 33% and SCARDBs had 43.1% NPA.

Business Share of RCBs in Total Banking Business in the Country

Scheduled commercial banks in the country are the biggest group of banks and they consist of public sector banks, private sector banks, small business banks, payment banks, local area banks, foreign banks and regional rural banks. This group is having over 90% share of banking business in the country. Remaining banks are the UCBs and Rural Coop Banks. The following chart shows the business share of banks in March 2020.

31-3-2020 (₹ in crores)	Assets	Deposits	Advances
Total Banking sector	1,98,98,496	1,52,01,156	1,13,37,453
Scheduled Commercial Banks-SCBs	1,80,14,425	1,39,75,045	1,03,01,897
Share of SCBs %	90.53	91.93	90.87
Urban coop banks	6,24,064	5,00,830	3,05,289
Share of UCB %	3.14	3.30	2.69
Rural coop banks	12,60,007	7,25,281	7,30,267
Share of RCBs %	6.33	4.77	6.44

We can observe that RCBs hold 6.33% share in total assets, 4.77% share in deposits and 6.44% share in advances.

9

Protection for Bank Depositors and Deposit Insurance

Government Ownership of Banks—Whether Deposits in Govt. Banks are Safe?

How safe are the deposits with the banks? This is an important question in the minds of account holders. Theoretically speaking govt. banks are considered safe as the govt. is the owner. However, there is no express guarantee provided by the govt. The status of the public sector banks is similar to other private banks in all respect except that in public sector banks, govt. is the owner. Initially Govt. of India held 100% capital of all govt. banks. Subsequently after the banking reforms were introduced and the govt. banks were in need of capital, Govt. of India allowed the public sector banks to tap the capital market for raising resources. At that time Govt. of India agreed to retain minimum 51% ownership of these banks. This represented the controlling interest in the public sector banks. Many public sector banks went public and raised capital from the market. In April 2021, after mergers, there are now 12 public sector banks.

Other than public sector banks, there are Regional Rural Banks created from the year 1975 onwards. The Regional Rural Banks were owned by the Central Government, the State Government and the Sponsor Bank (Any commercial bank can sponsor the regional rural banks) who held shares in the ratios—Central Government – 50%, State Government – 15%, and Sponsor Banks – 35%.

All the RRBs were sponsored by public sector banks except J&K Grameen Bank which was sponsored by J&K bank ltd. Though J&K bank ltd. is a private sector bank, it is promoted by Govt. of J&K which has 68.18% share in the bank as at June 2021. Hence RRBs can be treated in public sector only.

J&K bank is treated as private sector bank but the majority holding is with govt. Hence for practical purpose J&K bank is also a public sector bank.

All the Rural coop banks are cooperative credit societies registered under the coop society's acts of the states. They are owned by individual members and/or other coop societies. Hence, they are privately owned prior to the year 1951. However, in order to strengthen the capital base of these banks, provisions were made for capital contributions by state governments in the year 1954. At that time state govts. were asked to provide 51% share capital. This resulted in govt. stake in RCBs going up to 51% in most cases. Later a Task Force on Revival of Rural Cooperative Credit Institutions was appointed by GOI in August 2004. It submitted its report in February 2005 which was accepted by GOI. Under this report now the state govts. are advised to hold not more than 25% of the total capital of the rural coop banks and PACS. Besides capital contribution by governments in rural coop banks, governments have also invested funds as loan or grants in these banks. GOI has decided to keep rural coop banks in the system to take care of agriculture credit. Thus, rural coop banks are with the support of central and state governments.

IDBI bank was a public sector bank owned by Govt. of India. Govt. stake in this bank was transferred to LIC of India on June 2018 which took 51% stake in IDBI bank.

Life Insurance Corporation of India is a corporation owned by the Government of India. The Life Insurance Corporation of India was founded in 1956 when the Parliament of India passed the Life Insurance of India Act that nationalised the insurance business.

Since formation of IDBI bank it was a public sector bank. But when GOI transferred its stake to LIC of India in 2018, the bank is treated as a private sector bank. But govt. ownership indirectly through LIC of India continues. GOI has now in October 2021, decided to make an IPO issue and disinvest portion of its holding in LIC to public. But the majority control will remain with GOI. Hence for all practical purpose IDBI bank can be treated as public sector bank.

Govt. ownership is critical to consider the status of the bank. Though banks are limited companies registered under companies act, the govt. ownership in them makes a big difference in terms of their safety. Though govt. has not provided any express guarantee to these banks, it is obvious that govt. cannot allow these banks to close down. Govt. definitely has a moral responsibility, and in practice, it acts like a guarantee. Past history shows that govt. has always stepped in to protect its companies going burst. A sovereign govt. may not be in a position to disown its moral responsibility in the banking companies it has nationalised or it has created. Govt. can be absolved of this responsibility only when it privatises these companies or banks.

Why Govt. of India is continuing to have public sector banks in the country?

We may look for an answer to this in the history of bank nationalisations. Bank nationalisation was for social control on banks and to channelize the banking resources to segments of the economy that govt. considers important for national development. Loans to agriculture, small enterprises, small business and social lending for poverty alleviation programmes of the governments are the policy matters for the govt. Govt. has to take care of these segments of the society. It's well-known that these lending cannot be done through only moral suasions. Govt. will require using persuasion for the banks to lend. Govt. can use the infrastructure of banks to reach the target groups. However, Indian Govt. has already gone ahead with globalisation which may ultimately lead to free trade and free market conditions. The aim is to make the country a developed nation. The trend is to allow the market forces to decide and control the economy.

But it may not happen in the very near future. Our country may have to develop in an all-inclusive manner where the poor also get equal opportunity to face and make a living in the free and open economy. But for the interim period, some sort of hand-holding may be required. By definition, developed country is one which allows its citizens to act independently in all financial matters. The govt. will have nil or minimum interference in the trade and industry. The acid test for proclaiming developed status is when the currency of the country attains capital account convertibility status. Capital account convertibility is the status when the citizens are allowed to convert their local assets into foreign assets or vice versa without any restrictions. So far GOI has achieved only current account convertibility of Indian rupee. Financial sector reforms ushered in the year 1991 has capital account convertibility as one of its goals. RBI had appointed S.S. Tarapore Committee which submitted its report way back in May 1997.

At present the rupee is fully convertible on the current account, and only partially convertible on the capital account.

India is yet to achieve capital account convertibility. Its long since the committee has made its recommendations and set the time frame of years 2006 to 2011. But at present there is no move on this matter. This means that the capital account convertibility is still far away. This is mainly due to the weaknesses observed in the economy particularly after the year 2015, in terms of GDP growth, fiscal deficits of the govt. and rising NPA in banking sector.

We can observe that the concepts of priority sector lending by banks, lead bank schemes for the development of all districts of the country, govt. sponsored schemes for reaching out to the poor are all continuing.

Historically Govt. of India has moved away from socialist economic principles and now pursuing free market economy. In this direction, it has broken the monopolies of public sector and has created level playing field for the private sector. It is encouraging private sector to grow. Govt. is diluting the licencing regimes of the past and allowing private entrepreneurs to promote economic activities.

In banking system, govt. has encouraged private sector banks and foreign banks to increase their share in business. Private sector banks are growing very fast and taking away the sizeable share in business. The existing public sector banks are made to compete with private sector as level playing field has been created.

But the question is whether govt. will exit from banking in the near future?

Govt. has not declared its policy on this matter. After the financial sector reforms which specifically recommended freedom to open new private sector banks in the country, many private banks have come up.

Recently in 2019 GOI announced merger of some public sector banks to create bigger banks. By 1st April 2020 total number of public sector banks was reduced to 12 banks. In the budget proposal of 2021 GOI has indicated that two public sector banks will be privatised. This means that GOI is now considering disinvestments in banks and also other financial institutions.

The 2020-21 Union Budget had set a record divestment target of ₹ 2.1 lakh crore for the current fiscal ending on March 31, 2021. The target includes ₹ 1.20 lakh crore from the sale of shares of central public sector enterprises (CPSEs) and ₹ 90,000 crore from a share sale in public sector banks and financial institutions, including the listing of insurance behemoth LIC.

Disinvestment or divestment can be defined as the government's action of selling or liquidating its stake in a public sector unit asset or subsidiary. Generally, this is considered when PSUs start turning into liabilities and putting pressure on the government resources. In such cases, disinvestment helps to bring down the financial burden imposed by the inefficient PSUs on the public finances. The money raised by disinvestment can be put to better use. The recent decision of GOI to privatise Air India is a case in example to weed out loss making public sector units.

When we look back, Nationalisation of banks in 1969 and in 1980 has helped the country and bank credit was directed to agriculture and other priority sectors in the country. Govt. ownership of banks made it easy for the govt. to divert bank credit to help nation building. Subsequently, RBI has made the stipulations for priority sector lending and also fixed targets for different categories of banks to achieve. At present priority sector lending by banks is governed by the credit policy stipulations of RBI which is mandatory for banks.

We can observe that presently the credit requirements of priority sector borrowers are fully met by banks. RBI prescriptions to public sector banks and other commercial banks for priority sector lending are same. Hence there is no special target for public sector banks. In view of this, GOI can now think of disinvesting in public sector banks.

As such GOI has earlier approved to bring down its stake in public sector banks to 51% to enable these banks to raise capital from the public. This was done with a view to save govt. from additional contribution to capital of public sector banks in view of new capital norms under Basel Accords. Despite this, govt. is forced to recapitalise public sector banks to meet capital adequacy norms when they are burdened with bad loans.

Continuing with public sector banks may require GOI to meet future capital requirements of banks for two reasons. One is the increase in the bank credit over the years and other is to take care of bad loans. GOI cannot be expected to divert tax payer's money for this purpose. The option is to disinvest in public sector banks and allow private enterprises to take over these banks.

This change in the GOI view on public sector has started from the year 1991 when financial sector reforms were introduced. The present govt. is continuing with this policy on disinvestment of public sector undertakings. At present GOI is bringing out its yearly plan for disinvestment in its budget proposals. Disinvestments are carried out in phases and the proceeds are being used for financing new development projects.

Thus, it is clear now that the public sector banks will be slowly privatised over next few years. GOI has created six big public sector banks by mergers and we may presume that these six banks may remain in public sector for some time.

Under the present scenario govt. owned banks still have an edge over private sector banks as they are considered safer due to govt. backing and govt.'s moral stance.

Account holder has every reason to think himself fully secured for his deposits in the public sector banks including RRBs, Rural Coop Banks, IDBI Bank and J&K Bank.

Govt. Equity in Public Sector Banks

Govt. has already diluted its equity share in the public sector banks from 100%. Dilution was allowed after the financial sector reforms have been introduced from the year 1992 and GOI has agreed to reduce its holding with minimum of 51%. Public sector banks started public issues to collect equity from the public from the year 1994 onwards. At present the govt. share in public sector banks are as under:

Public sector Banks (Government Shareholding %, as of 30 June 2021)

S.N.	Name of the Bank	% age of GOI Shareholding 30-6-2021
1	State Bank of India	57.60
2	Punjab National Bank	73.01
3	Bank of Baroda	64.00
4	Canara Bank	69.33
5	Union Bank of India	83.50
6	Indian Bank	78.86
7	Bank of India	90.34
8	Central Bank of India	93.08
9	Bank of Maharashtra	93.33
10	Punjab & Sind Bank	97.07
11	Indian Overseas Bank	96.40
12	UCO Bank	95.39

Source: Wikipedia.

Thus, the public sector banks, in addition to govt. support for additional capital requirements, can also raise capital from the market at some appropriate time to strengthen their capital base.

Adopting the prudential norms and strengthening the capital base as per Basel Accord and the supervisory standard made applicable for the banks are with the purpose to safeguard the banks so that the depositors of the banks are protected. But this in itself may not protect the depositors of the banks in every eventuality. Banks are always exposed to business risks and however strong the measures to control and supervise the banks, it may not remove the risk of bank failures and the risk depositors of the bank are exposed to.

Till such time the public sector banks are continued in the country, the depositors of these banks may continue to feel secured. However, govt. should clarify this matter in view of the proposed bill with bail-in provision, whether this is applicable to public sector banks.

Deposit Insurance for Bank Deposits

Deposit insurance for bank depositors is now provided by many countries in the world. The insurance does not provide 100% cover of the depositors. It is only partial coverage as the idea behind the insurance coverage is to protect the householder depositors to some reasonable extent and save their hard-earned money from vanishing due to the bank failures. This insurance has evolved over the years during this century and generally at the behest of the governments or the central banks of the countries. The countries have developed different models of insurance suitable to their respective countries.

As per International Association of Deposit Insurers (IADI), deposit insurance schemes in some explicit forms are present in 145 countries (as of July 2019).

International Association of Deposit Insurers (IADI) is formed in 2002 to enhance the effectiveness of deposit insurance systems by promoting guidance and international cooperation. It is a body under the aegis of BIS Basel. India is a member of this association. IADI has revised and issued 16 Core Principles for Effective Deposit Insurance Systems in November 2014.

The important three core principles are as under:

Principle 1 – COVERAGE

Policymakers should define clearly the level and scope of deposit coverage. Coverage should be limited, credible and cover the large majority of depositors but leave a substantial amount of deposits exposed to market discipline. Deposit insurance coverage should be consistent with the deposit insurance system's public policy objectives and related design features.

Essential Criteria

1. Insured deposits are clearly and publicly defined in law or regulation and reflect the public policy objectives. This definition includes the level and scope of coverage. If certain types of deposits and depositors are ineligible for deposit protection, they are clearly specified, easily determined and do not affect the speed of reimbursement.

2. The level and scope of coverage are limited and are designed to be credible, so as to minimise the risk of runs on banks and do not undermine market discipline. The level and scope of coverage are set so that the large majority of depositors across banks are fully protected while leaving a substantial proportion of the value of deposits unprotected. In the event that a substantial proportion of the value of deposits is protected, moral hazard is mitigated by strong regulation and supervision, as well as by the other design features of the deposit insurance system.

Principle 2 – PUBLIC AWARENESS

In order to protect depositors and contribute to financial stability, it is essential that the public be informed on an ongoing basis about the benefits and limitations of the deposit insurance system.

Essential Criteria

1. The deposit insurer is responsible for promoting public awareness of the deposit insurance system, using a variety of communication tools on an ongoing basis as part of a comprehensive communication programme.

Principle 3 – REIMBURSING DEPOSITORS

The deposit insurance system should reimburse depositors' insured funds promptly, in order to contribute to financial stability. There should be a clear and unequivocal trigger for insured depositor reimbursement.

Essential Criteria

1. The deposit insurer is able to reimburse most insured depositors within seven working days. If the deposit insurer cannot currently meet this target, the deposit insurer has a credible plan in place to do so.

(Excerpts from Core Principles IADI)

As per the core principles, the deposit insurance 'Coverage should be limited, credible and cover the large majority of depositors but leave a substantial amount of deposits exposed to market discipline'. This is based on free market principles that total security to the bank depositors will make the banks to indulge in undue risky business and put the economy into trouble. This also means that the bank depositors will require to identify safe banks and weak banks for their dealings with the banks. Deposit insurance scheme shall cover the large majority of depositors as per this advice. Countries will have to fix the insurance coverage limit in their respective countries based on their country's needs and other factors prevailing.

Deposit Insurance in Our Country

Deposit insurance act was passed by the central govt. in the year 1961

Protection of depositor's money was engaging Govt. and RBI attention since 1938 or even earlier. In 1938, the Travancore National and Quilon Bank, the largest bank in the Travancore region, failed. This was followed by banking crisis in Bengal during the years 1946-48, but it was in 1960 when Laxmi Bank and the Palai Central Bank failed, govt. decided to create deposit insurance for protecting the depositors of the banks. The Deposit Insurance Corporation Act was passed in 1961 and the deposit insurance corporation was set up in the year 1962 as a subsidiary of RBI. India was the second country in the world to create deposit insurance to protect bank depositors. The first country was USA which created deposit insurance scheme in the year 1933.

The Reserve Bank also promoted a public limited company on January 14, 1971, named the Credit Guarantee Corporation of India Ltd. (CGCI). With a view to integrating the functions of deposit insurance and credit guarantee, the two organisations, viz. the DIC and the CGCI, were merged and the Deposit Insurance and Credit Guarantee Corporation (DICGC) came into existence on July 15, 1978. The Deposit Insurance Act, 1961 was amended and it was renamed as 'The Deposit Insurance and Credit Guarantee Corporation Act, 1961'.

Banks covered under deposit insurance scheme:

(i) All commercial banks including the branches of foreign banks functioning in India, Local Area Banks, Regional Rural Banks, Small Finance Banks and Payment Banks are covered under the Deposit Insurance Scheme.

(ii) All eligible co-operative banks as defined in Section 2(gg) of the DICGC Act are covered under the Deposit Insurance Scheme. At present all co-operative banks are covered under the Scheme.

The premiums for the insurance cover shall be paid by banks as under.

PREMIUM RATES PER DEPOSIT OF ₹ 100	
Date from	Premium (in ₹)
1-04-2020	0.12
1-04-2005	0.10
1-04-2004	0.08
1-07-1993	0.05
1-10-1971	0.04
1-01-1962	0.05

Insurance Coverage

Under the provisions of Section 16(1) of the DICGC Act, the insurance cover was limited to ₹ 1,500/- only per depositor(s) for deposits held by him (them) in the "same right and in the same capacity" in all the branches of the bank taken together. However, the Act also empowers the Corporation to raise this limit with the prior approval of the Central Government. Accordingly, the insurance limit was enhanced from time to time as follows:

- ₹ 5,000/- with effect from 1st January 1968
- ₹ 10,000/- with effect from 1st April 1970
- ₹ 20,000/- with effect from 1st January 1976
- ₹ 30,000/- with effect from 1st July 1980
- ₹ 1,00,000/- with effect from 1st May 1993
- ₹ 5,00,000/- from 4th February 2020

Under the deposit insurance scheme, all banks are included for the cover. Banks shall bear the premium for insurance of the deposits and banks cannot recover the same from depositors. The claim is payable in the event of the winding up or liquidation of an insured bank, and every depositor of the bank is entitled to payment of an amount equal to his deposits held by him in the same right and in the same capacity in all the branches of that bank put together, with a maximum of the limit set by the corporation. The limit is ₹ five lacs for each depositor of the bank at present (4-2-2020). This limit remained at ₹ one lac from the year 1993 till February 2020.

The insurance limit was enhanced to ₹ five lacs in February 2020 after the PMC bank, 5th largest urban coop bank, came into trouble in 2019. The trouble in this bank received wide media coverage as large numbers of account holders are affected. The bank was placed under direction by RBI and the matter is resolved only in the beginning of the year 2022. Govt. took notice that the deposit insurance protection of ₹ one lac is woefully insufficient compensation for the bank depositor and enhanced it to ₹ five lacs in February 2020.

Position of Deposit Insurance Cover as at March 31, 2021

DICGC in its annual report for year 2020-21 has shown the position of insured deposits as under:

Table 9.1: Insured Deposits

		Particulars As at the period end of[1]	Particulars As at the period end of[1]
		March 31, 2021	March 31, 2020
1	Total No. of Accounts (in crore)	252.6	235.0
2	Fully Protected Accounts[2] (in crore)	247.8	216.1 (231.0)
3	Percentage of 2 to 1	98.1	92.0 (98.3)
4	Assessable Deposits (₹ in crore)	1,49,67,770	1,34,88,910
5	Insured Deposits[3] (₹ in crore)	76,21,251	36,96,100 (68,71,500)
6	Percentage of 5 to 4	50.9	27.4 (50.9)

1. Based on deposit base of September 2020 and September 2019, i.e. six months prior to the reference date.
2. Refers to accounts covered by deposit insurance.
3. Data for March 2020 refers to ₹ 1 lakh deposit insurance cover while those in parentheses relate to ₹ 5 lakh deposit insurance cover estimated at ₹ 68,71,500 crore.

Source: DICGC

As per the annual report released by RBI the total insured deposits stood at ₹ 76,21,258 crore as at end-March 2021. This is 50.9 per cent of the total deposits of ₹ 1,49,67,776 crore with the banks. This means that around 49.1% of the amount deposited with banks does not enjoy the DICGC cover. This position is after the increase in insurance cover to ₹ 5 lacs from February 2020. Earlier to this, in the year 2018-19, the insurance cover was just 28.1% of the total deposits of the banks i.e., ₹ 33700 billion as against the total deposits of the banks at ₹ 120051 billion.

RBI has advised all banks to bring this insurance cover to the notice of account holders. Many banks are showing the insurance cover of ₹ five lacs per person from DICGC by printing it on the pass books as a notice to the depositors. RBI intention is good as it wants to educate the bank account holders on the risk that is inherent to bank deposits. We will discuss this matter little later in this chapter.

As per reports of DICGC in its annual accounts for the year ending March 2021, DICGC has paid claims to failed banks since its inception in 1962 to March 2021 as under:

	Type of banks	No. of failed banks	Total claims paid "₹ in millions"
1	Commercial banks	27	2959
2	Co-op banks	365	54669
	Total	392	57628

We may observe that failure of commercial banks is only 27 banks in past 58 years which is commendable. This is mainly due to the control and supervision of RBI over commercial banks. There was no major commercial bank failure in these years and RBI managed to save bank depositors by merging the troubled banks with stronger banks mostly public sector banks.

But the banks in coop sector continue to fail and the trend is alarming. These failures are in urban coop banks category only, Failure of urban coop banks regularly, underscores the weakness in the control systems on them. DICGC has stated that the claims settled during the financial year 2021 was ₹ 563.9 crore (₹ 5639 million). Further DICGC has approved to release insurance amount to beleaguered depositors of PMC bank in the beginning of the year 2022 and also to another 20 failed UCBs.

Further till the time the recent DICGC Amendment Act 2021 (August 2021) was passed, depositors of failed banks were made to wait for DICGC insurance settlement. When the banks were put under direction or moratorium by RBI restricting the withdrawals by the depositors up to certain limit, depositors are put to hardship for long time as they cannot withdraw money from the accounts even for their sustenance.

The present Amendment Act provides for DICGC to make payment of insured sum within 90 days from the date of issuance of directions on the banks by RBI. This will help the depositors of failed banks in future.

Deposit Insurance Covers in Other Countries of the World

Worldwide, 146 countries have deposit insurance schemes. Deposit insurance schemes are for the protections of bank depositors. Every country has evolved the scheme as suitable to its financial systems. Though the purpose is same to protect bank depositors in case of bank failures up to a set limit, the approaches are different by the countries. This is mainly due to the fact that the financial systems in most developed countries are complex in nature. Hence the deposit insurance scheme is country specific.

Let us study the schemes obtaining in few important countries. Some information on deposit insurance practices is collected from the relevant sites of the insurance authorities of the countries and is given in the following table.

We may observe that many countries have actively promoted or revised the schemes in current decade starting from the year 2001. In few cases, there are more than one deposit insurance schemes in operation concurrently.

Country	Deposit insurance	Cover	In ₹
USA	The Federal Deposit Insurance Corporation (FDIC) is an independent federal agency insuring deposits in U.S. banks and thrifts in the event of bank failures. The FDIC was created in 1933 to maintain public confidence and encourage stability in the financial system through the promotion of sound banking practices. As of 2018, the FDIC insures deposits up to $250,000 per depositor as long as the institution is a member firm. It is critical for consumers to confirm if their institution is FDIC insured.	$250,000	@73.22 18305000
UK	The Financial Services Compensation Scheme (FSCS) is the UK's statutory deposit insurance and investors compensation scheme for customers of authorised financial services firms. Deposits held in banks, building societies and credit unions (including in Northern Ireland) that are authorised by the PRA are protected up to £85,000. This includes, for example, eligible deposits in current accounts, savings accounts, cash ISAs (held with a deposit taker) or savings bonds.	£85,000	@104.74 8902900

Country	Deposit insurance	Cover	In ₹
	The deposit protection limit applies to the total eligible deposits of each person, per PRA-authorised firm. So for deposits in a joint account, this means that each account holder is protected up to the deposit protection limit, i.e. the total protection adds up to two times £85,000.		
China	China's deposit insurance scheme came into effect in May 2015. It covered commercial banks, rural cooperative banks and rural credit cooperatives.... The payout covers a deposit of no more than 500,000 yuan for each depositor in a bank. The insurers are required to pay premiums every six months under the scheme. (May 31, 2019)	500,000 yuan	@11.32 5660000
Singapore	**Singapore Deposit Insurance Corporation Ltd** In the event a Deposit Insurance (DI) Scheme member bank or finance company fails, all of your insured deposits with that member are aggregated and insured up to S$75,000 by the Singapore Deposit Insurance Corporation Limited (SDIC). Insured deposits held in trust and client accounts held by non-bank depositors are insured up to S$75,000 per account.	S$75,000	@54.40 4080000
Germany	Alongside the Deposit Protection Fund, there exists a statutory deposit protection scheme, the "Entschädigungseinrichtung deutscher Banken" [Compensation Scheme of German Banks, EdB], which was set up in 1998. The EdB performs the tasks of the compensation scheme called for under the German Deposit Guarantee Act (Einlagensicherungsgesetz, EinSiG) for the area of the private commercial banks and private building and loan associations. The protection provided by the EdB is limited to € 100,000 per depositor. The Deposit Protection Fund only covers deposits and depositors if and to the extent that these are not already covered by the EdB.	€ 100,000	@86.38 8638000

Country	Deposit insurance	Cover	In ₹
	The Deposit Protection Fund of the Association of German Banks secures the deposits of each and every customer at the private commercial banks up to a ceiling of 20% of the relevant liable capital of the respective bank as at the date of the last published annual financial statements. Please note that, due to banks' increased capital base, the deposit ceiling will be adjusted over the next few years. As a result, from 1 January 2020 it will be 15%, and from 1 January 2025, 8.75% of the liable capital of the Bank relevant for deposit protection. There is one exception: the protection ceiling for banks joining the scheme is in principle only € 250,000 up to the end of the third calendar year of their participation in the Deposit Protection Fund.		
Japan	The deposit insurance system in Japan is subject to the Deposit Insurance Law (enacted in 1971). Deposit Insurance Corporation of Japan (DICJ), which was established with funding from the government, the Bank of Japan, and private financial institutions, is a main body that operates the system with the purpose of operating Japan's deposit insurance system. From April 2005 onward, deposits which come under the category of deposit for payment and settlement purposes—the deposits that meet three requirements—bearing no interest, being redeemable on demand and being normally required payment and settlement services—are protected in full (permanent measures). Meanwhile the protection of deposits other than those for payment and settlement purposes is protected up to a maximum of ¥10 million in principal plus related interest thereon per depositor per financial institution (Note). Uncovered portion of the insured deposits (i.e. the portion of principal exceeding ¥10 million	¥10 million	@0.66 6600000

Country	Deposit insurance	Cover	In ₹
	for insured deposits other than deposits for payment and settlement purposes) as well as uninsured deposits plus interest thereon may be partially payable in accordance with the state of assets of a failed financial institution.		
France	**Protection for customers and the entire banking system** When a bank is no longer able to repay its customers' deposits, the Fonds de Garantie des Dépôts et de Résolution (FGDR) compensates customers in an amount up to €100,000 within 7 working days subject to certain conditions and limits. By protecting depositors, the deposit guarantee scheme helps to maintain confidence in the banking system and ensure its stability. The "DGSD2" directive adopted on 16 April 2014 (2014/49/EU), which was transposed into French law at the end of 2015 and includes 5 implementing decrees of 27 October 2015, introduced several significant improvements for depositors: All deposits covered by the guarantee are added up to determine the amount which the bank owes its customer. The FGDR pays compensation in this amount, up to €100,000 per person, per institution, within 7 working days.	€100,000	@86.38 8638000
Canada	Deposit insurance protects your savings if your financial institution fails. You don't have to apply or pay for deposit insurance. The Canada Deposit Insurance Corporation (CDIC) automatically insures your eligible deposits up to Can.$100,000. CDIC insures deposits held in Savings and chequing accounts. Sep 20, 2017	Can. $100,000	@58.05 5805000
Russia	The statutory individual bank deposit insurance system (DIS) is a special governmental programme of the Russian Federation implemented in compliance with the Federal Law dd. 23.12.2003 No. 177-FZ "On Insurance of Individual Deposits with the banks of the Russian Federation".	RUB 1,400,000	@0.99 1386000

Country	Deposit insurance	Cover	In ₹
	Upon occurrence of an insured event a deposit with the bank is to be compensated in size of 100% of the deposit amount with a bank, however, the total compensation shall not exceed RUB 1,400,000 (applicable to the insured events occurred after 29 December 2014). If a customer has more than one deposit with the same bank, the deposit compensation shall be paid pro rata the amounts of such deposits but the total compensation for all deposits should be no more than RUB 1,400,000. This condition is applicable to all deposits made by a depositor (in favour of a depositor) with one bank including those made for doing lawful business activities (except escrow accounts opened for making settlements under real estate transactions or settlements under shared construction participation agreements).		
Australia	From the year 2012, The Australian Government has guaranteed deposits up to Aus $250,000 in Authorised Deposit-taking Institutions (ADIs) such as bank, building society or credit union. This means that this money is guaranteed if anything happens to the ADI. The cap applies per person and per ADI. Oct 24, 2018	Aus $250,000	@53.43 13357500
Indonesia	IDIC is a legal independent institution which established based on the Law No. 24 of 2004 concerning Indonesia Deposit Insurance Corporation. The maximum amount of deposit insured by IDIC is Rp 2 billion per depositor per bank as of 13 October 2008. If a depositor has several accounts in one bank, the balance of all depositor's accounts will be cumulated to calculate the amount of deposit insured. However, in the early times of IDIC operational, IDIC insured fully amount of depositor's deposit. The amount of deposit insured will be deducted gradually until it reaches the maximum amount of Rp 2 billion.	Rp 2 billion	1rp=0.0051 ₹ 10000 rp= 50.78 ₹ 10156,000

Country	Deposit insurance	Cover	In ₹
	For conventional banks, the amount of deposit insured covers the initial funds and interest, while for Islamic banks, the initial and revenue sharing become the rights of their customers.		
Switzerland	Esisuisse is the deposit insurance scheme that guarantees client money held with Swiss branches of banks and securities firms. If a deposit is no longer available in the event of a bankruptcy, all clients have their savings repaid by the liquidator up to a maximum of CHF 100000. This limit applies per client and bank. The Swiss Banking Act of 2005 stipulates that all Swiss branches of banks and securities firms must have their preferential deposits protected by Esisuisse. If a bank or securities firm in Switzerland becomes insolvent, the other members of Esisuisse will immediately provide the required funds. This collective scheme ensures that the clients of such an insolvent bank have their protected deposits paid out to them within one month. Deposits totalling no more than CHF 100000 per depositor are protected. The banks receive reimbursement of their contributions at a later date when the insolvent bank is liquidated. Swiss Financial Market Supervisory Authority FINMA FINMA is Switzerland's independent financial-markets regulator. Its mandate is to supervise banks, insurance companies, exchanges, securities dealers, collective investment schemes, and their asset managers and fund management companies. It also regulates distributors and insurance intermediaries. It is charged with protecting creditors, investors and policyholders. FINMA is responsible for ensuring that Switzerland's financial markets function effectively.	CHF 100000	@80.05 8005000

Country	Deposit insurance	Cover	In ₹
Brazil	FGC is a private, non-profit organization that manages the safety net mechanism for depositors and investors in the Brazilian Financial System, up to the limits established by regulation, against its member financial institutions, in the event of intervention and extrajudicial liquidation and recognition, by the Central Bank of Brazil, of the insolvency of the member institution. FGC's member institutions are Caixa Econômica Federal, multiple banks, commercial banks, investment banks, development banks, credit, consumer credit and investment companies, real estate credit companies, mortgage companies and savings and loan associations operating in Brazil that fulfill one of the following requirements: • receive demand deposits, savings deposits or term deposits; • accept bills of exchange; • raise funds through the issuance and placement of real estate notes, mortgage notes, real estate letters of credit or agribusiness letters of credit; • raise funds through repurchase operations involving securities issued by related companies. FGC membership is mandatory in accordance with the Central Bank of Brazil. The maximum amount of guarantee per person against the same member institution or against all member institutions that are part of the same financial conglomerate is two hundred and fifty thousand reais (R$ 250,000.00).	R$ 250000	@14.08 3520000

From the above table we can understand how deposit insurance schemes are operated by the countries. We can compare the deposit insurance protection available to bank depositors in some important countries which are given in the table below to show the comparative position:

No.	Country	Deposit insurance cover limit	Exchange rate 31-8-2021	Value in Indian rupees
1	USA	$ 250,000	@73.22	18305,000
2	Australia	Aus $ 250,000	@53.43	13357,500
3	Indonesia	Rp 2 billion	10000 rp=50.78 Rs.	10156,000
4	UK	£ 85,000	@104.74	8902,900
5	Germany	€ 100,000	@86.38	8638,000
6	France	€ 100,000	@86.38	8638,000
7	Switzerland	CHF 100,000	@80.05	8005,000
8	Japan	¥ 10 million	@0.66	6600,000
9	Canada	Can. $ 100,000	@58.05	5805,000
10	China	Yuan 500,000	@11.32	5660,000
11	Singapore	S$ 75,000	@54.40	4080,000
12	Brazil	Reais 250,000	@14.08	3520,000
13	Russia	RUB 1,400,000	@0.99	1386,000
14	India	₹500000		500000

USA is having a protection limit for bank depositor which is highest at 183 lacs in terms Indian rupees. It is 133 lacs in Australia and 101 lacs in Indonesia. In UK and many other European countries, the limit is from 80 lacs to 89 lacs. At the bottom is Russia where the limit is over 13 lacs.

Five lac limit of our country is unbelievably low for a country which is now emerging as an economic power in the world. According to the information given by DICGC in its annual accounts for 2018-19, the deposit insurance fund it has is US $ 13.6 billion (over 970 billion rupees) as on March 31, 2019 and it is claimed that it is fourth largest in terms of value amongst the countries after USA (₹ 18305,000), Japan (₹ 6600,000) and Brazil (₹ 3520,000). We may compare the insurance limits in these three countries mentioned within brackets, which is very high.

As on March 31, 2021, the deposit insurance fund has further gone up and stood at ₹ 1,17,629 crore.

Deposit insurance cover is provided to safeguard the interests of bank depositors against bank closures. It is to impart stability in the financial system which is of paramount importance for any economy.

It is interesting to note that New Zealand at present has no deposit insurance scheme in operation. Now New Zealand is proposing to have deposit insurance for protecting the bank depositors. It is said that this country has now finalised its deposit insurance scheme after study and is proposing to fix insurance limit at New Zealand dollar 100000/- per depositor. This works out to equivalent of ₹ 51.40 lacs. This scheme is expected to be in place in the year 2023.

Indian experiences about bank failures are not different from the experiences of other countries over the world. In fact, as far as bank failures are concerned our record is little better in the past 50 years. There were no major bank failures in this period. This may be mainly due to public sector banks who till today have stronghold in banking business. RBI has been proactive in identifying weak banks and merging them with stronger banks. Probably the govt. is thinking that this is the strong point in the stability of country's financial system and has not given much importance to deposit insurance cover to bank depositors in recent times. We observe that while other countries have actively considered the need for depositor protection and have provided higher insurance cover in this decade, our govt. has not taken it seriously.

But there is need to look into the inadequacy insurance cover to bank depositors now. This is because since introducing banking reforms from the year 1991 many new private sector banks have come up. Few of them have grown in a short time to the list of top ten banks of the country. Many new Payments Banks and Small Finance Banks have been opened. Their share in banking business is continuously increasing now. Even if we presume that depositors of public sector banks are safe, the depositors of private sector banks also need the safety net for them.

Besides our banking system has a weak link in urban coop banks. Bank failure in this category of banks is a regular feature. Many of these urban coop banks are small banks. Hence the failure of a small coop bank does not receive public or media attention. But the depositors in these banks suffer and their hard-earned money is lost. DICGC cover available is not helping them as it is too low. Only when big coop bank runs into trouble, public and media become aware and it became news as in the case with Madhavpura mercantile coop bank in 2001 and PMC bank in the year 2019.

However, it must be clearly understood that govt. cannot be expected to take the risk/liability on itself to provide deposit insurance using tax payer's money. World over governments are not inclined to use tax payers' money to bail out bank depositors. This may not be possible for governments to do so. Cost of Deposit insurance may have to be borne by the banking system itself to attract deposits by providing safety nets. This is the reason for the premiums are borne by the banks. Govt. and RBI have supervisory responsibility to create a system and supervise it. Generally, this model is adopted by countries all over the world.

In the proposed Financial Sector Development and Regulation (Resolution) Bill, 2019 (FSDR) for creating resolution authority in terms of FSB recommendations, we observe that GOI is now proposing to handover deposit insurance to the resolution authority. It is also proposed to create deposit insurance fund under the resolution authority.

Keeping in mind the global developments to bring in stability of banking system it is pertinent in our country to resolve the issues as under:

What shall be the reasonable level for deposit insurance in the country? It shall be assessed keeping in mind the profile of bank depositors in the country and that majority of bank depositors shall get full insurance.

How the issue of govt. ownership of banks will be resolved? GOI refusing to protect bank depositors fully in public sector banks or banks controlled by govts. is unthinkable.

Can bail-in provision be made as a law and force bank depositors to sacrifice for the purpose of saving the banks? Can even public sector banks be saved this way?

Epilogue

We have studied the challenges the Indian banking has faced in the recent past more particularly after the year 2014 when BJP Govt. is established in the country.

Indian banking has come a long way with nationalization of banks in 1969 and 1980, and the subsequent move by the GOI for globalization of Indian economy in the year 1991. This was in the aftermath of forex reserve crisis faced by the country. Financial sector reforms and reforms in industrial environment were introduced with the purpose to open up the economy and make it to move towards free market economy. We observe that these reforms worked well to the benefit of the country and the economy surged ahead within a span of 10-15 years.

Financial sector reforms were aimed at bringing the financial sector of the country at par with the global financial sectors. Banking sector is the main sector in this and Indian banking was aligned to achieve global standard as it is imperative to transform the economy to global standard. GOI and RBI have fairly achieved their objectives in this. It was also aimed to make Indian currency as a 'free currency' and can be freely converted to any other global currency. This is also known as capital account convertibility of the currency. Though this was aimed at, for some reason it is delayed, and at present there appears to be no agenda for GOI and RBI for it.

As we have studied, Indian banking has now adopted all the required international standards and comply with KYC norms, anti-money laundering measures, Basel committee recommendations on capital structure of the banks, and the best international accounting and reporting systems. Prudential norms were introduced for banks. As Indian banking was public sector dominated, private banks were allowed to come up and foreign banks are encouraged to expand their base in the country.

We observe that politically India has become strong in the past five years and the Indian economy now ranks in the first four of global economies. Despite the effect of covid pandemic, country is poised to have highest GDP amongst all countries. India's exports are strong and the country has at present very comfortable forex reserves which is adequate to finance one full year's forex requirements of the country.

With the above background, we may now look at the immediate future challenges before the banking sector of the country.

1. Structure of Indian Banking

We have discussed the present structure of Indian banking. We now have public sector banks, private sector banks, foreign banks, small finance banks, payment banks, few local area banks, RRBs and banks in cooperative sectors i.e., UCBs and RCBs. GOI has now created 12 public sector banks out of which six banks are formed by mergers and they are the bigger PSBs. GOI has decided to handover two public sector banks to private parties. Though GOI has not made any policy statements, it appears that GOI may handover all six smaller PSBs to private parties in the near future retaining only the six bigger PSBs with it.

However, GOI may have to decide on the future of even these six bigger PSBs as to how long it will remain under GOI. We have also studied that govt. ownership of banks will, as per present practice and customs, force the GOI to bail-out them in case of difficulties, and also provide capital for their growth and stability.

Now this practice is looked down by the Financial Stability Board—a global forum, and it has advocated bail-in provision and quick resolution system for ailing banks and FIs. FSB has recommended that tax payers' money shall not be used by govts. to bail out banks and financial institutions in trouble.

As per the present system in all countries, bank depositors' interest shall be secured by deposit insurance schemes which shall not secure 100% risk for all depositors. As per guidelines, insurance cover shall be substantial but not full for any big deposit accounts.

Govt. ownership of banks will be an antithesis as govt. in such case cannot disown its obligation to secure the depositor's interest. Govt. cannot make pronunciations disowning its liability and tell the bank depositors of PSBs, to accept and share loss in case the bank runs into problem.

GOI has not yet introduced the legislation of Financial Sector Development and Regulation (Resolution) Bill, 2019 (FSDR) as required under FSB recommendations. It means GOI has not made up its mind on this bill. But sooner or later GOI has to decide on this bill which has the obnoxious bail-in provision for resolution purpose. This bill may be made a law and GOI may also decide to privatise all PSBs in a gradual manner over a period of time.

The proposed Financial Sector Development and Regulation (Resolution) Bill (FSDR) is important as it aims at quicker resolution of banks and FIs in trouble, to avoid repercussions on the national economy. The purpose is to set up a resolution authority with full powers to deal with sick banks and FIs and bring them back to health within shortest time possible. In case the sick bank or FI cannot be revived, then it must be closed immediately and the liquidation process conducted quickly so that the economy is not burdened to carry the failed bank or FI for long time.

Next few years may be crucial and when our country fully adopts FSB recommendations, it is likely that the banking sector of the country will move into private sector.

GOI will also require to review the present deposit insurance cover of ₹ 5 lacs and make it reasonable as it is still quite low as compared to other countries. This will be a real issue if GOI abstains from bail out of commercial banks (however GOI was forced to do it in Yes bank case in 2020). It is obvious that if any large commercial bank fails in future, the deposit insurance cover of ₹ 5 lacs will be inadequate and there will be serious disturbance in the banking system of country.

At present deposit insurance is provided by DICGC (subsidiary of RBI). The proposed Financial Sector Development and Regulation (Resolution) Bill (FSDR) has now indicated that this function will be looked after by the Resolution Authority to be created under the proposed bill.

2. Banks in Cooperative Sector

We have studied UCBs which are in private hands, and they are prone to failures and there is regular closing down of few of them every year. As discussed, GOI has now put them under the exclusive control of RBI and also made provisions for UCBs to get capital funds from public to strengthen these banks. These changes are introduced in the year 2021 and RBI has to watch the progress and the health of these banks to ensure that they remain safe and that the number of failures come down in future.

At present UCBs have the option of converting to commercial banking as Small Finance Banks or remain under co-op sector and improve their working. As there are more than 1500 UCBs at present, their status after the changes made in the legal provisions in 2021, will be known in next few years.

One major change made by RBI in the year 2021 will now affect the UCBs. Earlier UCBs were at par with commercial banks in terms of their credit portfolio. They had obligation of 40% lending to priority sector same as commercial banks. Now priority sector lending target is prescribed at 75% for UCBs which is same as for Small Finance Banks. Thus, UCBS are now equated with SFBs in their role and functions. They are now not comparable to commercial banks. UCBs shall now re-orient themselves as smaller banks and make necessary changes in their approach for lending.

GOI has also retained the status of RCBs in the country and made some provisions to strengthen them financially. GOI has also desired that these RCBs be run like the other banks in the country under same discipline and reposition themselves. The progress and success on this will be known in next few years.

GOI has now approved amalgamation of DCCBs with state coop banks. This will be subject to state govt. consent and RBI approval. Hence, we may see voluntary amalgamations of DCCBs with state coop banks in next few years. This will change the existing three tier set up for short-term lending by RCBs. At present there are PACs at ground level, DCCBs at district level and StCBs at state level. When all the DCCBs are merged with StCBs, as proposed now, there will be only two-tier system for short-term lending i.e., PACs and StCBs.

3. Capital Account Convertibility of Indian Rupee

The ultimate aim of any developing economy is to achieve full convertibility of its currency which includes both current account convertibility and capital account convertibility. It is the stage when the economy becomes a developed economy.

Capital account convertibility gives the option to citizens to hold assets anywhere in the world and also that the assets held in the country can be freely converted to foreign assets. This was one of the goals set by the country when it embarked on globalisation of Indian economy.

Govt. of India appointed a committee (S.S. Tarapore committee) in May 1997 to study and submit report on Capital Account Convertibility with recommendations.

The committee had observed and laid down three crucial pre-conditions for attaining CAC as under:

The committee recommended that before allowing full convertibility, nation shall ensure that macro-economic conditions are in good shape and the economy achieves certain goal posts as preparatory steps. They are:

- Govt. deficit to be controlled within 3.5%,
- inflation to be brought down below 3-5%,
- banks are strengthened by adequate capital and their NPAs to be under 5%, and CRR for the banking system to be at 3%.

In committee's views when these goal posts are reached, then it will be the right time to allow full convertibility.

A second committee, also chaired by S.S. Tarapore, was set up by the Reserve Bank of India in consultation with the Government of India in the year 2006 to review the position.

Tarapore committee II, has reviewed the progress made by the country and recommended a five-year roadmap, to be implemented over three phases, to relax regulations on capital account convertibility.

The Committee report, said the phase I should start from the fiscal (2006) while phase II should be implemented in the next two financial years (2007-09) and the last phase in the following two fiscals (2009-11).

Committee also made recommendations for further reforms in banking sector like encouraging setting up of new banks in private sector, encouraging foreign banks, strengthening of capital ratios for banks and compliance of Basel committee recommendations. It also recommended that all commercial banks should be subject to a single banking legislation and all banks, including public sector banks, should be incorporated under the Companies Act and made few other recommendations on other financial matters.

While Indian rupee achieved full current account convertibility in the year 1993, capital account convertibility is delayed and is yet to be announced.

However, much progress has been made in this direction. Inflation targeting has been made a law and GOI is now setting it. GOI is also controlling its budgetary deficits. Private banks and foreign banks are now free to start or expand business. Banking laws are streamlined. Bank capital requirements are now as per Basel committee recommendations. NPA level of banks were very comfortable before 2014 but increased thereafter. It is now coming down due to various measures initiated by GOI and RBI. Forex reserves of the country is now at comfortable level. Rupee exchange rates are free and market determined now.

We can expect that the country is steadily moving towards achieving capital account convertibility of Indian Rupee.

4. Supervision over Banks

RBI has the supervisory authority over banks in India and this authority is derived mainly from two Acts; Reserve Bank of

India Act of 1934 and Banking Regulation Act of 1949. Earlier to the year 2021, RBI authority on banks were different on commercial banks and the cooperative banks. While RBI had full authority on commercial banks, the cooperative banks were under dual control of RBI and state govts. Due to this reason RBI has ensured that no commercial bank in the country was closed. But urban coop banks have been the weak links and almost every year some UCBs were failing and are closed making their depositors to lose heavily. In the year 2021, GOI amended the laws and brought all coop banks under the direct supervision of RBI. Hopefully this will stop UCBs being closed due to better control on them.

Though legal provisions have now been made to safeguard cooperative banks, there is a long way to go as RBI shall be required to supervise all cooperative banks which are very large in numbers (more than 2000 banks). RBI is now required to supervise closely to ensure that timely actions are taken to arrest impending weaknesses in these banks. The main areas of concern will be the system in coop banks for sanction of loans and management functions, know your customer norms to be followed by these banks, prudential norms for accounting system, NPA control and provisioning for bad loans and CRAR requirements of these banks. This will be a challenging task for RBI in the next five years.

Index

G

H

I

J

K

L

M